Women in a World at War

Seven Dispatches from the Front

Madeleine Gagnon

Preface by Benoîte Groult
Introduction by Monique Durand

translated by
Phyllis Aronoff and Howard Scott

Talonbooks
2003

Talonbooks
P.O. Box 2076, Vancouver, British Columbia, Canada V6B 3S3
www.talonbooks.com

Typeset in Bembo and printed and bound in Canada.

First Printing: October 2003

Les femmes et la guerre was published in the original French by VLB
Éditeur in 2000.

National Library of Canada Cataloguing in Publication Data

Gagnon, Madeleine, 1938–
  Women in a world at war: seven dispatches from the front /
Madeleine Gagnon; translated by Phyllis Aronoff & Howard Scott.

  Translation of: Les femmes et la guerre.
  ISBN 0-88922-483-8

  1. Women and war. 2. War victims. I. Aronoff, Phyllis, 1945– II.
Scott, Howard, 1952– III. Title.
HQ1233.G3313 2003   303.6'6'082   C2003-910960-7

The publisher gratefully acknowledges the financial support of the
Canada Council for the Arts; the Government of Canada through the
Book Publishing Industry Development Program; and the Province of
British Columbia through the British Columbia Arts Council for our
publishing activities.

Acknowledgments

I would like to thank all of the following individuals and organizations.

The Canada Council for the Arts provided financial assistance in the form of a grant under the Millennium Arts Fund.

The following organizations contributed in various ways to this book: the Canadian International Development Agency; OXFAM-Québec; Médecins du Monde; Amnesty International; the Centre Québécois du PEN; KFOR, the NATO intervention force in Kosovo and Macedonia, especially the soldiers of the Canadian, Hungarian and French armies.

The following persons gave me support in one way or another: Marie-Francoise Allain, Jeanne Angelovska, Eliad Awwad, Samia Bamieh, Hoda Barakat, Souha Béchara, Nalah Chahal, Swaleha Niaz, Mujefira Donlagc, Henriette Duvinage, Claude Gorayeb, Liliane Ghazaly, Rita Giacomin, Salima Hashmi (Faiz), Naghma Imdad, Asma Jahangir, Josée Lambert, Rahmeh Mansour, Olga Murdzeva-Skarik, Veronique

Nahum-Bunch, Mirheta Omerovic, Martin Pâquette, Elmedina Podrug, Dalal Salameh, Seida Saric and her co-workers Aida and Divna, Marlène Selfani, Mohammad Tahseen, Sister Theodora and all the people interviewed in Sri Lanka who, for reasons of safety, chose to remain anonymous.

Monique Durand, my journalist colleague, was a marvellous strategist for our journey, during which she worked on a series of ten radio documentaries on women and war for Radio-Canada. These programs were broadcast in the summer and fall of 2000.

Preface

Few writers have been able to express the full horror of war. Few have been able to find a language that could convey all its dimensions. For it goes beyond words, official discourse, and novels and films, as beautiful as the latter may sometimes be.

This is probably why Madeleine Gagnon has chosen to express herself in the "black ink of poets," to use the lovely expression of the Quebec poet Paul Bélanger. Only poetry can take readers beyond appearances to penetrate the diverse but universal experience of women in wartime. Reading her words, we feel in our flesh the permanent anguish of the victims—whether in Bosnia or Kosovo, Israel or Palestine, Pakistan or Sri Lanka—the misery, the suffering, but also, in the depths of horror, rays of hope, hope of escaping the vicious spiral, the hope of the women who for a time fight side-by-side with their men in wars of independence, the hope of all these women that they will finally be recognized not only as mothers and servants but as autonomous, responsible human beings. And yet, what a pity it is to see what becomes of this hope!

Typical of these women is Dalal Salameh, a young Palestinian woman who is a member of the Legislative Council and who is "absolutely convinced" that the eighty-three men on the Council will include in the future constitution the demands of the women who share their battle.

A hope repeatedly thwarted, but the illusion is reborn, and many women survive only because they are "absolutely convinced" of a future of reconciliation and justice.

"We are utopians," writes Madeleine Gagnon, "Or else we wouldn't be here, we would not have undertaken this voyage." A voyage to a no man's land— in the most literal sense—where the desire to escape the absurd violence that spares nothing is taking form, in a moan or in a shout. Because "war, in this century of ashes, has changed. It no longer takes place man-to-man on a front defined by generals. There are no more fronts. Or rather, the front is everywhere."

And everywhere is where Madeleine Gagnon wanted to go. Not just to write another book, but so that we would understand that the oppression of one sex by the other is at the root of all violence, all war. So that, as an Iranian woman said, "the veils would fall not only from our faces, but also from our souls and hearts."

Pacifism and feminism have often been linked. But we must be suspicious of stereotypes. I was twenty years old during the war and, like many men and women who experienced the fall of France and the German occupation between 1939 and 1945, I cannot forget that France's honour rested entirely on the few men and women who chose to continue the fight alongside General de Gaulle or who joined the underground resistance against the Nazis.

I tend to think that pacifism does not come "naturally" to women, that they are not intrinsically peaceful, but rather that this image is a myth constructed around motherhood, a myth that has become second nature to women. Women's pacifism is simply one aspect of their exclusion from the public sphere. It is important to realize this. Because they have for millennia been barred from the three major forms of power—religious, political and military power— women have been forced to retreat to the values associated with the home. In the background, subservient to the gods—always male—of the great monotheistic religions, excluded from decision-making, deprived of education and freedom of expression, women were condemned to be among the mute victims of all wars. History was made without them.

From the dawn of Western civilization in the Greek city-states, women have been relegated to a single role in war: that of begging the gods for victory by the men, and then celebrating the men's victory or mourning their death. As for the Amazons that are often mentioned by feminists, they are not real, but rather creatures of myth, symbols of men's fear of women getting hold of their weapons.

The Middle Ages of feudalism and chivalry also excluded women from the use of weapons and the exercise of power. As shown in the monumental collection of essays, *A History of Women in the West*, edited by Georges Duby and Michelle Perrot, this was a markedly masculine period. Even courtesy was only a strategy of power, in which women were nothing but trophies.

Nor did the French Revolution do anything to change women's status as eternal minors. The aptly named *Declaration of the Rights of Man*[2] excluded women from the army and the legislature. The only equality women obtained in 1789 was the right to be guillotined just like the men.

Finally, closer to our time, totalitarian regimes, fascist or Nazi, reduced women to their role as wives and mothers. The Vichy government of Marshal Pétain harshly condemned women who strayed from the ideal of the "eternal feminine" and their "vocation of peace"—which in the circumstances was somewhat suspect. And women's contribution to the resistance against the German occupiers was for a long time minimized by a male-dominated hierarchy.

Far from subverting the sexual order of things, wars have always reinforced it. They accentuate male dominance and widen the gap between men and women. This is why all the progress we believe has been made in the common struggle with men is swept away

1. Georges Duby and Michelle Perrot, *A History of Women in the West*, 5 vol. (Cambridge, Mass.: Belknap Press of Harvard UP, 1992–1994).
2. Whose name we have not succeeded in changing in France, as they have in Quebec, to refer to "human rights."

when peace is restored. Women have always been cheated by wars and revolutions.

Madeleine Gagnon's book will leave no one untouched. Reading about such displays of everyday heroism and the capacity to transcend suffering forces us to question the very structures of society, which are based on a totally outmoded view of the role of women. We must of course strip war of its glory and its sanctity by challenging the idea that battle is honourable, as the French writer Christine de Pisan did in the fifteenth century. But our priority must be to attack traditional concepts of identity, which are at the root of both private and military violence. It is not in their maternal role (a fact of nature) that women should draw their reasons for opposition to war, but in their awareness of their worth and their self-esteem as full citizens. Peace is something that both sexes together must conquer and build day by day. Political reforms alone, even full equality before the law, will not change behaviour; it is the perceptions that men and women have of themselves that must be transformed.

The book you are about to read, which explores women's silence in history and shows their vast potential for change, should contribute to building something that women have often lacked in the past: solidarity, which alone will enable them to cast off the age-old yoke of patriarchy and misogyny.

This book is the farthest thing from what we hear in official speeches. It speaks in "another voice."

Benoîte Groult

Introduction

I wanted there to be some trace, not only in sound but in writing, some trace of what I knew would be a disturbing experience. I was convinced that literary writing would be better able than journalism or documentary writing to convey the depth and the inexpressibility of what I was going to see and hear. I dreamed that there would be a series of radio documents that would remain as an aural echo, but also that there would be a book, the words of which would take root in another garden of memory and irrigate another layer of the imaginary.

Radio-Canada had called for projects to mark the turn of the year 2000. I can still see the busy highway from Quebec City to Montreal that morning in the fall of 1997, as the two of us racked our brains for words that had loomed large in the twentieth century and would also figure in the twenty-first. Our pleasure in seeking, dreaming, imagining. This was a long time before we would have to weigh the reality, determine the time and budget available and tackle the logistics.

In the end the two words that remained on our lips were *women* and *war*. Because we felt the twentieth century would always be the century of women's revolution—at least in the Western world—and of two world wars and Auschwitz, the horror of which has exceeded everything previous centuries could have imagined and we believed the same two words would also permeate the twenty-first century. The women of the so-called developing countries would continue their slow quest for emancipation through education, control of fertility and economic growth, while the women of the rich countries would continue to occupy the centres of political, economic and cultural power. Armed conflict, terrorism, occupation, slaughter and war would continue on many existing fronts and on others still unsuspected. The "war to end all wars," "never again," "peace and love," these commitments of the twentieth century, would be betrayed, shattered and trampled on in Chechnya even before the first glimmers of the twenty-first century.

Our project was born. Women and war. We would try to think about war from a female point of view. Perhaps a key to understanding the phenomenon of war was to be found there.

I chose the writer Madeleine Gagnon for her way of writing and thinking about life and death, femaleness and maleness. She was someone who would be able to convey the great complexity of the world and of feelings, who would be able to translate into words the enigma of men and women marching in step in war and in love. Men holding weapons, doing the dirty work, killing, cutting throats, raping. Women not only innocent, not only victims, but in love with life and with their men—wombs of love and of war. Women and men with a pathological longing to belong. Madeleine Gagnon was also someone who would be able to bring forth, out of the disaster shrouding the world, a kind of hopeful light.

And so the journey took form, at first in atlases, maps, notes, grant applications and dreams, a lot of dreams. Until, in October 1999 on a late afternoon something like that autumn morning two years earlier on the highway from Quebec City to Montreal, a Swissair plane set down, plunging us into the tumult of the Skopje airport occupied by KFOR soldiers, and into the burning heart of our subject.

We were beginning a one-year voyage that would take us from the Balkans to the Middle East and then to South Asia. An exceptional year that culminated in a dense book by Madeleine Gagnon and a series of radio programs I produced. But that has barely begun to work itself into our fibres, to permeate our pores, to become truly our own—all these women and their wars, their blood, their tears, the landscapes of all these countries, slowly spreading a great veil of humanity over our lives.

Monique Durand
August 2000

BEFORE LEAVING

Before Leaving

She said, "Write that my name is Anna. Don't say where I come from. I want to live, I don't want to die." I met Anna in Toronto. Exiled there four years earlier, she was waiting, she said. Waiting for what? I asked. She didn't know. But she was sure that something or somebody would come. Why? "To deliver me from the terror," was her only answer.

She had known war. Ten years. She always repeated "ten years" like an incantation, swaying gently as if she were being rocked to a melody. Her body was a prayer sung very softly. She had not wanted me to go to her house. "I don't want to die," she had repeated. I invited her to my hotel, because she didn't want to meet in a public place either, where "there are deadly looks that continue the war here."

She had come to Canada four years ago with her husband and three youngest children. Her eldest son had died in combat, at least that's what they told her. "We never saw his body, maybe he will come back, maybe there was a mistake, or maybe they just said anything. Men who make war have no souls, how can you expect them to have words to speak the truth?"

She showed me a photograph of her dead son. "Call him Karim. He was twenty-two years old when he left. He's a beautiful child, don't you think?" She put the photograph back in her handbag after slipping it into a little case between her residency and health insurance cards, which she showed me proudly. "These cards are my country, you know, this is my new geography."

Before coming to Canada, they had stopped in France. In transit. She emphasized that word. "We would never have stayed there. France, Europe, they still smell of war. We needed an ocean to wash all that away." From her bag, she took out a book, which remained on her knees throughout the interview, I never found out why. I couldn't see the title, it was hidden by a worn leather cover. With her long, slender hands resting on it, the book seemed to be part of her, to be the soul of her words as the image of her dead son was their flesh.

She watched me closely with a raw, burning intensity. Rarely have eyes said so much. As if there was another field of vision beyond her gaze. Very far away. As if from another age. From another time. In that anonymous Toronto hotel room, the situation was suddenly reversed. I had presented myself with my questions about "women and war"; now it was she, Anna, who was asking me questions, asking them with her eyes alone, holding a photograph of a dead child and a book about which I would know nothing, not even the title.

I told her about my project. Told her what I wanted to understand through these peregrinations in several countries at war, including hers. Explained to her that I was perhaps an idealist, and certainly a romantic, to imagine I would be able, even in a very small way, to penetrate the mystery of women's role in relation to war—what they have to say about it, whether they have a stake in the death instinct in action, whether, although in a more subtle, more secret, more buried way than men, they have the same taste for blood in their mouths, the same morbid, death-dealing proclivity as far back as the dawn of our earthly memory.

And if they, too, were not humble artisans of the death instinct in action, although in the background of the deadly conflicts, wouldn't they, in the time immemorial of war, have conceived powerful strategies for stopping the deaths of war, have conceived their sons differently and not reared them to be those little soldiers who dominate daughters, sisters and sometimes mothers? Isn't the mothers' field of tears the inescapable counterpart of the fathers' field of honour?

Anna's eloquent silence encouraged me to continue. Sometimes she would fix her gaze on an imaginary point on the wall opposite, just above my head, and then look back into my eyes, her own eyes full of questions related to mine, and move her long, slender hands, amber-coloured in the slanting rays of light from the window. There were three of us in that neutral Toronto hotel room, she, the sun and I. Her hands moved lightly over the mysterious book.

And what if the great war from time immemorial was the war against women, Anna, the war that kills more women in the world than cancer or car accidents and almost as many as AIDS, kills them with blows, mutilation and rape, not to mention the millions of female fetuses consigned to limbo every year in countries where technological progress has made possible the "natural" selection of male children through ultrasound?

I want to understand the relationship between that great war and the others, Anna, to grasp through women's voices and through women's eyes the connections between the age-old wars and that primeval war, the one so little talked about. In the space of a book, I want to cultivate this field of enigmas, to survey its furrows like so many paths to the Other, to any other person whose words will meet mine at the crossroads of questioning without the actual words necessarily being the same, any other person who will mix their zones of shadow and light, their true fictions, with mine. I want to cast my ink on the paths sown in blood and nourish the strange soil. Far away. Elsewhere.

Then Anna said, "Women give life, men give death. Why?" Coming from her, this slogan from the feminist movement of thirty years ago surprised me. I didn't have time to say so, as she went on: "Is it a gift when it is death? What a terrible gift. As you know, there are two laws that have been used to justify all wars: the law of male supremacy and the law of primogeniture. I know no more about the former than you do. I know only that the gods of all religions are male and that the gods have always decided everything. You cannot change the order of things. The gods are immutable and eternal."

"But Anna, it was men who invented the gods. Every civilization, every religion has projected its fictions and myths, its fantasies of absolute domination, onto them." She shot me a withering look and then closed her eyes as if lowering a curtain between us, tenderly touched the book on her knees, and without looking at me again continued: "As for the other law, you know it too—or else reread *your* Bible. It is just as deeply etched on the clay tablets, it is inexorable, you cannot change it. The law of primogeniture is the law of blood, first of all, which is the basis of the family. It is the law of the soil, next, which is the foundation of the fatherland. In other words, first come, first served—first authority in the family or over human geopolitical territory.

"Mind you, the eldest are almost always punished. Think of Cain or Esau. But my son had not committed any of their sins. Had not denied or blasphemed or betrayed his position or his mission. It was simply, if I can put it this way, that he went to war, he defended a just cause, he believed in the god of his ancestors. He was able, since he became a man, to exercise due authority over his two younger sisters and even over me, his own mother, when my husband was not there, as it is written in our holy book. Maybe he paid for the sins of all the Cains, all the Esaus of the world? Maybe he spilled his blood for all the apostates, all the renegades the earth has begotten? Maybe my tears, mixed with the blood of my son, are seeding an earth where the fundamental rights I am talking about will be respected? If this is so, I will be happy to have lived."

In the hotel room, silence descended like a sheet of lead. Not a sound was heard between us. I would have to learn to write this silence. I phoned for room service. Before the waiter knocked on the door with our tea, I saw Anna become a perfect stranger again. She put the book back in her bag, took out a veil and put it back on, and disappeared far away behind the opaque fabric, her gaze vacant now and her smile gone, sitting straight, waiting, motionless. Absent.

After tea and before we took up our pens and datebooks to set another meeting, her eyes looking into mine grew huge and I read in them an immeasurable ocean of sadness. She smiled anyway and said: "Do not believe a word of all my theories. I will mourn my son to my last breath. Exile, even in your pampered country, will not change that. You are right. Continue your quest. Ask your questions. I will come back. To see you."

The day before our second meeting, I received a letter from Anna at my hotel. I was all the more troubled by it because what she said in it coincided exactly with what had been on my mind since the morning, summed up in one burning question: How to write women's silence?

As I knew from films and television, doctors and psychologists agree that, on one of the most horrific aspects of war—the wholesale rape of women by enemy soldiers—the women remain silent, they clam up. I understood that this silence should never be subjected to the force of questions. That these mouths had a right to secrecy. That the violently invaded vaginas had turned the tides of stillborn words back to the source of tears with the tides of blood, like so many aborted foetuses. I also realized, or at any rate I had the intuition, that abortion following a rape would be subject to the same unspoken reserve.

I remembered Edmond Jabès saying in *The Book of Questions* that silence is not a refusal to speak. I remembered that his own writing was nourished by silence and the desert, the ink of the words becoming an oasis, the source and breath of life. Would my written words on the wholesale rape of women—only recently recognized as a crime against humanity—and on the murder of civilians, men, old people, women and children, be faithful to those words I would not hear? Anna's letter coincided with these questions. Exactly.

You whose mothers and great-grandmothers, fathers and great-grandfathers, brothers and sisters, sons and daughters have not known war, receive these words of a poet I have always read in your language—with mine, it is the only one I know. My husband and my children have started to speak English, but I really believe I will die in Arabic even if I was to live another forty years in America. However, it is your language that leads me to an understanding, however slight, of the horror, especially when it is expressed through poetry, even in translation, because poetry is the only language that really takes one to the timeless shores of wisdom (please excuse my French). You may want to think about these lines:

Not from shyness, this silence of theirs;
nor from any hint of fear.

...

you built them a temple at listening's core.

Rilke, *Sonnets to Orpheus*

Do you know the great Lebanese poet Salah Stétié? This is quoted in his book *Réfraction du désert et du désir*. As for Rilke, I lost his books with my entire library in the fire after our house was shelled. I will see you tomorrow.

When Anna came back the next day, I gave her the complete works of Rilke, which I'd bought that morning in a bookstore. She had brought three pink roses for me. Had she guessed how much I love roses as she had guessed my thoughts the day before? I thanked her with my eyes while she looked at her gift with delight. We embraced like two old friends.

Then, without any transition, as if to cut short the emotion, Anna took her seat in the same place as the day before, in the armchair at an angle to the window, with the tall buildings of Toronto's downtown behind her and the line of Lake Ontario in the distance, and the same sunshine on her suntanned hands. She adopted the same position, straight-backed and dignified, took out the mysterious book and placed it on her knees, lowered her eyes to look at it, and then suddenly looked up, enveloping me in her gaze to lead me wordlessly to lands so remote that the neutral room I was in suddenly disappeared.

In the great calm that filled us both, I felt that the travels I had been dreaming of for months were beginning, drawing me toward their destination. I remembered reading Victor Segalen writing on this paradoxical state, probably just before his trip to China. I felt that a leave-taking was occurring before the actual departure. And it required a pause. To measure the distance between far away and here, I needed this period of suspension that could come only from another human presence, intensely there and at the same time already so strangely outside. I had to go from native-born to foreign-born, with another language buried deep in an almost unknown elsewhere within me, a language at once native and nationless, whose grammar poetry alone had sometimes allowed me to glimpse.

I could feel that Anna found herself, like me, in an in-between time, an in-between place. That we were both on the same path. Looking for what escaped us about war but that we both wanted to confront by going through elsewhere—where she was, where I was going—to return to what was most distant in us. To what was most secret.

Anna did not seem to want to talk. She was there, calm, composed. She radiated a serenity, a relaxation that suited me perfectly. I had awakened from an upsetting dream and had not yet had time to recover.

All the anxiety of leaving had focused on a single concern, as happens to me whenever I am beset by doubt. Will I be up to the project? Have I foreseen all the potential dangers? Will I be able to find the answers to the questions I am asking in these war-torn countries?

I said to Anna, "I'm not going away to write a book. I'm going to meet women who have experienced or are experiencing war. If I write a book, it is to better understand, to better see what they have seen, to better hear what they tell me. Only writing will enable me to understand what happens between them and me." She answered, "I know," and went back to her thoughts.

I went back to my dream. I was at the airport in Dorval and I was about to leave. When I went to show the customs officer my plane ticket and passport, I realized that I had forgotten the safari (or reporter's) jacket, with the dozens of pockets, that my friends C. and S. had given me. I rushed out of the terminal, hailed a taxi, and shouted to the driver to take me back to my home in Montreal, fast. He understood right away, driving like a maniac and almost getting us killed in the traffic on the way to my street. But then, as happens in dreams, my home wasn't where I live now, but a former apartment where I lived a long time ago, a dilapidated building in a run-down neighbourhood. I was looking for that little beige jacket that I felt I couldn't leave without. I found myself in a gloomy old street that seemed to have been burned and pillaged. The taxi had disappeared. Suddenly I was wearing a white veil on my head. I tried to shout—to whom?—"No, I don't want to leave this way," but the words caught in my throat. I woke up.

I told my dream to Anna, who lost her impassive look. She said, "Listen to mine. I have been wanting to tell you about it since this morning. Last night I felt like I was dying, suffocating, but fortunately day came and the light let me leave the labyrinth where I slept. Before telling you my dream, I have to tell you something quite real. The all-too-real tragedy of my life. My son Karim, as you know, was born as a result of a rape by an enemy soldier. Our troops had hit them hard. His division was in retreat. They were like animals caught in a trap. They attacked everything that moved on the road, human or animal. I was eighteen. I was with a friend, coming back from the neighbouring village. We had gone to visit her mother in the hospital. We had brought her apples and a few flowers gathered in the fields along the way.

"Even though it was wartime, no one among our friends or families had yet been affected, and we headed home singing. We could hear shooting in the distance, on the other side of the hills surrounding our town, it seemed to come from the end of the world, from a million miles away. All of a sudden, a pack of rabid dogs that were human in name only was rushing toward us. It happened so fast. My girlfriend was torn from my arms by the pack. I heard her heart-rending screams. I found out afterwards that they had torn her to pieces. As for me, one of them took me in a monstrous assault. He left me for dead in a field. I had to make my way home during the night. I didn't want to be seen.

"My mother nursed me for a long time. In secret. She made up a story for my father, my brothers, my cousins and family friends, I forget what it was. Only a few women knew. Because of the dishonour, you understand. A month later, I married a cousin who had been chosen for me. He never knew, he still doesn't. On the day of the wedding, there were no visible wounds. Things heal so quickly at that age. For the wedding night, my mother gave me a bottle of heifer's blood that I surreptitiously poured on the white sheet.

"Last night is the first time I've dreamt about it ... Karim came out of my belly bloody, with a knife in his hand. Although he was just a baby, he was a soldier. He looked at me, crying and enraged. I kissed him and said, 'You will go off to war. You will kill the soldier who sired you. You will bring me back his beast's eyes, I want to burn them on hot coals. You will bring me back his vicious tongue, I want to tear it out with my own hands. You will bring me back his sex of iron, I want to impale it, then light it like a fuse and throw it down the well. Avenge us, Karim. Restore the honour of our house.' Karim looked at me so sadly, as if in terror. He said, 'I do not want to kill my father. I want to kill, but who? I want to get myself killed in the war.'"

Anna had spoken without pause, as if far away. She came back to me, exhausted, her eyes hollow and dark-circled, looking suddenly like an old woman. She swore me to secrecy and said, "I don't know why I've trusted you. Maybe because you have the courage to look at the other side of things. Maybe because I sense your fear, too, and your warlike instincts. Maybe because you're a poet and you build your house on doubt. Maybe we women need to be reassured by uncertainty. Maybe ... "

Before leaving, she made me promise to write her from France, where I would stay between the major trips. I told her that I had actually already dreamed of writing the first part of my book for her, calling it "Before Leaving," and that I was delighted by her request.

She put the book back in her bag and took out the veil. I went down with her and watched her rush off into the crowded street. In the distance, with the veil in the wind against the dark background of the lake, she looked like a great peaceful bird from foreign lands imagined in a dream.

Like the madwoman in *India Song* spouting untranslatable words all along the dark roads of the Mekong, Rabia, a Kosovar refugee I met yesterday in Paris, now speaks a language indecipherable by everyone, including her own family. They say that before the fateful night when she saw her husband and her two sons murdered and her fourteen-year-old daughter raped, she was a quiet woman with a radiant smile—everyone who knows her mentions that radiance. Then, at dawn, with the sunrise, a flood of words rose within her, submerging her. She pours them out all day, day after day, in a continuous torrent. At night, she sleeps peacefully, a smile on her lips, say her cousins, who have taken her in.

There are twelve of them living in a tiny, shabby apartment. They don't want to go back to Kosovo. Zake, the eldest, who speaks French, told me, "We do not want to walk on the unhealed wounds of our land. We do not want to walk on the flesh of our dead." They don't want to hospitalize Rabia either, as was suggested to them. They have also refused the medication a psychiatrist prescribed. "We do not understand her language," her cousin Barbuka said, "But we understand ours better since she has been talking this way. Our tongue is black, you know. Day after day, night after night, ashes rained down on it. No medication can change ashes into water."

Anna, as promised, I am writing you from Paris. During my meeting with Rabia and her family, I couldn't help making a connection between your two destinies as exiles. To grasp the horror of war, both of you have buried your mother tongue very far away, at the end of the road to foreignness—you in the language of the Other, that of the French and of poetry, Rabia in an invented language that comes from who knows where, that she alone seems to know but that she is nonetheless eager to pour out to whoever is willing to listen. Your days are calm, you said, and your nights filled with nightmares, one after another. Rabia's days are filled with tumult and her nights seem freed of all fear.

Before the war, Rabia was a seamstress. Her cousin Barbuka told me she now screams at the very sight of a needle or thread or scissors. Last week, they were walking together in the streets of Paris. Rabia saw an old sewing machine in the window of a secondhand store. She bolted and ran ahead, panic-stricken, making sounds like an animal with its throat cut. When Barbuka caught up with her, she touched her and took her in her arms, but only the soft humming of a song from her childhood would calm Rabia and bring her back to the chanting of her invented monologue.

Before your war, you taught French in a college in your country. It was through poetry that you led your students to my language, which you speak so well. Your degrees and those of your accountant husband are not recognized in my country today. Both of you janitors in that Toronto forest of apartment towers from which, you said, "the stars are invisible," you have to go back to school, and your few days off are spent going over what you already know, while your daughters come home from class weighed down not only with homework, but also with the mean, sarcastic comments they're subjected to just because they are different. That, too, is war, Anna, and it is everywhere. There's no country that's free of the pain of living. If there were one, we would all have taken refuge there. By "we" I mean those people who desire peace with every fibre of their being.

I'm in Paris, Anna, in this in-between place I've chosen, between my land of origin and the wounded lands I want to immerse myself in and understand. I needed this pause, this space between—neither home nor completely elsewhere—in order to open up the maps before crossing the territories. To achieve the right distance, I needed this intermediate space between the starting point and the places of arrival. A space where the dream of understanding the hunger for war is possible. Yesterday I remembered the bellicose words of an old feminist activist twenty years ago, who asserted with absolute conviction that the death instinct does not exist in women—can you imagine? Just like in the dream you told me, Anna, as long as we women do not confront our murderous desires in the depths of the dark territories that nourish our flesh, war will continue, even though we are not its architects, even though we are most often victims. We are not innocent. We're boiling with rage beneath the ashes.

The ashes of wars are everywhere, Anna. As you know. We came together in that knowledge. The women I will see in the wounded lands will have that wisdom, whatever their madness. I heard it behind Rabia's invented language. Beyond her indecipherable words that came from terror, I picked up the monstrous litany that had been dormant within her and that the horror had awakened. At that exact moment, a shiver went through my heart. Rabia had struck my own chords of cruelty. I looked at her. There was a glimmer of light in her eyes. For that instant, she was no longer in madness, she had found the language of the gods, a music that made her sing. In that home of misery and exile, a balm of joy touched us all. Zake uncorked the bottle I had brought. We clinked our plastic glasses. Rabia took a sip, beaming, and immediately fled back into her soliloquy of fear.

The women I will meet, Anna, will have the gift of ubiquity. Of the heart and mind. They will be able to split themselves in two. Will be able to take bypasses to go from the elsewhere of war that falls upon them, for which they are not guilty, to the here of conflict that lies within them, for which they are responsible. I want to understand that, Anna, that tenuous, nebulous place, that time of going back and forth between the far and the near, to understand that in the other, to better grasp it in myself. That pass, that channel, that gorge, that road, that strait. That opening.

The women I will meet will also have the gift of intuitive memory. They will not recite what they have read in history books. They will not harp on the ready-made theories that for centuries have encircled and enchained us, the edifying discourse on violence and its effects, the fuzzy utopian visions of a peace in some rosy future. I want something new, Anna. I want something real. Some surprise. I want something other. In that other, I want to find myself, as humanity changes me into myself. Indirectly, I am quoting Mallarmé, one of your favourite writers, who is very dear to me as well.

The women I will meet will be poets. Even if they do not have that status. That stature. Even if they do not know it. Especially if they do not know it, perhaps. And the men I will meet will be their lovers. Even if they have not made love to them. Will be loving to them. These men will not be guilty of rape. But responsible for all the rapes of the world. Within them. There where, by winding and uncertain paths, they have desired, even if only once, to re-enter by force into the bodies of their mothers, from which they were—but do they remember?—so cruelly expelled.

I want to meet these women, these men. There where the other in me is met. In all my raw memory. In my intuited memory, and even in my invented memory, for there is a truth of fiction, as you know, a truth marked by extraordinary images hidden in the subterranean paths of the soul. But how, tell me, to make these obscure obvious things clear to those people who are called wise, who carry the torch of reason for all, warriors and victims, and shine the proud light high over the fields and scrub of the fray, upon the absolute carnage that has outraged man's world since its beginnings—how to go about it, tell me, and how to write it?

Others have given up, but I lend my pen to this challenge. I am leaving to walk on the burned roads, to sow the lands with my song, to harvest hope from the soil of despair, death and abdication. I will dance, Anna, I swear to you, and will give words to what no longer has any.

Anna, I am in Paris, in this in-between place, as I said. Between Montreal, my city of departure, and those cities, towns and villages where I will soon arrive. I recite their names in my reveries. Skopje, Pristina, Sarajevo. Jerusalem, Bethlehem, Nazareth, Jericho. Beirut, Istanbul, Karachi, Islamabad, Colombo. I recite their names to myself as one says the name of an unborn child very low, rocking it. I give them life within me before they whisper their lives to me. For months, I have been gathering information. I have been reading, looking at images, and unfolding maps a hundred times, becoming familiar with the places. But

I know very well that, while they are totally imaginary now, they will impose their laws and their desires on me in the test on the ground. A very real test of the laws and desires and customs of the inhabitants of those lands.

I am in this in-between place, this time to be born and these spaces to be discovered. I am not at the centre of the world. Every big city in the world, Paris perhaps more than any other, thinks it is the centre of the world. I've seen the same thing, in other ways, in New York, London, Berlin and Rome. The same is true, I know, of Beijing or Tokyo, Hong Kong or Moscow. There is a megalo-discourse in every megalopolis that has become a capital through the accidents of history. Listen to what Victor Segalen says in *Équipée* about major rivers, which applies perfectly to the great capitals of the world: "The River also possesses that lyrical quality par excellence that is the voluble expression of itself, and a splendid ignorance of everything that is not itself."

When I hear or read certain high-profile Paris intellectuals, sons of the great proud century of the Enlightenment—beacons of civilization!—I know that war is not only intertwined with the bodily instincts of destruction. It is also, and perhaps primarily, in the arrogant domination of the spirit. The spirit of war precedes the act of war. The spirit of war begins when one vision of society sees itself as the model for the Other. Whoever the Other is, and whatever the culture of the Other.

Anna, I come from no centre of the world, and that is a blessing, I believe. My ignorance is real, but it will never have the arrogance of those who dominate the spirit. Coming from a non-country, Quebec, that has always dreamed of belonging to itself without ever really winning that goal, and will remain in its beautiful dream, a non-conqueror until the end of time, I feel I have more right to enter into the intelligence of the Other, wherever he may be. Elsewhere. Wherever she may be. And whatever their language. A language that will be able, with its strange words like poetry, to speak of the unnameable when death in all its forms deliberately destroys life.

Paris is not the centre of the world and I am not at the centre of Paris. To face the horror that I will soon be close to, I've made a point of giving myself a daily dose of happiness. Last night, I dreamed I was a prisoner of a dangerous forest whose only promise was the impossibility of leaving once you had entered it. "That's exactly what I've got into with this trip," I said to myself. I took a few steps anyway. To see. You never know. A sterile refusal to move has not at any time in my life been my response to danger. Suddenly, ahead of me in the suffocating blackness, a flash of light drew me forward. There was a well, with a quartz mine in it; the stone was pure, smooth, already cut with a fleshing knife, and it came off piece by piece, like so many sculptures.

Those splendid objects were, for the time of my dream, my dose of happiness, like the place where I've been staying since I arrived. Not at the centre, as I said.

On the outskirts. At the city limits, off-centre, in the twentieth arrondissement. I didn't know this Paris. I had come to it as a tourist, but now I'm living here. I'm in a village in the city, more in the in-between place I told you about than if I were at the centre. I like this paradox, this already-elsewhere, this working-class neighbourhood where so many peoples of the earth, including yours, have landed up.

I am living at the intersection of three villages, Belleville, Ménilmontant and Saint-Fargeau, which were forcibly annexed to Paris in the mid-nineteenth century. This is where, at the time my grandparents were born, the revolution of the Communards started, and that of the first trade unionists, and that of the utopian socialists, and that of the anarchists against the bourgeoisie and the church. This enraged people that already contained in its ranks Jewish and Arab exiles whose brothers and sisters elsewhere, on their native soil, were being oppressed by murderous racist powers, this motley people thirsting for egalitarian justice but also for revenge, was subdued through murder and torture by the centralizing power of Versailles. The Republic was founded in blood. The monuments in the squares and the cemeteries here have wiped away its traces. That was yesterday, in 1871.

The Père-Lachaise, Belleville and Charonne cemeteries tell of the carnage in their own way. The history books, too. But nothing and no one talks about the war waged against women during those months of civil war. Thousands were raped by the combatants on all sides, and not only by the Prussians, who waited at the city gates for their chance to attack, including attacking the bodies of women when the opportunity arose. There are descendants of the Prussian rapists here, you can still see it in the hair colour, the skin colour, but they don't know it anymore. There are also offspring of native rapes, who are equally unaware, the mothers of that time having been trapped in the same guilty secrecy of shame as women today in other latitudes. I asked a few of the local residents to tell me about that war that took place in this neighbourhood not so very long ago. Nobody knows anything about it any more. No one remembers. Their grandparents told them nothing. The speeches of the Republic have wrapped them in a shawl of forgetting.

I met an old woman who was born in 1912. Her mother, the product of a rape in those strange years, had talked about it. She had sworn her daughter to secrecy. The daughter asked for anonymity, and I promised it. In her home, I had access to some amazing files. Over the years of her long life, she had gone through piles of documents in the public libraries and official archives. Letters, personal diaries, items in the newspapers, legal testimony, accounts by historians and ethnologists, but all on the same subject: the rape of women and girls in recent wars—since the revolution of 1789. Amazing!

In the beginning, she copied all those documents by hand. Later she used a photocopier, which she was grateful for. A passion, you'll say, an obsession. The woman, whom I do not want to betray or to name, told me, "This was my way of healing myself from the war of which I was born. If everyone did as I did, this mess would no longer exist."

She never wanted to marry. "And even less to have children," she said. She has loved once, only once—a Jewish woman who was deported in 1942 and whom she never saw again. Lucid and stoic, she contemplates the documents in her personal archive. She still lives alone. A friend does her shopping for her, cooks her meals, does her cleaning and laundry. She will leave quietly by the little door of her dilapidated but very cosy apartment. She will take her place near her mother in the cemetery not far from here. She believes neither in God nor in the devil and has never cried. She has known sadness only one time, and that time lasted for years—when they came for her love, and later when she knew her love had died in Auschwitz. She said to me, "How, Madeleine"—she too calls me by my first name—"could I have known tears? My mother swallowed them all when I was in her womb."

How did I come to meet her? The story would be too long. Perhaps one day I'll write a novel about her. And why did she trust me? Why was I the first person she told and then showed her secrets to? I don't know. I preserve that mystery along with the strength to live and go on that she gave me.

I forgot to tell you. The old woman wants to see me again. I've promised to go back there. She said when I was already walking out the door, "Come back, I'll tell you about the father I never knew. If my mother is the product of my grandmother's rape, I'm the product of chance. That's what Maman said. She was forty years old when I was born. I was her only child. Like me, she hadn't wanted marriage or children. She said it had been love at first sight with my father, who was much younger than she was. She became pregnant with me. He went away, she didn't know where. Later she learned that he had died in the Great War. At Verdun. He's buried there. One day my mother took me on a trip. I was twelve years old. To my father's grave. A small slab, a name, two dates, that was the picture of my father. My mother said, 'He was so handsome, I fell head over heels.' You see, I'm the product of chance. Of my mother's great sorrow. Of my father's good looks. Of my mother falling head over heels."

Anna, I must go now. In three days, I leave for the first major trip. The Balkans. Skopje. Pristina. Sarajevo. Very soon, I will face the test of reality. Other images will be born. Other words. Other dreams. I will live in another memory. And my own, the light turned down low, will have to accept forgetting. If sometimes I feel lost on the tumultuous roads still marked by strife, I will light my way, I promise, with "the black ink of the poets," as the Quebec poet Paul Bélanger has written. Here is *Trois chants funèbres pour le Kosovo*, by Ismail Kadaré. You will like it, I promise. I'm happy to learn from your last letter that you are slowly rebuilding your library, one book at a time.

MACEDONIA

Macedonia

First, the view from the airplane, which must have been invented so that painters could take in the landscape in a single glance, in one swoop—painters have the souls of birds, as da Vinci understood. This unfamiliar Macedonian land I had imagined only from reading books on ancient history, so old that it was another world to me when my village in young French America could be crossed in a single bound and grasped immediately through its familiar tales and landscapes.

But here, as the Swissair Boeing begins its spiralling descent, the arid autumn landscape burned by a thousand summer suns, the smothering plain nestled among mountains, the pastures with their herds like ants, the multitude of paths taken by humans and animals through the valley, the bell towers and minarets crowded together over a millennium of migrations already foreshadow a country that can hardly be grasped, a country of mixed peoples, with identities, icons and flags always close to the surface—a country we will soon discover.

When our huge albatross alights on the runway, our eyes round as portholes are presented with the test of reality, the hard reality we had repressed beneath the bucolic image—the omnipresent (and all-powerful) KFOR[3] army surrounding the airfield, the khaki trucks, planes, helicopters and jeeps with their busy, disciplined soldiers standing on newly created berms that follow the contours of the hills and mountains. In the distance as in a set for a cinemascope movie, sentinels planted like stakes, leaning on rifles, looking from a distance like the little G.I. Joes of my sons' childhood games. I cannot ignore it any longer. War, real war, occurred not far from here such a short time ago. As our friend Olga, whom we met later, and who runs a peace studies centre at the University of Skopje, said, "The Kosovo war? We are in it, Madam. Now. Here." That was at our first meeting. Later, she called me by my first name, which she welcomed into her language, transposed, and transfused through the filter of affection, and I became Magdalena.

My colleague and I go down a small stairway onto the tarmac. I take with me the image of the haggard face of the charming young flight attendant rushing in tears toward the tail of the plane after the other passengers had got off, and stopping beside us—she needed to talk, to confide her sorrow to witnesses, who knows? "Is there anything we can do to help you?" I asked her, and in a rush between sobs, she said, "This is

---

3.   International peacekeeping force in Kosovo, whose rear
     bases are located in Macedonia.

my country and I don't recognize it anymore. It isn't my country anymore." And she turned away again and ran to the back of the plane and stood there, alone, her head against the wall of the Boeing that had become her boundary.

On the tarmac, amid the KFOR soldiers and just as many Macedonian police, carrying the image of the young flight attendant exiled from nowhere, no homeland, I hear in my head the voice of Anastasia, a woman from here, singing "The Death of Alexander," about their great mythic hero: "In sorrow I was born. In sadness I will die. On my tombstone, please write, my only sorrow, you will write." I take away that image like a talisman, and that song, before being swallowed up by the crowd in the miserable air terminal. Searching for the mountain that separates us from Kosovo to the north, far above the heads of the little soldiers dug in on KFOR's berms, I look up into the sky for the barrier of war, which we will see two days later from the top of the other mountain, to the south, Mount Vodno, which overlooks Skopje—Vodno, which, as Olga will tell us, "means in your language 'where there is water,'" because dozens of streams pour down the mountain to form the long Vardar River that flows from north to south into nearby Greece, where it's called the Axios but it's the same river. "There shouldn't be two countries," Olga will add, "nor three or four, there should be no borders, we are all citizens, no ethnic groups, and especially no religions, we are all citizens." I will see that wall of war between Macedonia and Kosovo, it's called Montenegro but it isn't the country of Montenegro, it's the mountain of the same name, because it's black, Black Mountain, with its dense forest of evergreens. And suddenly, against that threatening north, we will see a rainbow, swathed in mist in the slanting rays of the setting sun. "That's good luck, perhaps good luck for peace," Olga will murmur as if to herself.

At the terminal, there are as many policemen inside as out, and other men in civilian clothes, looking like secret agents in American movies of the Cold War era, grey men dressed all in black who all have the same mask in place of a face, whose dull eyes seem to be looking nowhere and yet see everything. On their belts, they're wearing walkie-talkies—they've got their guns in the inside pockets of their old-fashioned jackets, that's for sure—and they seem to have violence buried deep inside where we have hearts. They send shivers down our spines and yet I'm dripping with sweat in this bustling heat where we're shrouded in cigarette smoke. I will not look at those agents anymore.

But how can I forget that the war is a stone's throw away, or that it's the reason we've come here? That's the question I ask myself during the long wait at the customs post while a motley crowd of nervous, exhausted men, women and children push every which way, refusing to line up obediently despite the repeated admonitions of a policeman, whose angry shouts resound in the heavy, fetid air. All of us in the same migratory boat, clutching our passports like precious treasures, looking enviously at the privileged few with badges on their coats who, with smug smiles, go straight through—they are ethnic Macedonians or UN officials or members of NGOs[4] come to work in the region. We will wait a long time. Our heads full of questions and our eyes looking everywhere except at the agents, who give us the chills and whom we will not look at any more, our bodies stuck to each other, swaying in this swell of bodies, of breath mingling, we wait, the uneasiness of uncertainty mixed with the quiet, naive assurance that a Canadian passport opens all the doors in the world. And we go through.

On the other side, there are two glass doors behind which a thousand pairs of eyes in faces gaunt and grey with smoke are staring at us, the two most foreign of the group. How can we open these doors and cross this other border, and what do these people feel toward us? We push our way into the crush and in a cacophony of broken English we hear, "Taxis … fifty dollars … forty dollars … thirty dollars … taxis to Skopje." I'm smiling all around and saying "thank you, thank you," when a pleasant-looking man approaches us and almost sings, "Twenty dollars." He takes our baggage and we follow him to his old car. His name is Mirko, he wears a cross around his neck, and we ask, "You're Macedonian?" in English, of course, the only language we will speak here except among "cultivated people who speak French, a language of class," as Suzana will say later. And Mirko, fingering the cross at his neck, answers, "I am a Macedonian. But Orthodox."

---

4.   Non-governmental organizations.

On the other side too, it's war, religions, territories, divergent versions of history, as we very soon learn. War that speaks to us in the language of the Other, which they all seem to know, they've picked up American English, its words, its music blaring everywhere, its food—McDonald's and Coca-Cola are here as elsewhere —yet it is in that language that they all tell us of their rejection of America, its imperialism, and its thirst for power that provoked the Balkan war, dividing and conquering, carving up, region by region. The Americans are the new Turks, they all tell us in American to the sound of rock and roll, we lived under the yoke of the Ottoman Empire for five centuries, we will endure the new empire, we have a gift for suffering and in spite of everything will preserve our culture, the oldest in the world—and they are certain of it. What is NATO doing on our territory, what are the KFOR soldiers planning? Everyone, Europeans, Canadians, friendly peoples, you have been manipulated by the regents of imperialist terror in Washington (they say "Vashington"). There must be some good Americans, democrats, self-management socialists, citizens, but we don't know them. What are the KFOR soldiers planning if not the occupation of all our countries for a long time? "Go tell your people when you return, write it," Joana said to me in French, "Tell them that in Washington they are preparing for war here, tell them that we will suffer as they did in Bosnia and Kosovo. Tell them we are suffering now."

Never in our lives have we seen so many women crying and so many men smoking and talking endlessly in low voices. At times shouts echo from hill to hill and suddenly die out, disappearing as mysteriously as they came, like the fog that covers everything for days and suddenly lifts to reveal a magnificent methylene blue light above the ochre of the city, the crimson of the roofs. These gentle, gracious people stroll in the squares in the evening holding their children's hands and singing and laughing with them, eating ice-cream or sipping Coca-Cola, the children joyful, like all children, walking by the thousands at nightfall with parents who never scold them or hit them. Unlike in Paris, where it's commonplace for harried mothers to pick up the children at school, then rush through the shopping, then the homework, and then to bed, here the fall of evening seems to be a long moment of tender enjoyment and peace for everyone. When our questions about the Other finally dare to take form, we do not understand how there can be so much hatred. The Other, for the many Macedonian women and a few Macedonian men (all pacifists) we meet, is first the USA and NATO, whose KFOR troops are seen as a threat here, but above all, the Other is the Albanians, whether they come from Albania or Kosovo or have been Macedonian for centuries.

We do not understand the reasons for the words we hear a thousand times, "They are not civilized," *they* being, of course, the Albanians, from Albania, Kosovo, or Macedonia, and when we ask what they mean by "civilized," they all answer as if the same words came naturally to everyone's lips and had been taken in with their mothers' milk, as if these words circulated in their very blood, they answer with the same tautology: "They have no civilization." To our questioning looks, they all offer the same anecdotes as explanation—the only thing Albanians want to do is make children, usually ten per family, they can't dress them decently or educate them. "They have no education, no civilization," their only goal is to multiply in order to settle on our lands, in the west, from north to south, which is just what they're doing, driving us back toward the interior and further east near the Bulgarians, who, like them, made deals with the Nazis in World War II. They were fascists, supporting the Italians, who are just like them, except that the Italians have been civilized for a long time, but like them, they're corrupt, gangsters, and you'll see, with the help of NATO and KFOR, under the control of the USA, they'll carve up our little Macedonia region by region as they build their Greater Albania. We will be nothing more than a memory of civilization, we who invented the Renaissance long before Italy and Giotto. Go see the monastery of Saint Panteleimon, look at its superb frescoes from the twelfth century, and you'll understand the genius of our civilization.

And when we mention the Greater Serbia of Milosevic and the other bloodthirsty nationalists, when we dare to raise the issue of the terror in Kosovo, the ethnic cleansing, the denial of basic rights such as the right to education in their own language, the massacres, the burning and plundering of Kosovar Albanian towns and villages, when we speak of all the crimes against humanity committed just on the other side of Black Mountain to these peace-loving Macedonian women, the four rape camps set up by the Serb militias during the war, veritable brothels where young Albanian women were used as sexual cannon fodder, prisoners of the fantasies of their brutish tormentors, they reply, as nice as can be, that those supposed atrocities are propaganda fabrications of which, alas, we, like everyone in the West, have been the naive victims.

One of them, Katika, the only one we met who acknowledged the obvious, and who seemed to suffer in her own flesh the economic, political, cultural and sexual sufferings inflicted on the Kosovars and the Albanians in her country, said, weeping, "If the world were run by women, there would be no war." And when we asked her to say more, she answered with a flood of tears—where does all this salt water come from in the bodies of Macedonian women? A young musicologist working at the folklore center at the university collecting her people's old music, which, before independence in 1991, was "despised by the civilized people, the intellectuals," Katika suddenly sang us a lullaby from the time of the Ottoman occupation, one that grandmothers used to croon to their children: "The child of her Turkish mistress at her breast, Iana cursed it as she rocked it: 'Child of my mistress that today I rock, tomorrow, God willing, when my people are avenged, I will mourn your death. Because to the village festival I cannot go, to see my betrothed and to dance. Drink my milk today, I love you and you know it. But, God willing, I will mourn your death tomorrow when my people are avenged. I am your mama's slave, she is my mistress who forces me to stay here, close to you.'"

The same Katika, a little later, said to us point blank:
"Don't go across the Vardar River in the east to the
Albanian town with the big bazaar and all the mosques.
Don't cross any of the bridges separating us from them.
I suffer with them, but here, at home, on my side, with
my fellow Macedonians. I went there just once and I
was afraid, it still makes me shiver. All the men were
undressing me with their eyes. I know very well they
wouldn't have done anything to me—contrary to
what's said about them, they aren't rapists. But their eyes
were like hot coals burning through my body. And all
those Muslim women, those hordes of silent women
wearing scarves and ankle-length coats, they too stared
at me with so much hatred, I swear, I saw the hatred,
and I ran back to the bridge and across the Vardar,
breathless, and returned home, frightened to death."

And yet Katika is tall, sturdy and strong. We could
hardly understand. Where does this fear come from,
where does this desire come from, and what layers of
history are they buried under? We are thinking of this
mystery, the source of myth, as we cross the river the
next day, as we walk past the souks in the big bazaar,
penetrating deep into the maze of little streets teeming
with people busy selling things that seem to come from
every corner of the world—American and African
clothing, Turkish antiques, Greek and Italian jewellery,
French lamps, Swiss and German electrical appliances,
old-fashioned tinsmith's tools, Chinese sewing
machines and Japanese silks. We get a little lost in the
tin-roofed labyrinth of the food market, where there
are sheep hanging by their feet dripping blood in the

potted plants on the cobblestones, eggs by the dozen, and tons of all kinds of beans, rice and flour, beside mountains of peppers of all colours, garlic and onions. We lose our way, but the sun in the west, setting between Mount Vodno and Black Mountain, will guide us, and so will the ancient mosque we glimpsed as we came in, with its roof of broken tiles and its crumbling stone, its flowing sands measuring time for us.

We eat there, in the centre of a still-sunny square. Dozens of half-starved cats and weary-looking wasps fight over what we leave, we chase them away with the backs of our hands, making the hissing sound that's the same in every language. They leave as they came, to go beg elsewhere where the same fate awaits them. They didn't attack us, any more than the looks did. We only encountered busy men there, sometimes bent under their burdens but always answering our greetings with a smile and a friendly wave of the hand. As for the women, the young and less young all walk together, wearing those silk scarves and long fitted coats of fine serge in dark colours, they hold hands or walk arm in arm, apparently telling each other funny stories, they laugh together, sharing secrets in that language that eludes us, that sounds like a polyphonic choir. Discreetly, barely looking at them, we listen to their spoken songs and their laughter. From time to time, one of them, older, gives us a little smile with a hint of gentle mischief in the corner of her eye. We do not see what Katika experienced here. Was she in a different world from ours? Do the same geographic spaces contain as many hidden countries as there are souls walking in them? Will we tell Katika about this? Will we even see her again?

We leave gentle Macedonia with more questions than we came with, we will unfold them slowly, one by one, in the weeks and months to come, in keeping with the slowness of time in this young independent country, young and yet so old in its culture. Is that why the hands of the watches and clocks here move so much more slowly? We observed this again and again, whenever we checked the time, as if each day, eternally unwinding its minutes towards night, counted as four, and in a single week there we lived a whole month.

We take away with us the longing for an earlier time, a pure time, that seems to exist in all of them, accompanied by their music, sober and melancholy. That time of purity is always before today, before the loss of their Macedonia in Greece, before the Ottoman occupation, or before the dismemberment of Yugoslavia, the "self-managed, non-Bolshevik federation, far from Moscow, but just as far from American capitalism" that they all seem to miss, even those who voted yes in the referendum on independence. Along with the sweetness of life in this country, we will remember this mad desire for a time before, mixed with the terrible fear of what will happen after NATO leaves, and the pacifism expressed by all the women (and some men), combined with the rejection of the Other we are now going to visit.

We will have as a talisman a card Olga gave us on Mount Vodno, showing fragments of a fresco from the monastery of Saint Panteleimon, their great saint and model, who was martyred very young, his throat slit by the Turks. The fresco, Olga says, is "the apple of our eyes," like the entire monastery, "a sheer masterpiece from 1164, which by pure miracle escaped the earthquake of 1963, when Skopje was given its second name, Solidarity, because the Macedonians helped each other so much and showed such great courage." Olga tells us about the fragment of the fresco "The Mourning of Jesus Christ." At the top, the angels are preparing his way to paradise. Then, three apostles and Mary Magdalene are crying and kissing his bare feet and his hands. Then Jesus himself, naked in death, a veil over his sex, in the arms of Mary, his mother, who is crying. And not only in her arms, Olga says. "Look at her legs. They are open as in childbirth. She has her arms around her son's head and chest. Between her open legs, look, she is putting her son's body back into her own belly. Look, she is giving him life again. It will be another birth."

Olga continues, telling us about the Mothers' Movement Against War at the beginning of the wars that led to the break-up of Yugoslavia. "We didn't want our sons to go kill their brothers or be killed by them in Croatia." Women from all over Yugoslavia joined the movement, from Belgrade, Skopje, Sarajevo, Vukovar, Pristina. In the evenings they went to their town squares and army barracks with lighted candles, as in church. And they wept together, saying, "We want all our sons to come home." Olga adds, "I don't know if our demonstrations had any impact. Fighters love war.

How can you expect them to be moved by our tears? Tell me, if women hate war, why do they continue to raise fighters?"

Young Katika gave us her view of one of those nights when the group Women Against War cried together, holding lighted candles. It was nine years ago, when Katika was twenty, in the big central square of Skopje: "All the little flames, the long plaintive cry, the great cacophony of tears, it was dreadful, frightening. My mother was there among them. An old woman dragged me by force into that insane crowd. It was so violent, I was afraid, I ran all the way home and I cried all alone, my head buried in the pillows so I wouldn't hear what was outside. Women and war? I have just one thing to say: men or women, you have to fight when you're attacked."

KOSOVO

Kosovo

In the opaque Pristina night while sleepers toss and turn, gunshots rip through the black silence, post-war settlings of accounts that begin at nightfall in the unlighted streets and lanes. And night falls early—it's November, winter, but we wouldn't think so, accustomed as we are to measuring time by the cold. Here the days are hot and the hills that wind around the city are bathed in ochre and blue sunlight. Here the days are peaceful.

People come and go about their business, strolling to the sounds of music and car horns as they do in towns all over the world. The visible scars of the recent barbarism do not dim the sparkle of joy in the eyes and smiles turned toward the thousands of foreigners who have come since June to take part in their deliverance and the reconstruction of their ravaged country. But every night, when the spitting of bullets takes us back to the horror of the events the Albanian Kosovars went through over weeks, months and years that seemed to them a hellish eternity, we try to summon sleep with a litany of the names of their towns and villages in their

language. We no longer say Kosovo or Pristina in the
Serbian language, which is to them a murderous language
—we pronounce them "Kosova" and "Prishtina," and
we fall asleep all the same, our heads buffeted by that
other mournful sound that resonates from hill to hill,
the barking of hungry dogs, silent and invisible in the
daytime, whose language of the night echoes that of the
scattered belligerents, reminding sheltered humans of
the madness the dogs were witness to in their way, the
madness we try to forget during the dark hours so we
can find rest, because in the early morning, we will set
out again for the test of reality while the dogs sleep.

No, there was no war in Macedonia, our Skopje
pacifists had some crazy ideas, no, they have
experienced neither rapes nor mass graves nor looting
and shelling of houses nor the Serb expulsion of
Albanians from their universities, their schools and their
churches, nor the denial of all basic human rights for a
very long time, since Belgrade withdrew their
territory's status as an autonomous province. Yes, there
are some wars that are justified! Confronted with
attempts at ethnic cleansing by conquering armies and
peoples, confronted with murderous strategies for a
"final solution," other armies must intervene. There was
the absolute crime of the Shoah, which was thought to
be the last, the ultimate, and then East Timor, then
Rwanda, then Chechnya, and then Chiapas, and again
and again in other places—yes, a war to save the native
peoples of North and South America would have been
justified, yes, all the "civilizations" of the earth, the
languages, customs, religions and peoples, have a right

to exist, and no "civilization" is superior to another, and when we think that, it is the spirit of war that is moving us, men and women. War begins in the mind and the atrocities and the weapons come after, they are merely the tools.

To cross the border between Macedonia and Kosovo is to change worlds, to go from a state of peace, where everything thrives under the sun, to a state of war, where devastation reigns. Mirko, the kindest of men, had taken us by taxi to the border, but Mirko, who had not been back to Pristina since the war, couldn't go through the disorderly roadblocks staffed by irate Macedonian police and, on the other side, KFOR troops and UN military police, made up of men and a few women from dozens of countries under the authority, there at the Deneral Jancovic post, of the Greek forces. Mirko regretfully left us there, among a group of toothless, smoking Albanian taxi drivers who wrangled over us, potential customers. How had these wily, ragged Albanians suckled on war, who could communicate among themselves only by fighting and hurting each other, got around the Macedonian police roadblock? Two Macedonian boys of about twelve (why weren't they in school?) communicated in their language of signs and English numbers—"five dollars"—that they would walk the two kilometres to the Kosovar post with us. They loaded our baggage into their construction wheelbarrows, tying it on with old twine, and we set out on foot across the dusty ground, under a blazing sun, passing the long convoy of KFOR troops, UN and NGO vehicles, and a few anonymous civilians. But two

Hungarian soldiers, seeing our KFOR badges, invited us
to climb into their big khaki truck—salutations to you
two good Samaritans, and long live Hungary. It took us
two hours, at a snail's pace but in safety, to get to the
other side, where some Albanian boys greeted us with
the V-for-victory sign, laughter and words of welcome
that we understood despite the unfamiliar language.
The boys, at the windows, only had eyes for the
Hungarian soldiers' impressive rifles lying between the
seats, their shiny wooden butts touching our legs,
"Kalashnikov, Kalashnikov," they said, enraptured, they
would have loved to touch it, but the Hungarian soldiers forbade it. We smiled and said "no, no" as we
might have done with our own sons, they would have
loved to play with that weapon, as the boys of Pristina
play after school in packs in the yards and concrete
squares with balls or with toy rifles that look decep-
tively like the real ones and that go bang-bang like the
ones the big boys have.

Monday, November 1, All Saints' Day, and a day of
commemoration of their dead in the recent war, the
schools are out and the boys of Pristina spend the day
playing war while the girls, also outside and also
wearing American jeans and shoes made in Third World
countries, sing and play with household objects and
musical instruments they have made themselves from
whatever they've found in the piles of refuse everywhere in battered Pristina.

Sometimes the older boys play police—they've
managed to find whistles among the junk in the
makeshift stalls of the black market of the destitute,

where cartons of American cigarettes are stacked in pyramids. With whistle blasts and barked orders, these teenagers, dressed in the soccer uniforms of the world's major teams, have cleared the back yards of smaller kids or quiet girls. These boys who have not known Albanian police—the police here were Serb, and now they are international—have created their own, imitating the others, making their own law, and the mothers go by with their bags of groceries and smile at them, knowing that these boys will not be arrested by the Serb police, who took thousands of their fathers, their older brothers, their uncles and cousins to torture and often to death at the main police station downtown, which was practically destroyed by NATO bombs, and whose shell we see from our window.

When school lets out, they have only two short hours to play outside before the fall of the hard night, they brighten the city with their shouting, the girls sneak back, whispering a thousand secrets to each other and watching the littlest boys, who timidly approach the bigger ones, but nobody will hurt them. When they see us, all of them, whatever their ages, stare at the KFOR badges that have gained us entry to their territory, even the toddlers greet us with the victory sign and the ones who can talk all say, "Hi, hello, what is your name?" We tell them our names and smile, and I say in my own language, French, "Vive le Kosovo libre!" From the smiles that light up their faces, we see that they understand, their sufferings and privations have given them the gift of languages, they will never forget this polyglot host of foreigners in the khaki KFOR trucks and the gleaming white vans of the UN, Médecins du Monde, and three hundred and twenty NGOs, who move about their city so recently besieged by the Serbs and bombed by NATO planes. They will always remember these people in uniforms or strange outfits, with safari jackets and hiking boots, cameras, tape recorders, computers, notebooks. They will remember all these people who've left their countries whose names the children have seen only in the dry geography of schoolbooks, all these people they welcomed as liberators—which explains the jubilant atmosphere of this devastated city, the children's joy in being alive and playing, beyond the horror they have witnessed. They will not forget, will tell the story to their children and grandchildren, who will perhaps forgive their tormentors if they repent and atone.

While the girls and boys who have escaped the turmoil take advantage of the last rays of sun, flocks of crows cross the city from one hill to another. Late every afternoon they unfurl a long black sheet across the sky. It's as if their cawings herald the mournful sounds to follow—they resonate like a brass section, the raspy notes blending together to become a symphony, wave after wave, an overture that soon gives way to the guns and the dogs. But the crows choose to blend their aria with the cries of the children big and small, which grow louder as they pass. Do the children know that no other city in the world has as many crows as theirs? Did these companions of their days' last games still fly under the bombs? We will ask the children.

We asked our new friend Arta, who is thirteen years old but could be twenty—she's so tall, so deep, and her words are so beautiful. She already speaks four languages, including English, which she enjoys practising with us, and she'll start French later, she told us. Arta is vivacious, she looks like the great Semitic beauties of the Old Testament. She is Albanian and proud of it. She recounts the recent history of her oppressed people with such grave intelligence. When we asked about the crows, she seemed to feel there was some Western madness in us and quickly brought us back to her own questions, told us about their former school, from which they were driven by the Serbs, of the kilometres she walked to the clandestine Albanian school she had to go to for six years, about *their own* school—she stressed the possessive—empty of Serbs since the war, to which she had finally returned, about the extra hour she could now sleep in the morning because of the nearness of *her* school, about her aunt, her father's sister, who was killed by the Serbs, about all the parents of friends who were also killed. In the towns and villages and the countryside, where they all have family, there are orphans everywhere, parents without children, children without parents, Arta said, "In our hearts, we weep for our dead, and in our minds, we are putting a lot of knowledge and many languages, to rebuild our Kosova, we want to make it a jewel." Arta passed on thanks from her father, who doesn't speak our languages, he said that with the money from the apartment he is renting us, he can pay for private English lessons for his daughter. He's an electrician, poorly paid like all Kosovar tradesmen, since the high, well-paid positions were all taken over by the Serbs, but he's educated, except that, starting in 1989, the Albanians were systematically driven out of the civil service, the university and the hospitals, and had to do forced labour, except for a few crooked gangster collaborators—the way it's always been everywhere.

Looking at Arta, her ardent joy combined with a deep seriousness, with the sadness that passes like a fog over the eyes of all the children here, we realize that this maturity has been forged out of a people's pain and that the hardships give them a heightened awareness, a generosity of knowledge. What can we say to our spoiled children in our countries abounding in riches, in despicably complacent peace, how can we answer their questions that are unaware of the existential void? Is it necessary to suffer so much to become responsible, and so young? I heard Arta describe the horrors she and her people had experienced, and I heard the questions springing up in my mind. There was a long moment of silence in which it seemed to me that she had understood everything—and then that disarming smile of hers, common to the children here, that smile under their often tragic eyes and over their sorrows.

In the evening, the youngsters play, setting off firecrackers in the deserted streets of the city, imitating the sound of gunfire, frightening us so that we begin to wonder, are they real ones this time?—all the more so because the sirens of the police cars and ambulances are constantly howling, and already the yelping is starting, at the hour of the wolf, when the music of the crows has fallen silent and so have the joyful young voices. In the apartment without electric light, heat or running water, like all the others around us, I wonder what pushed us to this war, and to war in general, and what women have to do with it. I suddenly remember the words of a French friend, a brilliant journalist we met here: "I'm fascinated by war. I don't think that's morbid, but I'm fascinated." And deep down inside, I answer, "Me too," thinking of women who are unconditional pacifists, regardless of the circumstances, holier-than-thou types who say violence and murderous instincts are men's business only … which reminds me of two dreams of the previous night.

In the first one, an old Albanian woman killed herself by putting a gun in her mouth and pulling the trigger, and some men placed her in a cardboard coffin—there was no more wood or metal. She was old, and I was within her with my pain at the human catastrophe and she contained all the young Albanian women who had been raped during the dirty war of the Serb soldiers and militias. I was her, because I think of rape as a violent intrusion, of the mouth as well, from which words normally flow. In my mind were etched the words of that wonderful Albanian girl, Anda, a law student at the University of Pristina who was working with other women at the little aid centre for women and children in Kosovo—there would soon be other centres everywhere here, thanks to the financial help of Italian and Swedish women—"There were hundreds and hundreds of rapes here by the Serb soldiers and militiamen, you know. Rape is a weapon of war. They knew the mentality of the Albanian people, they knew that a virgin who was raped would not be able to find a husband, they knew that a married woman who was raped would be abandoned by her husband and his family, they knew that the women wouldn't say anything in the investigations by the International Criminal Tribunal. Because to be raped is shameful and the women feel guilty for the acts of those who knew that the best way to destabilize the Albanian population would be to destroy the family unit, our great strength. They knew our mentality well."

I was that old woman and I was capable of shooting any rapist bastard, of loading a gun, holding a revolver without shaking, even though I don't have a sex that's erect like a rifle, even though I'm not male. Faced with the nauseating fact that I slept in one of the beds of the Grand Hotel of Pristina before finding this apartment, before learning from Anda that the hotel had been a brothel for the rape of Albanian women, the only way not to be her, not to turn the weapon against myself, in my mouth that words come from, that has drunk milk and given kisses, the only way not to sink into absolute despair is to replace the gun with a pen, to find other words in the unfathomable mouth of writing. I came here to write, and to write is to see better and hear better. To write is to bear witness—and may the sceptics of the "highly civilized" countries keep away. Bearing witness doesn't sound good to them anymore, it sounds Catholic or sentimental, I've read it too many times. I am of every religion in the world and of none, I belong to no sect and believe in no dogma, I who have the good fortune not to have been raped come to countries at war to bear witness, to write of the harm done by war to women and children and innocent men.

In the other dream, I was being threatened by a group of Serbs dressed as Nazis, but no, it was not me they wanted to hurt. In front of my eyes they killed an Albanian, they placed him on my back and went at him with knives, his hands were hanging over my shoulders and down my chest, they turned colder and colder, his blood was dripping onto my feet, he was dying. I was him and not him, holding on my back the fate of all the Albanians, and in order to no longer carry that burden, like the cross of Christ from my childhood, I laid him down on the ground. I found a weapon on him, hidden in his clothing, I loaded it with several bullets without shaking, and spun around, killing the Serb soldiers dressed as Nazis one after another.

All the counsellors, all the shrinks of all the NGOs in the world who come here to treat the emotional wounds of the victims won't do any good unless they plumb the violence they carry deep down inside their own labyrinths.

Deep in the great book of sleep, the release of violence, page by page, prevents acting out. It is the only solution. There will be no peace as long as people resist their dreams, as long as they double-lock the door to the labyrinth, as long as the eyes of the soul, whose eyelids are sewn shut with steel thread, cannot see, deep within them, written out in full, the call to murder, as long as the ears, sealed like tombs, cannot hear the primordial animal instincts cried out line by line. But here, as everywhere in the East since the Bolshevik revolution, shrinks are banned, Freud forbidden and his writings burned, dreams and fantasies censored along with all religious or secular mythologies, all those fictions dangerous to socialist-realist peoples, lumped together in the same dustbin of history, the Western snakepit, petit-bourgeois individualism. From Lenin to Stalin through Hoxha and even Tito, all the same in this—the great book of sleep with its cortege of ghosts crying revenge had to remain hermetically sealed. They did not want to know that after the exhausting gallops through the violent forests of the black night, at dawn there is brightness that heals the real assaults of the test of reality, refused to admit, throughout this long century, that in the morning "one is silent again, but one carries the bright words in oneself," as Rainer Maria Rilke wrote in the *Lay of the Love and Death of Cornet Christopher Rilke*, refused to understand that those bright words are carried in oneself throughout the violence, page by page, carried like embryos to the edge of birth.

There are no talk therapies in Kosovo, we were told by the French psychoanalyst we met at the clinic run by Médecins du Monde, who was in charge of reestabishing the only psychiatric hospital in the country. There are one or two neuropsychiatrists, who treat patients with chemical or physical strait-jackets. The patients, held there in restraints, disoriented, are violent animals, often beaten, or catatonic zombies going through their whole lives with no concept of time or space, alone and alike in the midst of the herd, abandoned, for whatever reasons, "in the worst medieval conditions," as we were told by our psycho-analyst guide, who tries to start again at the beginning with each of them, to make diagnoses with a view to diversified treatments. Some of them were left in these places by mothers who were raped, who refused to raise these offspring of Serb men—"I would rather be killed than carry the child of a Serb," one of them told us. Some lost their minds after repeated torture sessions. Others, like mad people all over the world, have always been mad—that is what is written on paper yellowed and soiled by the years. There are no talk therapies, we are told, as well, by the women who run the aid centre for women and children, and in any case the women here would not be able to talk about rape—it's the shame, the fear of repudiation, they feel they are guilty. They are at least given counselling to make them understand it's not their fault, but in vain, they feel guilty, they want abortions without their husbands knowing—when they still have husbands. Fortunately the hospitals and clinics in Kosovo do abortions with-out hesitation, but they always do a brutal D and C, which injures or weakens these poor women's uteri. The mother of a fifteen-year-old girl told us, and repeated it twice, "I would rather my daughter be killed than raped by a Serb." We did not want to believe it was less painful to her to imagine her daughter dead, but we had to believe it since it was so often confirmed by others. We had to understand, had to go still further on the painful path of battered bodies and minds, to learn that often the women had not been able to get abortions, because, after raping them, the Serbs held them prisoner until after the fifth month of pregnancy. The heartbroken women would be released on the roads, where they would give birth in pain among the convoys of refugees, walled up in their silence and the silence of all, piercing it only with their screams during the arduous labour of childbirth in the arms of some silent midwife, not wanting to become attached to this *child of a Serb*, which they would nevertheless nurse at the breast, life being stronger than anything. But the infant would suck the milk of hatred, until, on the return from exile in the camps of Albania or Macedonia, it was abandoned on the doorstep of an orphanage or the psychiatric hospital, and the rapist who had wanted to set the belly of a Kosovar woman on fire with his pure Slav blood would perhaps one day, at a turn in his road of ashes, meet a son who would murder him.

One of our young friends, Xhelal, who had lived in Switzerland for three years and had returned last winter, like so many others, to fight in the ranks of the UCK (Kosovo Liberation Army), had tears in his eyes when we talked about his women compatriots who were raped. So taboo was the very word to him that he averted his gaze, unable to utter it or talk about it. We respected that embarrassment, our silence joined with his for infinite seconds. Suddenly he took a letter from his pocket and unfolded it to read to us. It was the story of a friend of his, Sevda, who, with her husband, Esat, had fled the war in Bosnia. "They had lived in Sarajevo, and they came to Kosovo in 1993, at the very beginning of the Serbs' other war. Here Esat, like me, joined the men of the UCK. He was killed in the first weeks, in an ambush in the mountains of Suva Reka, and my friend Sevda, who loved him more than anything in the world, could not stay here anymore and says she will never come back. She went to Sweden to stay with friends of friends. Before leaving, she gave me this paper, it is a passage from St. Augustine's *Confessions*, which she studied among the Catholic Croats at the University of Sarajevo before the war."

My friend Xhelal, very dear to my heart, keep this text as a talisman, it will tell you why I am leaving, why I am leaving my Esat in the scorched earth of Kosovo, we who had left so many friends in that of Sarajevo.

I was astonished to see other mortals alive since he was dead, the one I had loved as if he would never die; and I was even more astonished, with him dead, to be alive myself, I who was his other self ... Yes, I felt that his soul and mine were one soul in two bodies; that is why I had a horror of life, I no longer wanted to live, reduced to half of myself. And perhaps I was afraid to die only for fear that he whom I had loved so much would die completely.

You see, Xhelal, what Augustine's friend was to him, Esat was to me. I am not totally leaving my Kosovo, half of me is buried there with him.

We listen to Xhelal, who looks like an angel, but
when he shows us his photographs of himself in
uniform, Kalashnikov in hand, he looks tough as nails
and we don't recognize him. Xhelal replies that he is
two people, one, the gentle one we know, and the
other, a violent one, who surprised even himself the
first time he put on the uniform, carried the rifle, and
took the oath "to kill all the Serbs of the earth, down
to the last one" in front of his comrades. War makes
human beings double, it causes a split in them. That's
why some go mad afterwards, they cannot put the two
images back together again, like those raped women
who become detached from themselves and talk about
the horrors they experienced as if it were others who
suffered them. And in order to understand and
sympathize, we have to try to slip into that in-between
place that is barely perceptible but that opens onto a
yawning abyss, that place between self and Other in
them and in ourselves. And how can we comprehend
the extraordinary decision of that raped girl, Fatime,
who was taken away to one of the brothels set up by
the Serbs after the death of Reshat, her fiancé, Fatime,
who left for Germany with a group of refugees,
determined to continue her pregnancy to term, to
bring the "child of a Serb" into the world and raise it
without anybody ever knowing its origin? What will
become of this son or daughter of Slavic-Kosovar
lineage, how will Fatime answer if, as an adolescent, he
or she one day asks for an explanation, how will she
accept his violence, if it's a boy, or her melancholy, if it's
a girl? But does Fatime, who left for Germany for the

sole purpose of bringing her child into the world and raising it, all traces of torture seemingly obliterated when she laid her hands on her warm belly to feel life moving within her, the only life remaining to her, like a treasure being carried away—does Fatime ask herself these questions?

After nightfall, against the ultra-contemporary music of KFOR's helicopters and supersonic planes, the gunshots from a city bled dry, and the barking of the starving dogs that sound as if they've turned back into wolves, I hear the generous words of Samka, the nurse at the aid centre for women and children. She talks continuously, her words are such a balm to her, her stories and anecdotes that she knits for us, stitch by stitch, plain and purl, trying to make them into one piece that holds together, a fabric without holes, knitting back together for us and for herself what was once unravelled every which way, wanting to put a little meaning into the recent chaos in which all reason vanished. Samka talks continuously, but coherently and clearly. Suddenly the flood stops, she turns towards the wall, her head on her folded arm, and another flood takes over from the words, a flood of tears that she hides from us but that we hear. Then, abruptly, she wipes her nose and turns towards us, her grief blown over like a storm, she looks us straight in the eye, and a cloud of anger passes quickly across her gaze. I think I hear within me the words she has censored out of politeness: "What are you doing here, you cannot know, even if I told you for a thousand years, you could never know." But no, I am mistaken, this time it is hatred we are seeing on her face, and she says, through young Anda, her interpreter and ours: "You know, the NATO leaders and Kouchner, at the UN, are creating plans for ethnic reunification in their nice big notebooks and on their expensive computers, but it will be a complete tragedy if they force us to live with the Serbs. We can no longer live together with our tormentors, they will put us through hell, every day will be an eternity of torture for us. If the Serbs are there, we will never be able to bind our wounds, to forget a little, to sleep peacefully sometimes ... "

As much as we are not racist and we believe that all the peoples of the earth are equal, that one ethnic group is as good as another, and that every language is a treasure, as much as we are pacifist, stateless and without borders in spirit, we feel, just as much, that well-intentioned ideologues are completely mistaken, are falling into the pure utopianism of the now-dimmed Enlightenment if they believe that, from one day to the next, victims and executioners can share the same land, the same house, the same table, the same bed. Their commendable intentions of bi-, tri- or multi-ethnic territories are completely utopian, and we know the way to human hell is paved with good intentions. We know it would have been unthinkable after the Shoah to force the Jewish victims to live side by side with their Nazi executioners. If it is true—and it is true—that a great many of the victims could no longer "write after Auschwitz," to make them live on the same soil as their tormentors would have been to force them to relive their ordeal. We say all this to Zamka, adding that it takes generations before the victims are able to forgive the executioners, and besides, as Vladimir Jankélévitch wrote in *L'Imprescriptible*, only the immediate victims can forgive, and they are dead. But still, just for the great-grandchildren of the victims to be able to talk to the great-grandchildren of the executioners, the executioners would have to have atoned, made amends and asked forgiveness. The representatives of the UN, NATO, the European Union and the NGOs, not to mention all the well-intentioned ideologues, should know that, on the territory of genocide, multi-ethnicity is a completely different matter, that there are contaminated, mined areas where executioners and victims can be blown up, together or separately. Their combined presence on the still-burning soil is a time bomb, and if anyone should leave, it is obviously the executioners. If anyone should lick and bind their wounds, peaceful and alone, it is obviously the victims. We say this to Zamka with the help of the ears and mouth of our young interpreter, Anda, a law student who works in this centre "to remake life." The cloud of rage and hatred has left Zamka's face and Anda smiles with a salty mist over her eyes. Zamka comes and kisses us and says, "You know, it will take a long time for them to understand, but in the meantime they are protecting us."

The following day, we are crossing the Drenica Valley, its beauty now tragic with the light shining down from the mountains on the charred and plundered houses but also on the fields freshly ploughed by Albanian Kosovars who have returned from the camps to bury their dead, rebuild their red brick houses and work the land, and on the kilometres of hillside vineyards that the Serb owners quickly abandoned on the arrival of the KFOR troops, taking care to mine them so that the delicious *kaberne sovinjon* will not flow again for a long time. We think again of the words of young Anda: "There was no hatred between the Serbs and us before, before the years of propaganda by the Belgrade butchers and their allies. My best friend is Serb, she's a refugee in Belgrade and will probably never come back, she feels too guilty about what they did to us. She sent me an e-mail message here at the centre after I came back from Albania. We were together at university. She said she was so happy, so relieved to know I was alive. I didn't reply, I can't, I can't find the words, but I still love her. We—young people and women—we didn't want this war, even the few women who joined our comrades in the UCK and took up arms. Women love the life they give too much to kill, but we had to defend ourselves. Now that they have worked in solidarity, side by side with our warriors, maybe things will change in the home, maybe they will no longer be subservient to men, maybe they will no longer be mere breeders, objects of their men's desires. We will work so that they can go to school, they need to be educated as much as boys. One day, now that the schools belong to us and are no longer clandestine, now that parents are not tortured or imprisoned just for sending their children to school, one day we will no longer spend our time searching for our disappeared, whose images you see posted on every tree. One day the Albanian girls and women of Kosovo will take off their scarves and long coats, the signs of their submission to their male masters. And if things don't change, then I will change countries. I don't want to get married if things are like that. I will never obey a man, even one from my clan, even if I cherish him with all my heart."We carry within us these words of hope from Anda, a blond, blooming young Albanian woman of mixed Turkish blood, and we think every twenty-year-old girl in our overstuffed countries should hear them. These words of hope echo over the devastated, mined valley of Drenica and in this brand-new car of Médecins du Monde, with the young Albanian driver and Merite the interpreter, who is twenty-five years old, like the driver and like Anda, and vibrant and lovely. We have been invited to the gynecology clinic in the village of Malisheve, by Henriette, a French mid-wife in her fifties, free and courageous.

In the clinic, we encounter all the misery of the world. We see a procession of some forty women, all of whom are poor and have experienced the mass deportation and the camps, and some of whom have lost their men—fathers, husbands, brothers or sons, dead or disappeared. But they don't talk about them, they haven't come here for that, they are here for their troubles of the belly and of children. Almost all of them have too many children and would like abortions, here, right away, "with just an injection," without their husbands knowing, but Henriette tells them it's done in the hospital in Pristina, and when she deems it appropriate, she writes them referrals. Others want IUDs or they want her to remove the ones they have had without medical supervision for six years, which are causing them stomach pains, kidney pains, yellow discharges, infections. Many, trembling, dark circles under their eyes, come for pregnancy tests; a few burst out laughing in relief when they hear they are not pregnant; others are stricken to hear that they are; some, very few, are happy to learn they are going have a child, but they want a boy, "because a girl is nothing, abort it if it's a girl, please, doctor, if I don't have a boy, I will never be able to exercise a mother-in-law's power over a daughter-in-law or have any control of money," because boys inherit and girls don't, so it is the mother and father of the boy who control the lineage. "I'll die without that power," says one of them. "I have been subservient all my life to the authority of my husband and my mother-in-law. My father-in-law threw stones at me whenever he felt like it. I want to have my turn to exercise authority over my daughter-in-law. Give me a boy."

Another, who already has four girls, says, "I have no children, give me something." Henriette the midwife answers, "But you have four children!" and she repeats, "I have no children, I have no boys." And then an already-old woman—who we learn is only thirty-four, misery makes them fade so early—this already-old woman who was once beautiful, you can see it, and who is bowed under the heavy burden of life, says she is sterile. Henriette tested both of them at the Pristina hospital and proved that it's the husband who is sterile. She tries to explain, but the woman doesn't understand. She says it's impossible, that her husband has been beating her for eight years, every time he takes her violently and her belly does not grow big, that he will beat her again tonight when she comes back "with no treatment from the French woman doctor for the barren womb that gives him no son" and denies him power over his dreamed-of line. Merite, her compatriot, Henriette's interpreter and assistant, tries in vain to make her understand the reproductive process. The others continue in procession. One, who is older, forty-four, with thirteen children, wants an IUD. Another, thirty-three, beaten down by life, with eight children already, wants an abortion, but has no money and no husband, he died when she was in the deportation camp with her family, and an abortion costs money, "and where would I put this baby, with the house burned down, the animals scattered, the land mined?" Henriette is sure it was a rape, and she will see about an abortion. A last one comes to tell her sorrow, she's "sterile," with only two girls, "sterile," because with no sons, her husband has come back from the camp and said, "That's it, your sister-in-law has found me another wife." That is how things are always settled, Merite tells us when we are alone, and she weeps for all the others who have no more tears left, only yellow liquid that seeps from them. They all are infected, Henriette says, they "have relations at their husbands' will, without any hygiene for either of them." Like young Anda, Merite

weeps torrents of tears. Merite is twenty-six years old:
"I do not want to be mistreated by a husband, I do not
want a cruel mother-in-law or a father-in-law who
throws stones at me. I am ashamed, ashamed of my
people, ashamed of this misery. It is a war within the
war, what goes on in their homes. It is a war of men
against women. I will leave if things do not change. I do
not want to obey or to wear the clothing of our
submission"—she's dressed like young women all over
the world and is beautifully made-up in the Ottoman
style—"It is a war within the war. I will work to change
things. The girls will go to school now that our Serb
tormenters are gone. If things do not change and if the
corruption of our men continues, I will leave."

The four of us talk, Henriette, Merite, my colleague
and I, friends contemplating the sufferings of a people,
the atrocities we've witnessed. Suddenly there's a burst
of laughter from Merite across the poor, shabby little
room where we are sitting, Henriette's makeshift office.
My colleague and I had stayed because the women all
wanted us to be there, they had asked Henriette to let
us, they didn't even want us to leave during the
examinations. They took our hands and placed them on
their bellies and told us their stories as if we understood
their language, and we answered in ours, beyond the
translatable, but above all in the untranslatable. We heard
their sorrows, and they, our shocked compassion. They
took my colleague's microphone and spoke into it. We
said Quebec and Canada and they laughed, satisfaction
in their eyes, because they would be heard there, very
far away, elsewhere, and perhaps be healed by it, you

never know. With my pen I discreetly took notes, and when I stopped, they pulled the notebook out of my jacket and leaned over my shoulder, looking with wonder at the sight of their miserable fate in writing.

Merite's laughter resounded across the little examination room because the very last patient had just come in, with a baby in her arms in swaddling clothes covered with a blue satin quilt embroidered with little bears and red and white rabbits—she was eighteen and radiant. She said, and Merite translated for us, laughing, "It's a boy, he is called Clinton, we named him Clinton because it was Clinton who brought us back to our country." Clinton is five weeks old, in perfect health, cries like all babies in the world—they all have the same language before languages separate them—and weighs four kilos, two grams. He was conceived in desolation but after the horror, after the NATO troops had moved in here, probably to stay for a long time.

As we left Malisheve, the sun was setting in an orange ball across the valley, and in the half-light of dusk we could make out the skeleton of the humble primary school burned by the Serbs, but the sound of hammering and the shadows of men on the roof working to rebuild it came down to the battered road from which we were silently looking at the holes the bombs had dug in the vineyard. Our young driver, Arbem, who offered us a Coke, did not want to be paid, he said, in English, "I am paid by Médecins du Monde, who, like Henriette, have come to help my people. I am happy to give them a little gift." Later, on the way back,

Merite told him, in their language, what she remembered of the day.

Tomorrow we will leave for Muschtich, near Suva Reka, and perhaps go to Prizren, which they say is magnificent, unlike Pristina. We will continue our trip and, strangely, when we return home, this image of Kosovo at nightfall will cheer us until our last look at the inhuman condition.

Bosnia-Herzegovina

Bosnia-Herzegovina

Stone and concrete ruins greet us on our entry into Sarajevo, although they are modestly veiled in mist, and soon there is a curtain of rain between them and us in the dark late-afternoon. The devastated city does not show its charred and dismembered bodies to all comers, it jealously guards its secrets from voyeuristic intruders. But this first welcome by the ruins speaks to us in ash-covered words that we learn to read although we will never see the words of the National Library, which was shelled by the Serb army, its books, manuscripts and archives all vanished in smoke. We see from its gutted walls, which are still standing, that it rose proudly in the centre of the old Muslim city. In this monument built in the imperial style under the Austro-Hungarian occupation, we will seek the stigmata of history, of the wrath of history towards the Bosnian Slavs who converted to Islam under the Ottoman Empire, we will try to capture the dead words of their Turkish, Austrian and Hungarian ancestors and of the many other peoples transplanted to Bosnia and mixed with them, who have created the richness and beauty of this multi-ethnic land. We will imagine, beyond this bombed-out treasure, what was and what remains, what still exists of a people the Serb war criminals Milosevic, Karadzic, Mladic, et al. tried to murder, body and soul, during those endless years when they wreaked havoc under the impotent gaze of the disarmed forces of UNPROFOR,[5] when the plan of "ethnic cleansing" against the Bosnian Muslims had been perfectly obvious for a long time.

As we stroll through the blackness of the ruins, we try to grasp the unimaginable, to understand why and how these Bosnian Muslims were pushed from every direction into a murderous holy war, attacked both by the Orthodox Serbs, in Sarajevo, Srebrenica and elsewhere in their territories, and by the Catholic Croats, mainly in Mostar, another long-suffering city. That first night, when the only answers the earth offers are mass graves and mined fields, we send our questions up to the stars that shine down on hundreds of minarets, dozens of Orthodox churches and the strange Catholic cathedral, newly restored, that dominates the new city. The only answer is the silence of the thousands of dead, the thousands displaced within the territory of Bosnia, the thousands of refugees outside its borders, scattered to the four winds, the silence foreshadowing the "immense depression of the survivors," in the words of so many women we meet. The men, say the women, have become catatonic, and no longer talk about that.

---

5.   The United Nations Protection Force in the former Yugoslavia.

Because they were defeated? Because they feel guilty? Because they did not die heroes? The women can't say. Faced with the great void, they make hypotheses, predictions. One, whose name is Mirheta and who is twenty-four, says, "I took up arms after the burning of my village, Visegrad, and my house. I went to the mountains with my father, who was killed in the fighting. I have been wearing the scarf since his death. I had cut off my hair and put on the cap and uniform of the soldiers, who called me 'little guy.' I had a hand grenade always ready to throw, and a dagger in my belt. I almost died of cold, of hunger, of fear. I saw so many of my people die. And yet I do not despair, I comfort my mother and my brothers as best I can, I've almost stopped having nightmares. Though I freeze in the apartment where we squat in Sarajevo, though I am hungry, though I study by candlelight, I am not discouraged. So, what is the matter with our men that they retreat into silence? Although we fear the return of the Serb former owners, who will throw us out to sell the apartment and go back to the Republika Srpska,[6] where we come from and where they do not let us return, I am not disheartened. What right do the men of my people have to give up? Although my mother cries out every night in her dreams because she can never go back to the

---

6. The Bosnian Serb Republic; following the Dayton accord, which was signed in Paris in December 1995, Bosnia and Herzegovina was divided into two geopolitical entities: the Muslim-Croat Federation which occupies 51 percent of the territory, and the Bosnian Serb Republic, which occupies the rest.

grave of her husband buried in Republika Srpska, I am
not overcome with grief. Why are they?"

In the morning, under the fog that hides the hills and
mountains in the distance, I remember what Valida told
us the day before. She and Mumo had come to pick us
up at the airport and had taken us on a "tour of the
ruins" with the cheerfulness of people going to a comic
opera, I didn't know why. Valida had talked about an old
Muslim woman who, after the war, had killed herself
with a bullet in the mouth. So my dream from Kosovo
had really happened here. I will place this dream among
so many phrases heard subsequently, I will unfold it like
a letter in the pocket of my heart. I will also remember
this story of Mirheta's. Before the war, in her village, her
best friend was Serb, her name was Emma, they lost
touch with each other during the war, and after the war
Emma committed suicide, hanged herself, "because she
was guilty of having a father who was a paramilitary
who killed Muslims." Mirheta concluded, "I prefer to
mourn my father dead in combat than to have to hang
myself for a parent who is a murderer." In the morning
under the fog, these words resonant with death are with
us as we descend the side of the hill to the deepest part
of the basin where Sarajevo lies, to the shore of the
Miljacka River, its bronze-coloured water flowing in
the mist. As we cross one of its many bridges with no
name posted, we hear a polyphonic quartet made up of
the muezzins' voices from the chimney-shaped
minarets, the pealing of the bells of the cathedral, the
church bells in minor keys and the hammering of
reconstruction. The bronze water flows gently through
it all, bringing back the memory of what Valida said in

the most devastated area of the old city, facing the
mountain dotted with stones and shadows: "We call this
place Hiroshima now." And in front of the ruins of
stone, of concrete, and of souls, on the little bridge
spanning the Miljacka, I promise myself that I will
write *Sarajevo, mon amour.*

At the middle of the bridge, we suddenly come upon
a plaque with this inscription engraved on it: "A drop
of my blood was shed so that Bosnia may live." It was
for the first victim of the war, Suada Dilberovic, a
young woman who fell there under Serb fire during a
peaceful demonstration in 1992. Drops of blood, drops
of water from the river, drops of ink mix together on
the bridge, which is now named after Suada Dilberovic.

In the misty ruins of battered Sarajevo—which "has
kept its soul," as those who knew it before the carnage
say—among the faded pastel colours of the buildings,
along the streets lively with bistros and cafés, through a
labyrinthine bazaar filled with a thousand discoveries, a
thousand lives that are being reborn in spite of everything, and a thousand memories on display—including
postcards for tourists, with photographs of the ruins of
libraries, university, bridges, maternity hospital, schools,
etc., which we don't buy, incapable of distancing
ourselves, through these fixed images, from the feverish
reality that totally absorbs us—we walk for hours on
the pink and ochre paving stones cut in hundreds of
different ways. Treading these mosaics from another
time, we walk through elsewhere by the mere fact that
our footsteps are in the patterns. We walk past the

Markale Market, where a hundred and forty civilians were killed by a shell fired by the Serb army in 1995. "That was not war," said Mirheta, "War is between two armies. That was the deliberate murder of unarmed civilians. We were like the Jews in the Shoah. It was not by chance that they even set up their guns in the middle of the Jewish cemetery, on the southeast hill. They profaned and destroyed the Jewish cemetery to set up the weapons of our death." The hatred was so strong, so extreme, that a Serb mother whose name I won't reveal, married to a Muslim, left her husband at the beginning of the war and went to Serbia, left him alone with their two daughters, "because they have Muslim blood in their veins," she wrote in a note. She never returned, never sent news, and the two teenage girls "lost their wings to fly in life," Xenana, a psychologist, told us. "What can I do but comfort them? The father died during the war, and they are with their paternal aunt, who went mad after losing two sons and her husband. What can I do, with no supervisor to talk to, nobody to help me?" Walking past the market, which we refused to enter out of respect, we spend a long time looking at the well-fed people filling their baskets and shopping bags, their arms laden with the many-coloured flowers that grow in abundance in the gardens and surrounding suburbs, the children with their wide eyes filled with unanswered questions, smiling, holding ice-creams or pastries. I wonder, thinking of the Serb mother who abandoned her daughters with their "impure blood," if the women, who of course have less blood on their hands, are not also in the war, in its spirit, in its ferment, sewn into it with the thread of racism and ethnic hatred. From Macedonia and Kosovo to Sarajevo, I have heard such bitter, hate-filled words from them—about the "uncivilized"Albanians, the Slovenes,"rich Catholics of the former Yugoslavia who stole the woods and the mines of Bosnia and then wanted only to pull out and declare their independence," the Croats, "all of them Ustachi in the pay of Rome," the Serbs, "practically all of them Chetniks,[7] renegade royalists and nationalists," or the Macedonians, "cowards corrupted by their Albanian neighbours." I've heard so much hatred, it seems to come from a bottomless well, so much resentment, bitterness, rancour, that to understand even a little I have to look for the repressed and analyze its turns and returns. From the severed tongues of the Bolshevik period, the languages of extinct religions and empires, to the supposedly peaceful half-century under the big umbrella of neutralizing Titoism, when terror and suspicion reigned supreme, as they did everywhere in the so-called communist East—secret agents, double agents, wiretapping, private conversations recorded, freedom of speech flouted, freedom of expression crushed, arbitrary arrests, imprisonment, torture, minds under surveillance—tongues severed that, now, like dragons of old breathing flames in all directions, proclaim to anyone who will listen the decades and the centuries of suppressed antipathies.

---

7. The Chetniks and the Ustachi were extreme Serb and Croat Nationalists allied with the Nazis in World War II.

Facing the carnage, the human ruins and the ruins of stone, I had sought solidarities, I had hoped to find alliances, sympathies that I still believed must exist between the Bosnian Muslims five years after the war and the Kosovar Muslims with one foot still in the abyss of genocide—but no, I was wrong. "*We* are Slavs, *we* are civilized." (That word again! one more time and I'll get mad!) "*They're* Albanians, that *wild* people—how do you say in French, *sauvages*. Our shared religion does not matter now, we have nothing in common with those barbarians!" And true to myself, inside, I sided with the "savages," as I often did in my own country, where we have so much to learn from the Amerindians if only we would take off the blinkers of an arrogant white culture. I developed a keen affection for the most outcast of the outcast in the former Yugoslavia, where it seems people drink hatred with their soup. What propaganda was concocted, how, and for how many years, even before the apartheid imposed on the Albanian Kosovars, during a decade under the yoke of Belgrade? We will ask these questions of a group of women historians we are to meet.

The night after hearing the hatred spewed from the mouths of so many women who are nonetheless so gentle, who swear that, in their flesh and the flesh of their loved ones, they are the grieving victims of the most treacherous discrimination, I dreamed I had lost my shoes and couldn't go out or walk anymore, it was the end of the adventure and I was packing my bags to return home, but in my anxiety at being unable to leave for lack of shoes, I heard myself singing, "My shoes cannot travel anymore ... ,"[8] which woke me with a start.

Again in the morning, we had to go through the fog—will we ever see the sun here, and the blue sky?—to find our landmarks in the half-light with our inner compass and sextant, to track down some sign of the continuity of the world, to try to decipher in the ruins and wounds of war, beyond the raw hatred, the signs of life, hope and humanity. To follow the path written within paradox, to imagine that the words gone up in smoke in the burning of the National Library had spared a few letters, which fell back down with the ashes, a strange alphabet gathered by passers-by in the form of a future poem, to think that other manuscripts will be written, other books will see the light of day, new archives will again bear witness, that the ordeal by fire of people and of paper will set ablaze words newborn in the *auto-da-fé*. Listening to the familiar sounds of the market, the bazaar, the schoolyards, the single little tram that circles the city endlessly, and the workmen involved in reconstruction under the super-vision of SFOR[9] soldiers speaking every language, we move forward, remembering another story of burned books, told by some Bosnians who took refuge from

---

8. A well-known song by Félix Leclerc, the father of the Quebec *chansonniers*, begins, "My shoes have travelled a lot" (tr. note: our translation).
9. The international Stabilization Force in Bosnia and Herzegovina.

the war in western Canada. They had been so frozen during the interminable siege of Sarajevo—they couldn't find any more trees to burn on the denuded hillsides from which Serb snipers were firing shells and bullets, and they had burned every stick of furniture in their house—that they finally resigned themselves to sacrificing the treasures of a huge library, one by one, books, journals, encyclopedias, and finally, dictionaries in twelve languages, ancient and modern. Their memory of war is of *that* most of all, of a library that kept them from dying but whose loss killed part of their soul. "After we lost this family heritage, there was nothing more to keep us in Sarajevo. We wanted to go elsewhere, very far away, and the farthest elsewhere was Canada, the great plains of the West where you can see forever, where we could imagine losing ourselves and never coming back." If there is no longer any road visible on the horizon, we will dig underground to move forward, we will write underground paragraphs like the tunnel bored under Mount Igman by the local people during the war that allowed them to get through the natural fortress of the Dinaric Alps, which were occupied by the Serb army, to smuggle food, drugs and weapons, but also people wanting to escape, in one direction or the other. To this ingenious feat of amateur engineering on which women worked as well as men—"that is why we are so proud of it," said Hanifa, because it wove a "new solidarity" between the women and the men—we will dedicate our few chapters stolen from the shadows, although it is midday.

She is sitting on a stool at the back of a common room in that ridiculous shack that serves as a psychiatric shelter. She is there, absent, in the midst of all the exiles in their own country—women and men who have seen too much, heard too much, suffered too much, and whom the Centre for Torture Victims, Sarajevo, cannot hold or help. The attendants told us She did not need chemical drugs, She doesn't shout, sleeps and eats well, is not violent, doesn't bother anybody, She only raves quietly in her corner, from sunup to sundown. I approach her slowly, hear her litany in a language I don't recognize, I don't know Serbo-Croatian, but only the Serbs still use that term, the Croats now say Croato-Serb, and the others, the few neutral Yugoslavs and the Muslims, say Bosnian—you mustn't ever make a mistake here, you have to pay attention to who it is you're talking to. She is raving in Bosnian, then, since She's wearing a scarf, blue like her eyes. I see a wisp of jet-black hair. In fact She looks like a vestal virgin of ancient Asia Minor as imagined in children's books. My heart in my mouth, I step forward. She doesn't see me and continues her monologue, facing a dirty window that looks out on greyness, on nothing at all, but She seems to see something there that escapes me. She turns suddenly and looks me straight in the eye, her eyes are far from crazy. Abruptly her tone changes, and She says in a rush: "Never call me by my name, do not give me a nickname either, if you write about me, call me X." She speaks excellent French, and had heard me say when I came in that I wrote books. I say, "If I call you She, will that be alright?" She says yes, and continues: "I was raped and tortured by five Chetniks during the war. I had taken refuge in the forest with my brother. One night, my brother had gone to look for something to eat and they took me. I will not tell you the details, but it was the end of the world in my whole body. I do not want anybody to write what they did to me, it would make a pervert tremble. My brother found me the next morning in the bushes. He spent many days and nights bandaging my wounds and setting my bones. Write that not all Muslims repudiate their raped sisters or wives—my brother loved me as no one else did, neither my mother or father nor my fiancé, who died in combat, loved me as he did. I loved him for months with all my heart, all my body. It was not incest, and if it was, I don't care, it was pure healing kindness. Then my brother was killed too. It took me days to find his body, I finally found it curled up in a hole from a shell. I washed him from head to foot with water from the brook nearby, mixed with my tears and my kisses, then I dug him a different grave from the hole from the shell, I lay down on him, I sang him all the lullabies of our childhood. I don't know how long I stayed there, but one morning some people from my village came. They buried my brother and put a round stone on his grave. We went down to Sarajevo like mad people. It was hell there too. After the war, Bosnian soldiers came to find as many dead as they could. My brother was taken with the others to the big new cemetery over there on the hill, to the west, which I can see when the fog lifts." She falls silent, turns her blue eyes away, and goes back to her chanting, facing the dirty grey window that all day long connects her to her dead love, her lost brother.

The attendants asked me what we could have said to each other, but I didn't answer, only smiled, keeping her confidences for the writing. That's what She wanted, She wanted her story to be printed on a blank page, wanted her body and that of her brother to be laid down together, for their fluids to touch once again, the salt of tears, sperm and blood, the sweetness of milk and kisses, absorbed through ink.

When I saw her again—because She wanted me to come back—the scenario was at first the same, with her on her stool at the back of the gloomy room, the same dirty grey window through which She looked out towards the earthen bed of her beloved brother on the bare hill, addressing her delirious lament to him alone. She suddenly turned and said to me: "After you left, that night, I dreamed for the first time. Write that. Not far from me there was a Serb woman, about your age— I figure you're forty-five—she was dressed in black, like all Serb women, and she tried to kill me just with her look. She was the mother of one of the rapists who were my tormentors. There was a Bosnian peasant nearby, carrying a huge pitchfork as a weapon, which he handed to me, saying, 'Avenge yourself, it is the only solution, but in dreams alone. We must put an end to war.' I grabbed the pitchfork and drove it into the belly of that rapist's mother, I saw the blood and viscera pour out, and the peasant said, 'It is the rapist shit, the rapist's mother you are freeing yourself of by killing.' He talked like a professor I had at the university before the war— we don't know now if he's dead or alive, he disappeared. I have always been against violence and yet, look what I dreamed of. I no longer feel guilty, I woke up happy that morning. Why did I attack the mother and not the rapist? That is my only question. If God existed, and if I *really* believed in Him, He would be a God of dreams. He would help us to penetrate our great mysteries of the night. Do not see this scarf on my head as a sign of faith. It is my wedding veil, mine alone since the death of my brother. It is the sign of our marriage bond, the ring with which I encircle my spirit to celebrate our wedding beyond the grave, beyond life. No religion can comfort me, neither yours nor mine. I would embrace one whose God was a man and a woman, made flesh to love each other eternally."

No, no religion was ever that of a couple who love each other as She imagined. Here they have for so long been a source of discord, the reason and unreason for all the disunity. Here and elsewhere, people have burned, plundered, murdered, ruined the land, against a backdrop of beliefs, misbeliefs and unbeliefs, so many bloody crusades in the name of imaginary gods, so many swords raised, pyres built. Anna the Wise told me yesterday, "I will believe in a religion when women are admitted into the hierarchies of priests. All the monotheisms discriminate against the female half of humanity. Allah, Jesus Christ, Yahweh, if they really exist, have all erected the same fundamental apartheid as dogma—they are all the same, dominant men. The Greeks were no better, they put women at the bottom of their ladder of wisdom. Among them, love between males was valued more than love between male and female, because it was purer, greater, not soiled by the blood and milk of

women, those breeders of a lesser kind. And the
Romans, yes, they did have a few female goddesses, but
look what they made of them. I am supposed to be a
Muslim. Go see how we are treated in the mosques. I
don't care about their Koran. The men are in front for
the ablutions and the prayers, the women behind and to
the side, not entitled to enter the holy place if we have
our period. Impure, our period—and their sperm, is it
pure? Look at them when they all bend over, their
heads to the ground, their bums in the air, what
aggression! And when they stand up as one man, it is as
if they are going to war, all they need is guns. You know,
I've been trapped here since the war. Before, we didn't
even know who was Serb, who was Croat, and who was
Muslim. Why this massive return to religious practice?
They attacked us for *that*, so I suppose we wanted to
know what *that* consisted of. They attacked us for *that*
with weapons, so we made a weapon of *that*. I want to
leave this land of holy war and martyrs. I'm *déclassé*. You
know, during the Communist period, we had no right
to speak or to be political agnostics. We got rid of
Communism, but only on the surface. We still have no
right to say what we think. All of the former Yugoslavia,
all of Bosnia, is a political prison, tell that to Amnesty
International. They should come here with hordes of
psychologists, ethnologists and historians, or else only
with poets, only those who can get to the bottom of
things, to the heart of being. Tell them, or else we will
all go blind and deaf, with no language to speak.
Meanwhile, I want to go away, but where? Maybe to
France, where they tell me that thought and words are

supreme, but there are many countries where people who are *déclassé* like me can breathe. I hear yours is among them."

Anna, a bright young lawyer who would like to continue her studies in France—but where will she find the money?—added (and I carry these words within me, walking in the streets of dark Sarajevo to the Bosnia Women for Women Centre), "In my veins flows the blood of all the ethnic groups of the world, and all the religions." On her mother's side, she had Moorish ancestors, who came from Spain in the sixteenth century, but since they had "Jewish blood," they were persecuted by the Arabs and also the Christians; on her father's side, there were Turks and Hungarians. This is the ancestry that fed the great Slavic river flowing through Bosnia, and under Ottoman rule, Bosnia became mainly Muslim. Anna said, "I am all of them, and alone here, of no ethnic group, no identified religion." There is no place here for the continent of solitude that she demands. "Marriage and love do not interest me either. All women, Serb, Croat or Muslim, are subordinate to their men, and if the men die, they still obey their memory, their posthumous orders. It is that slavery that is the root of all war, it is war within war. We will never get out of it, we must get out of here."

We go into the Women for Women Centre, which was built thanks to the generous donations and the ongoing presence of American feminist groups. I see posted on the wall, in big letters in Bosnian, a photocopied excerpt from the Universal Declaration of Human Rights, the section on women's rights. "It's a start," says the lawyer Aida, who is in charge of educating women on their rights, receiving their grievances, and recommending solutions. Also posted on the walls are quotations from Kate Millett, Margaret Mead, Simone de Beauvoir, and so many others we quoted in the sixties and seventies. Yes, it's a start, a place through which dozens of women have passed since the war, where things can be said in confidentiality—the directors insist on that—where sufferings and complaints burst forth in the form of shouted words or weeping, so much conjugal and family violence, which all the women say has intensified as a result of the war. One woman dared to express doubts as to whether this was an effect of the war, she said: "This violence has existed for a long time, the beatings, the injuries, the rapes, the alcoholism of our men, but no one talked about it, it was not done. These centres were prohibited by Communism, or by our husbands. But today when Communism has fallen and so many of our men have died, when we find ourselves the heads of families, since we have shown our capacity for resistance and for education during the long war, we have found the courage to fight on our own behalf, not with weapons, but with words, which are learned even more readily than prayers. Since we have tested our endurance under coercion and oppression, in war as in our families, we are filled with energy, guts, determination." Suddenly, after the weeping and the continuous floods of words, which were translated by our friend Mirheta, the women, who were sitting in a circle and led by Divna, a psychologist, and Aida, the lawyer, burst out laughing.

We will make that laughter ours as we will their tears—
we need no interpreter to understand it, we know that
humour, "the politeness of despair," grows even in the
soil of abjection. Each one of them has cobbled
together a comical anecdote on the obscenity—they
have the black humour of the Jews, they make themselves the butt of their jokes, they laugh till they cry, and
then they just cry. This off-centre centre in the suburbs
of Sarajevo, built on the side of a hill among the mined
vineyards and stubborn gardens—oh, how beautiful
these yellow November roses are!—not far from the
devastated Jewish cemetery from which the snipers
started out, will soon let the cool evening in through its
walls. We go out into the night after affectionate good-
byes, saying we will come back again, with the dream
of She, with Anna's words coiled in her desire to leave,
with the sounds of a foreign language that have become
familiar through laughter and tears, with a melody of a
secular mass for a new time entwined around our
hearts, we go out into another night in Sarajevo.

Like people, cities have distinctive smells. Those of
Sarajevo in the autumn damp permeate my body's
memory, bathing mucous membranes and open pores
in fresh water, Turkish coffee, chestnuts roasted along
the sidewalks, black tobacco and mingled wet wood
and slate from brush fires or hearth fires, the aromas
capture my mind, then in the same breath set it adrift.
We continue our walk. An old man sitting by the
bronze fountain over there is feeding a huge flock of
pigeons, smoking his nargileh, from which emanate

fragrances of rosewater and hashish, he motions to us and smiles mockingly, and we walk towards him. He sings, saying it's for us, and Mirheta translates: "Foreigners, you will never know anything about it, the war is our business. If we want to die, you will never know why. All my dead I have mourned, and yet, see, I am happy. So many enemies have I killed, and my child's heart I have kept." We leave the old man after singing for him in return, as he asked—the two of us spontaneously broke into song with "L'hiver a chassé l'hirondelle,"[10] he started to cry, said he liked to cry, especially since the war, then he imitated the sound of sniper fire. We looked where he was pointing—snipers had shot dozens of holes in the Olympic rings of Zetra Stadium. We heard the old man's voice echo from the paving stones: "The Chetniks' aim was true. Well, we will take our revenge." In the distance we saw him turn back to his pigeons and his nargileh, then an old woman, laden with all kinds of bags, crossed the square towards him with a heavy step, put her raggedy arms around him like a young lover, kissed him. She turned towards us, and through the screen of grey drizzle, her smile lit up the whole city, and with it, us.

Sitting at a table at the Michele Café, on the second floor, where it's quieter, easier to talk, we are eight women—one Serb, five Bosnians (that is what those who are called Muslims by the UN call themselves), and

---

10. A popular Quebec country music song (Winter has chased away the swallows).

the two of us, my colleague Monique and I—there are
Liliana, Mujefira, Elmedina, Aida, Xenana and Mirheta,
and they call us Monica and Magdalena, all feminine
first names here end in *a*. We have come with our questions and they with theirs, the words mixed with laughter, even when they tell of the worst horrors. The
women are alone, without men, the younger ones don't
want any, the others are mostly war widows. Only one
still has her husband, she says, "He's wonderful, I'm free
with him," and the others burst out laughing as if they
don't believe it, and the happy wife, just as cheerful as
they, says, "You may not believe me, but my husband is
my best friend. It's true he wasn't raised according to
the discriminatory principles of this place, he was educated in France and then Canada." They look far off
into the distance, their gaze carried by the blue wreaths
of cigarette smoke and the steam from the coffee,
towards the horizon of fabulous lands. "It's hard to
imagine," says one, "that the women there are equal to
the men." "Impossible," adds another, and then they all
talk at once and their voices sound like voices in
dreams, rambling, exultant, as if in another dimension.
We come back down to earth and say to them, "You
know, it's not heaven in our country. Things are certainly more fair between men and women, but it's not
heaven either, there are still a lot of rapes and violence
against women. Every town, every village has its battered women's shelter." They say, "That's fantastic, at
least you have that. Here, only the town of Mostar has
such a place, and only since the war, because before the
war, no one talked about these things." Aida adds, "At
least, it's a start."

In Mostar, those who still have their men meet once a week, without the men's knowledge, just to talk about the problems of the two wars, the war the men, women and children of this supposedly Muslim people have suffered through together and the war they never dared to call by that name, that has been going on inside the homes from time immemorial. "We are naming it for the first time," they say, "this war of the sexes. We want it to end once and for all. Let our men learn to treat us as equals, or we will learn to defend ourselves. But not with weapons, we don't want that—no more violence, we're pacifists, we want dialogue between them and us, at our place, at our Women for Women Centre. And these meeting places will spread over the whole territory of Bosnia-Herzegovina. At our place, we talk in front of a Serb psychologist, we confide in her, and yet her people tried to destroy ours, we lost Serb friends and neighbours, because where we came from we saw them attacking our people, betraying them to the militia, driving them from their houses, we saw them killing. How can you expect us to forgive? The 'international community,' as they say everywhere—what a funny expression—would like us once again to become a multi-ethnic land, Serbs, Croats and Bosnians mixed together. How can you expect us to share the soil, the streets, the buildings of our executioners? The 'international community' is dreaming. We should just be left alone by ourselves for a time, to heal our wounds, to rebuild peace with the men we still have." And Mujefira, the historian of the group, adds: "You know why the Serbs, and a lot of Croats too, could feel so free to commit atrocities throughout the former Yugoslavia?

Those militaristic peoples have never seen their bloodthirsty leaders punished for their crimes. After World
War II, they acted as they do after every war, they
calmly returned home in complete impunity, leaving it
to their sons to prepare the next plan of attack. Here,
we never had anything like the Nuremberg trials,
nobody ever punished those murderers or established
the true extent of the atrocities committed. We have no
official memory of Greater Serbia's genocidal impulses.
We are asked to forgive, but how can we forgive
shadows? To forgive, you have to have public trials of
those who committed atrocities. They would have to
ask our forgiveness, after acknowledging their mistakes
and, if possible, making reparation. We would also have
to have fair history courses here—under the
supervision of UNESCO, for example. The textbooks
should be written in collaboration by historians from
here and historians from Western Europe and America.
All the history textbooks for Serb, Croat, Bosnian,
Slovene, Macedonian and Montenegrin students—I
don't know about the ones in Kosovo—all those history
books are propaganda. Our young people are taught
hatred of others and respect only for the victims among
their own people." The women concur with Mujefira's
words, and the discussion continues in all directions. We
listen, trying to grasp this complex reality that assails
them on all sides, to enter into this logic of despair in
which joy, ultimately, seems to prevail. We tell them this
and they answer, "Yes, that is how it is, even during the
war, especially during the war, there was joy in us." We're
at a complete loss to understand.

"Even during the war, there was joy in us, believe it or not," says Elmedina, "I was happier during the war," and they all agree. "During the war we had one goal, to survive, during the war, we had one hope, that there would be peace after the war. There was that total purpose and hope. But after the war, now, there is nothing, there is no peace here after the war, no peace, *nothing*, and no hope that this *nothing* will be followed by something. If something better than peace exists, there are no words to say it—no words, no dreams, no thoughts, *nothing*. The people who remain have no ambitions, we squabble over trifles. The Serbs come back and humiliate us with impunity. Our leaders are corrupt, winning votes is just a way for them to gain power. We are paid starvation wages. Our teachers, intellectuals and artists are depressed, they want to go away, to think in peace, create in peace, somewhere else. Family violence has doubled, delinquency and suicide are common. During the war, people did not commit suicide, they fought to survive. In fact, we had little daily goals that motivated us—for example, to cross what we called Sniper Alley, a wide-open boulevard completely visible by the Serbs, between our residential neighbourhoods and downtown. Sniper Alley separated me from the university, and that was my own goal during the five years of war, to continue my studies at the university—my faculty's building was, miraculously, spared—to cross that boulevard of death every morning and every evening, to study every day, to not get killed. That was my goal, and every night before going to sleep, I was happy to have defied death once again, to have, in a way, won.

Today, there are no more goals, except perhaps just to survive the surrounding melancholy, the *nothing* stretching ahead of us."

Nobody contradicts Elmedina's words and they add more in the same vein. One of them had as her only ongoing goal to make herself up nicely every morning, after going out on the perilous quest for water in the Bosnian scrub on the hillside, to return home to dress in her most beautiful clothes and make herself up for the day, "to be beautiful in the midst of disaster, that was my daily goal, my challenge for myself, every day when I got up, surrounded by children, my mother, and my cousins and aunts who were stranded there. There were sixteen of us living in a two-room apartment. From time to time, through our clandestine networks, we learned that one of our men, a father, husband or brother, had died in combat. Each day when I got up, I remembered the words I had read somewhere, I forget where: 'the epitome of love for a woman is to put on her make-up for a blind man.' In front of my mirror, with these words in my head, I would smile and make myself desirable, for no one and for the whole world. In this land of fire and blood, our hell, that was my dearest goal." They all had stories of their "goals of war." For one, it was keeping the children occupied with reading or games—there was no more school—telling them stories in the shelters, taking them with her to look for firewood when it wasn't too dangerous. "They would cut thin branches and make toys with them, little houses, cars, rifles or dolls. We let them have fun, even if it resulted in less wood for the fire. When we were all together, after eating what we gleaned wherever we could, the grandmothers would sing them lullabies, doing their best not to cry, and would rock the littlest ones, stroke their hair, and show them the sunbeams coming in through the window. Or in the evening, by candlelight, they would make a shadow theatre on the wall with their hands. They would say, 'Do not be afraid. You think those noises you hear outside are shells or snipers, but no, no, tonight the stars are having a party and that is how they sing. They dance and talk loudly because it is their Christmas. The stars have never known war. They are friends with the moon. Look at the crescent moon there, over the hill, the moon is playing with the lightning thrown by the stars. One day we will all be stars.' That is what the grand-mothers would say, and when terrible news came of fathers, uncles or brothers killed, piercing their hearts like snipers' bullets, they would not tell the children. But the next morning in the light of day, in front of the mirror, they would realize that their hair had turned completely white and there were new furrows lining their cheeks and their hands. The children would see their newly old grandmothers and ask 'Why are your hands filled with roots, why is your hair covered with the veil of the moon?' and they would answer, 'Because soon, we too will be stars.'"

Elmedina retells the story of a friend, never seen again, who had set herself the goal of going on foot every morning down the eight kilometres to her work and coming back up every evening, but the bank where she had worked no longer existed, it had been bombed, and the men had joined the guerrillas and the women were staying at home, but she made the trip back and forth every day for five years. It was her survival goal, she would rather walk to her former workplace and do nothing than be passive. Elmedina adds: "She was doing something. *Doing nothing* is more active than not doing anything, do you understand?" Other stories unfolded as the women's memories were freed, they wanted so much to talk, were so elated to have witnesses, that they had coffee after coffee, cigarette after cigarette, their laughter mingling with the muted music. We asked them why English and American songs were always played here instead of their own, and they answered, "Because in ours, Bosnian or Serb or Croat, there are those words that we understand. The least word can offend someone, stir up antagonism, the least metaphor can rekindle the differences. We want a rest from all that. English is neutral, we don't understand the words, and when we make out some of them, they don't concern us, don't reopen our wounds." But why is English so popular everywhere in the Balkans, instead of French or Spanish or Italian, or the language of any other people who have done them no harm? The youngest, Mirheta, answers, and everyone at the table agrees: "We all have to learn English anyway, it is the universal language, and besides, it is the English, the Americans and the Canadians who came here to save us from our murderers at the time of UNPROFOR. All the French and Dutch soldiers did was watch us being killed by the Serbs or sometimes by the Croats.

Listening to English and speaking it is a way of saying thank you."

The afternoon ends to the sounds of Elton John, with our offering of a round of cakes. Mirheta has picked a huge one, with cream and chocolate, a real treat because she was so hungry during the war. "This is happiness!" she says, her face beaming under the emerald green scarf she has worn since her father's death in combat, her cheeks turning rosy, she is entirely absorbed in savouring her dessert. Mujefira, the eldest of the group, orders her another one, her pleasure is contagious, she is obviously still very hungry, living in a miserable room where she squats with her two student brothers and her sick mother, how do they manage with no money? Mirheta says, "It is a miracle, we are surviving thanks to a miracle from my father up there, and the great Muhammad who protects us all." Before the war, they weren't religious in her family, and she made no distinction between Orthodox, Catholic and Muslim, did not know who among her friends was Serb or Croat—"We were all Bosnian"—before the ethnic cleansing. All the women around the table agree with what she says, but Valida, who has just joined us, says, "We are not guilty, but we are all responsible, we should have seen it coming, should not have elected those killers." No one answers. This little party at the café will soon end, and each one will return to the dark silence that awaits her outside. I see a shadow pass over the face of Liliana, who is Serb, listening to the others since the beginning, she keeps her secrets to herself. What did she see, fleeing along the roads of Bosnia at the beginning of the war, what has she heard in Belgrade, from which she recently returned? A cloak of sadness has fallen over her, I see her put her coat over her shoulders, and she shivers. What will the women from the executioners' side and those from the victims' side have to say to each other? Mirheta continues, "I learned the writings of the Great Prophet when I was with the guerrillas; I studied them with my comrades-in-arms, at night, in the cold of the mountains, hidden deep in the woods. We would hear the shells falling and the bullets whistling, would see the flames in our villages in the distance, and in the morning we would gather our dead. Allah became my only hope, they had killed all our other sources of hope." Mirheta has finished eating her cakes, she puts her emerald scarf back in place, singing very softly, just for herself, a song that sounds like a psalm. "Insh'Allah!" we hear, echoed by the voice of Elmedina, who, fiery-eyed, declares in a strong voice that we do not recognize as hers: "I will never be able to speak to Serbs, I have nothing to say to them, even our former friends, I will not talk to them anymore, even you, Liliana, I have nothing to say to you. Leave us alone with our silence. You, the Serbs, have nothing to do but repent and make amends. If you open your mouths to speak to us, ask our forgiveness, and respect our silence if we do not give you that forgiveness." And Liliana leaves.

As we get up from the table, Mujefira says, "All the peoples of the earth are not ready to live together. Some, even in the same territory, need a great distance before being able just to look at each other again. How can you expect us, the Bosnians, to get along with the Serbs? For centuries, the garden they preferred to cultivate has been war. For centuries, we have been peaceful, preferring, for example, to convert to Islam rather that confront the Turkish conquerors of the time, always choosing mixed blood over what is called racial purity. Do you know that for Serb mothers, the day their sons leave for military service is a major festive occasion, while for Bosnian mothers, that day has always been one of mourning?" Mirheta says, "Yes, that's true, but give them a chance to change." And Aida, who bravely takes part in the work of the Women for Women Centre, adds: "That's it, exactly, all of us women together, regardless of our ethnic group, want to change, starting by helping women to fight for their own rights, so that they free themselves from the war within the family, so that they finally give up their status as slaves of their men. We believe that the war of the sexes is the underlying basis of all war."

We leave each other, disappearing into the night, looking for the stars through the thick fog. It's cold.

From texts and images on film, I had constructed a city in my mind, a city that vanished when confronted with reality, scattered to the four corners of memory, and now I walk within my own ruins. This is the soul of Sarajevo, this impulse shared by the city and those who know it, this house of cards that is continually being demolished and rebuilt, this mutual attraction towards a plenitude based on absence, this magnet bonded to

lack. It shows us what was but is no longer, it seeks its
reference points, its cardinal points, and I seek mine, but
the fog makes it impossible. I find myself in the early
morning confronting the area called Hiroshima, led
here by my footsteps. No one lives here now. I pick up
the cards and start again, will I finally rebuild this
beloved city, or was it only my "castle in Bosnia," the
one I wrote about some years ago in a radio piece,
L'Amour de Mati, the one that was more real than life,
more faithful to what it was. Will I be able to reassemble
the fragments, the scattered pieces? A voice takes me
back to the project that brought me here, I had
forgotten it and it had remained buried on the fringes,
carried by those people that chance placed in my path.
The voice says in French: "During the war, there was a
'shared presence' among us, death. We recognized one
another by the sole fact of our being alive. But this,
now, is neither death nor life, it is *nothing*. We no longer
recognize one another. On the other side of the war, we
found not peace, but emptiness." She had seen me
looking, as she was, at the crescent moon between the
cathedral and the mosque, just over the chestnut tree. "I
recognized you because you are a foreigner here. Since
our shared presence has disappeared, I no longer
recognize anybody and I do not speak anymore." I
remember thinking then that I must reconcile myself to
what this city has become, foreign to itself, that is what
it is asking for—yes, cities have souls, some more than
others—and that is what it wants. Did I say this to the
well-dressed old lady with "rings on every finger"? I
don't remember. But in the early morning, facing the

Hiroshima neighbourhood, I again saw the scene when, for the first time here, the sun suddenly came out, burning off the fog, I've never seen such an explosion, have never seen the veil of the temple torn away—in an instant, Sarajevo became a huge nave open to the sky, with all the reference points finally there, the denuded mountains and hills finally showing their habitats, their well-worn furrows, their directions, very far, beyond the ruins, their horizons.

Finally we are able to climb up beyond the suburbs, to circle the city and see it from above, to get out of the basin and follow the bronze thread of the Miljacka, to climb up, but not on foot—forget walking, too many mined areas and not enough time now. We choose a taxi that will be our guide, Mirheta comes along, it is the first time she will see her city as a whole, she never had the means to make this excursion. In their language, Bosnian, they have quietly negotiated a price that suits us. We set out in the sun as if on holiday, we even have a picnic. Sarajevo is giving us the gift of its light for our last day—there has been endless mist during our stay, we were patient, and it's as if the city wants to thank us. Our driver, Milovan, first drives all around the city, he says, "To understand where we are going, we must know where we are coming from," with Mirheta translating. We ask our questions, and then she asks us not to talk anymore, insisting in a tone we haven't heard from her before. This twenty-four-year-old girl suddenly has the authority of a veteran, the pride of a member of the resistance. "We must not talk anymore, we must look," she says, and we comply. It's true, the silence among the four of us lets the ruins make their plea. I look at Mirheta's face close-up—a certain hardness, an immense gravity. She is obviously taking the measure of what she has never before seen as a whole, the thousands of unhealed wounds of a city where she ended up with her mother and brothers after they were driven out of the village of Visegrad in Republika Srpska, which is now inaccessible, and made their way through the forest and the camps. Milovan names each devastated place, we look and listen, taking in the topography of this city, the encirclement of its hills and mountains by the Serb army. We see concretely that it was practically impossible to get out or in. As we in our turn take the measure of the battlefield and the front, we hear Milovan's voice: "The residents of Sarajevo were under siege for five years, we survived one thousand, eight hundred and twenty-seven days under siege. Longer than St. Petersburg in World War II, longer than any other city. We broke all the records." There is pride in his voice, and a smile in his eyes. In the light, Mirheta once again becomes the vivacious girl we know. The two of them suddenly start singing a song of patriotic resistance—they had spoken and recognized each other. Milovan says, "I was a soldier with the Bosnian guerrillas," and they sing. It's not a military anthem, it's more like a lullaby:

> A coffin floats down the river.
> Mama, tonight I will not come home for dinner,
> For in heaven I will eat.

A coffin floats down the river.
Tell my mother I love so much,
No, no, tonight I am not coming home for dinner.

Mirheta continues, speaking to Milovan and translating her words for us: "I say thank you to the men who defended my country, I thank myself too. To the others, I have nothing to say. Their fighters were not soldiers, they were war criminals. Only one thing interests me concerning them, and that is to have news of their arrest and then their conviction by the International Criminal Court for the former Yugoslavia." Milovan adds, "In Banja Luka I had friends, in Vukovar, cousins. The Chetnik butchers massacred just as many there as here. We have our networks of information. Those cities were subjected to the same carnage as ours was. Your newspapers talk about the Croat massacres in Krajina. It is true, there were settlings of accounts against the Serbs after the ethnic cleansing in Eastern Slovenia, where the war criminals wanted to expand Serbia. The Croats took their revenge in Krajina, it is true, but that has nothing to do with the planned horror of Greater Serbia, neither in the scale of the carnage nor in the number of people killed or driven out. The figures are there, it was unprecedented. Tell them that in Canada, tell it everywhere you go. Even if they are fewer, if there are criminals among the Croats, they should be punished too." Mirheta goes further: "I was told that there were war criminals among the Bosnian Muslims. I have trouble believing it, but if it turns out one day to be true, they should be punished too. We must put an end to impunity, it is the only way to start living again here."

We reach the crest of the hills, and we can make out the shape of the mountains in the distance. Milovan announces: "From here, I have my plan. No more talk of money. I will take you to see the real war. I am not counting my time anymore." He turns off the engine and says, "Let's get out and stop for a while here. I want to show you where we have come from, down there." We are in the hills of Sedrenik, not far from the historic Kasarna, the main barracks, which was used by the Serb army and has recently been taken over by the new Bosnian army. A sentry is watching us through his field glasses, and we smile and wave in case he sees us up there in his solitude. Mirheta muses—why these words have come to her at this precise moment, we don't know—"If half of the governments and half of the armies were women, there would be no more wars." We ask her why she says that, and she answers, "I don't know, but I know." Milovan agrees, then adds mischievously, and she translates for us, laughing: "It is true, but you are forgetting Mrs. Thatcher."

Between the Kasarna and the city, we see, a little above us, an old woman sitting on a stump in an empty field, muttering, watching her herd of goats grazing on the dry autumn grass as if there was nothing out of the ordinary. Like the old woman, they don't worry about the mines there, as everywhere else, although yellow plastic ribbons put up by SFOR indicate the danger. The old woman must not know that language of obstacles, the terrain suits her and her goats and she has taken it.

Or perhaps she does know that she could be blown up with her herd, perhaps she has decided that this field adjacent to the new cemetery with its white stakes marking a common grave will be the site of her swan song, perhaps she chose this final resting place to be beside her old man who lies sleeping there, perhaps her murmured incantations among her goats are a last oath dedicated to her man, a final rosary as the hours pass, a bouquet of wishes on the common grave with no inscriptions or flowers—who knows? She hasn't seen us, or maybe she senses our presence but she is in her own elsewhere, where we will never be. We look away, respecting the intimacy of her resting place under the sky. Milovan traces a circle with his arm, and says: "Before, this was called the City of Seven Hills, now it is the City of Seven Cemeteries. There are many dead here, and these hills that were once sylvan masterpieces are bare, with no trees. But they gave us wood to warm ourselves and it is thanks to them that we are alive." I say, "It could be called the City with Seven Lives," and they agree, smiling. Then I remember *The Seven Books of Wisdom*, written in the thirteenth century by the Jewish philosopher Abraham Abulafia, who was driven out of Arabia and went to Spain, where he wrote his major work, which was banned by the dominant Thomist philosophy and came to light again only in the twentieth century. The road to hope is so long, and the scorched earth of the Balkans offers us a small shortcut to it.

Back on the road again, Milovan takes us to the site of "the real war," as he says. We drive along a narrow rocky road to the beginning of a track that snakes

among more barren fields, more fallow hills, more herds
grazing, more cemeteries filled with white wooden
stakes, against a backdrop of bare shrubs. We follow him
down on foot, carefully placing our feet on the
concrete slabs, terrified of mines. We notice furrows
filled with young shoots, wild lilies among the debris.
Pointing to excavations that look recent, Milovan
declares in a subdued, solemn voice, "There, those were
our trenches. With my comrades, I created them. We
were dug in there when they fired, and we counter-
attacked." So that was "the real war." It was his war,
where he had fought and come out victorious, where
he had witnessed the Serbs fleeing after the Croats had
finally joined forces with the Muslims against their
mutual enemy. Mirheta asks him what makes him
happiest, having helped defeat the Serbs or having got
out alive. He answers, "I am happy that peace has
returned." Then he says that Mirheta was right, that this
mess would never have happened if the world were run
by women, that women are better, they "have a better
morality than men." He knows something about this,
he says, because his mother was the bravest and most
gentle person and his wife, who has just died of cancer,
"may Allah take her soul!" was the most magnificent
creature in the world, "like a goddess fallen into the
rotten world of men." We express our condolences to
him. His eyes fill with tears, and he shakes his head. With
him we embrace the whole surrounding countryside.
He is reliving his war. He will talk to us for a good two
hours, he has so much to tell, the words tumble out,
eloquent, as if they had been awaiting this moment for

a long time. Mirheta translates, adding her own stories in counterpoint. Beside the trenches of death, these two have became very close, like old friends finally unburdened of their shared secrets of hard times.

When he points to the huge playing field of his adolescence, there on the left below, now a cemetery, they both cry. There were all kinds of games: soccer, baseball, rugby. When he tells us the story of the cherry tree, and then the story of the rabbit, Mirheta is so enthralled that she translates very fast, talking at the same time as he does, their voices intertwining harmoniously above the city. They are both facing the slowly setting sun, and their eyes, his black, hers blue, reflect its rays, burning embers against the backdrop of devastation. The cherry tree is in front of us. Milovan tells how, that noon, it was filled with sun, the red cherries swollen with juice. He and his comrades saw some young boys heading for the tree. The boys were famished. The men had just enough time to shout, "Don't go there!" The snipers above took aim at the cherry tree. The men saw it all from their hiding place. A ten-year-old boy had not heard, or maybe he didn't believe them, or maybe he was too hungry. He climbed the tree and in an instant was cut down. He was moaning and bleeding to death, and nobody could go out in the open to help him. A long time later, they were able to bury him in the presence of his family. "Real warriors would never attack a hungry child, they were not real soldiers," continues Milovan. "They would get drunk and take drugs, sometimes we would hear them raving and laughing at their posts, shouting and howling like wolves in the night. That cherry tree you see there is not the one I am talking about. That one was cut down after the war. Nobody here could stand seeing that tree of death anymore."

Milovan mimes the story of the rabbit crossing the hill on the Serb side as if he were really hunting. He was so hungry, having lived on grass for days, and the rabbit was so plump—"when I think about it, I am hungry again, it hurts here," Milovan says, pointing to his stomach—he almost decided to run after it and catch it. "I knew how to do it." It still makes him salivate, and he says, "I almost decided to die in order to eat." But life, once again, won out.

We drive slowly back down to Sarajevo after learning about his war, the deadly one, "the real war." Milovan takes the winding streets through the rebuilding, pleased by the energy of his people at work. After such a short time, he rejoices, there are already dozens of houses presenting their red tiles to the caress of the sun's last rays. The city is crimson, its river mauve. We hear the clatter from kitchens and cafés, the purring of cats, the sound of pigeons' wings. We say goodbye at a taxi stand. Sarajevo is clad in beauty on this very last evening, tonight she has taken off her veil forever. We tell each other we will always be friends. Let us give Mirheta the last word. She says: "Thank you, Milovan, for what you did during the war. You know, I could never have carried a gun." He answers: "You women do very well just as you are, it is from you alone that we will learn peace." We slowly walk away, blowing kisses until we turn the corner.

ISRAEL AND PALESTINE

Israel and Palestine

How can I understand the ago-old conflict between that people of the desert, the Semites, and that people of the sea, the Phoenicians, the one that invented the writing of the Book and the other that created phonetic spelling? How can I tread the soil of these lands where more blood has flowed than water or mother's milk, where the clash of weapons has never been silenced, even in the sacred places where the three monotheistic religions, Jewish, Christian and Muslim, were born, where no generation in written memory has ever known peace despite the presence of the three transcendent deities, despite the incessant invocation of the three sublime names, Yahweh, Christ and Allah, despite the desperate appeals to their heavenly illumination in the dark chaos of the ever-renewed despair of war? Looking at the two peoples, the people of Israel—which in 1948 got its own state, finally, following the Shoah, regained its paradise lost, its promised land, after centuries of exile and wandering—and the people of Palestine—dispossessed since the same fateful date, driven into other territories, then subjected to Israeli occupation, suffering in its turn the hardship of diaspora, half its population confined by military force in refugee camps—how can I "write after Auschwitz" if not by giving my ink, as others have given their blood, to these new victims, the Palestinians? In my mind is the thought that the history of these peoples is too huge for such a small space, that there is a disproportion between historical time and a tiny geography that cannot contain the immeasurable greatness that only the desert, like a mother, once encompassed.

The desert calls us, but it will have to wait. One no longer enters the Holy Land from that direction, one enters the Land of War from its liquid side, from the west, by way of the Mediterranean, a jewel of turquoise waters and jade-green corals, the new fortress from which American warships protect the sacred territory, as do the roaring jets of Tzahal, the Israeli military, which are constantly breaking the sound barrier and our eardrums. One no longer comes to it slowly, on the back of a camel, from the land of sand, the true measure of the immeasurable time of immemorial places. One arrives there, having absorbed it in the blink of an eye, at Ben Gurion Airport, named for the pioneer hero. This is Tel Aviv, the shining modern city built to celebrate the return, far from the ruins of the Temple and the suffocating memories like old nightmares. Tel Aviv, where soft sands washed by soft waves lie at the feet of the proud buildings, the stately fashionable hotels. But it is so close to Jaffa, the ancient legendary oasis of the Palestinians, who fled in panic and disarray in 1948. Jaffa, which gave its sumptuous abandoned villas to the new occupants. Jaffa, which is still there, its colonnades, porticoes and gardens the vestiges of what it was then. I contemplate it, trying to adapt the ancient image to the new one, and I am filled with longing. Jaffa gives itself to my gaze, an old woman who is no longer a great beauty, who has been unveiled and stripped, and who weeps all the Palestinian tears of past and present, which fall and feed the Levantine Sea.

We come in over the Levantine Sea to enter Israel-Palestine. We will learn very quickly, from people and maps, that the occupied territories in the centre of the country are called Judea and Samaria by the Israelis, Palestine by the others, and that they include East Jerusalem, Bethlehem, Jericho, Ramallah, and, further away, towards Egypt, the Gaza Strip, and, towards Syria, the Golan Heights. We will see that the centre is dotted with little islands encircled by Tzahal, although the Palestinian Authority has its police force there and, recently, its Parliament, which is made up of eighty-three men and five women. We will see this Palestine that is cut up between Jerusalem and the area west of the Jordan River—called the West Bank on English-language maps and Cisjordanie on French maps—a territory captured in 1967 by Israel from Jordan, which had occupied it until then. We will learn that, in the Six-Day War between the Arab countries and Israel, the lands of the centre, the east and the northeast were taken from the Palestinians, as those of the west had been in 1948 and those of the northwest were later, during the war in Lebanon. We will not be surprised to learn that the word Israel does not appear on the maps of the neighbouring countries, Jordan, Syria and Lebanon, but, in its place, Palestine, the name of the Holy Land of our childhood, when we were told the thousand-and-one stories of the Old Testament, the thousand-and-one days and nights that took the place of comic books and movies. Never in a thousand years would I have imagined, in our innocent America, that Palestine would soon drink from the fountain of suffering, never would I have known—as a little Catholic girl in French Canada, which was then Roman Catholic —that the Jews of Europe were then experiencing their Gethsemane in the Nazi death camps. We enter Israel-Palestine by the ancient road of the dead, arriving in ancient Jaffa enveloped in a shawl of warmth, that we carry everywhere with us, covering our hearts, cradling us.

On the sparkling beaches of Tel Aviv-Jaffa, we see only one bird, a white heron. Looking for gulls or gannets, we ask people why only the white heron bears witness to the time before. "Before," we are told, is always "before 1948" here, and not "before Christ" or "before the Shoah," as we would have thought at first. We get different answers to our question. An Israeli taxi driver says, "There are no more birds because there is too much industry." Someone else says, "Because all the coastal birds followed the Palestinians into exile." We leave for Jerusalem, claimed as their capital by both peoples. We imagine the colonies of birds returning singing one day with the three million, six hundred thousand Palestinian refugees who have been kept in the camps now for three generations, and with the two million others scattered in the neighbouring countries but also very far away in the rest of the world. We imagine this concert being given for the two peoples, now reconciled, each in its tiny territory, each in its huge historical time, each with its God, its synagogue or mosque, or no God at all for those who don't want any. We dream that the birds will carry in their beaks official passports for the Palestinians, who have all been deprived of them. And that, returning from the diaspora with their human masters, the birds will circle the Wailing Wall, now more commonly called the Western Wall, on the west side of the city, the rich part, where there are no Palestinians, and from the combined beating of all their wings, the wall will suddenly crumble to dust, for like the one in Berlin, it will no longer have any reason for being, for there will be no more reason, ever, to wail.

We enter Jerusalem through the poorer neighbourhoods of the Hassidic west, we see the ultra-orthodox Jews, the men in their black fur-trimmed hats, or *shtreimels*, and the women, who also wear head coverings or wigs. Our taxi driver, a non-practising Jew, hates them, he calls them "cowboys" and says, "They make me ashamed, they're cowboys, look at their *shtreimels* and their guns. You don't think they carry guns? They hide them under their coats. They are dangerous." He adds, "My wife will never wear the wig of the pious, I wouldn't let her, I have given her complete freedom, she had better use it or I will take another wife." He seems very angry. "I'm the son of Ashkenazim, we're free Europeans, we don't come from the eastern countries like those narrow-minded Sefardim who are making Israel poor." We remain silent, we know from reading it—but seeing and hearing is a different thing—that the major ethnic conflict between Israelis and Palestinians, and between Jews and Arabs, is coupled with another conflict, an intra-ethnic one that was buried for ages, between those who come from the East and North Africa, who are poorer and have less power, and those who come from the West, who are richer and are in control of the country, like the rich everywhere. We head towards the centre of Jerusalem, near the old city, where we have chosen to stay. The sun is setting, and we can see the famous Western Wall, the ochre of the stones bathed in pink light that turns scarlet as it moves slowly across the golden dome of the Mosque of Omar, defying religious boundaries. Then our eyes return to the wall, which will be there for a long time yet, for the people of this world are not done with wailing. A woman dressed in black crosses the street where our car is stopped, looks at us, and says in Yiddish—our driver translates—"Look at the ruined woman that I am. To me, both sides are making war. Look at me and never forget, my name is Jerusalem, write it down so you never forget it." We smile and enter our temporary home here.

We enter the old city by the Zion Gate, with Jeannette, a French woman who has been living in Jerusalem for many years and who wanted to accompany us here. A cleaning woman at the Notre Dame Pontifical Institute, she was born in Paris, where she married an Arab, but a Christian, "a Greek Orthodox

Christian," she says, "and I'm Roman Catholic." Here
identity is defined first of all in terms of religion. She
wants to take us to the Christian side of the old city,
saying, "That's where you must start, you're French
from Canada, you're Christians." We follow her along
the Via Dolorosa. She says, "There He fell the first
time," and there the second time, and so on to the
fourteenth station of the Way of the Cross. We don't see
anything, only time-worn stones on which the famous
stations on the way to the Church of the Holy
Sepulchre have been carved in Roman numerals.
Jeannette crosses herself each time, as she must have
done so often. Blinded by the colourful, noisy crowd
walking in the congested lanes of the bazaar, we see
nothing. Everything is for sale here—Catholic,
Protestant, Orthodox, Melchite, Maronite, Chaldean,
Syrian and Armenian relics, as many kinds of souvenirs
as there are Christian sects, with the prices shouted for
all to hear, but there are also fruits and vegetables,
American shoes, T-shirts, kebabs, hamburgers, hot dogs
and Coke, and junk from all over the world, cheap
jewellery, camels carved from olive wood, seconds of
designer bags—so many things that you can't see the
sky, such a cacophony that you can't hear the events
that took place here two thousand years ago echoing
from the old stone. The poor weeping men and women
of that time who went down the long road of death
with their hero bowed under his cross have been
replaced by the money-changers of the temple from all
over the world and the mob of the hungry. They cry
out their prices in Arabic, or in English, the language of

tourism. Hebrew is heard on other side, where we will
go tomorrow. Jeannette continues her prayers and her
signs of the cross. Her hand in her pocket, she is saying
her beads, and I remember the rosaries that my
ancestors cherished even in their deathbed, when they
stammered the holy words to the pangs of mortal
agony, to their last breath. I look at Jeannette, who
appears transported, as if on the verge of ecstasy. She has
the dishevelled hair of an old woman, and deep lines
like so many furrows carved by sorrow. She says, "I have
four boys," her toothless mouth smiling proudly, and
adds, "and I have one daughter," a shadow suddenly
passing over her face. "A daughter—it will be slavery
for her, submission to her husband, her mother-in-law,
all her in-laws. The only way for her to escape it will be
to become a saint, to pray a lot, all the time." Jeannette
has given her daughter a special first name, Véronique.
"Come, I'll take you to the Holy Sepulchre. Make a
wish and it will be granted." Not wanting to disappoint
our friend, we continue on to the Church of the Holy
Sepulchre. We can hardly see it for the mobs of tourists,
each group with its guide with a megaphone, each
person with a video camera. We try to make our way
through the teeming mass of pilgrims. "There's *the*
door," Jeannette says, "It's there they placed His
sepulchre." She's out of breath, excited as a little girl,
and behind the old mask, I perceive the beautiful face
of the young girl she once was, I see the freshness of her
sixteen years, her skin white as milk, her eyes ultra-
marine blue, I see that sweet Parisian girl of thirty-five
years ago, who fell madly in love with her Greek

Orthodox Christian Arab and followed him here on a long way of the cross that she retraces as one replays one's life, one's *via dolorosa*. But we will not enter by the little stone door through which the tourists are disappearing. Gently, we inform Jeannette that we will take a calmer path, away from the circus of religiosity, a less travelled road that runs along the wall to the Damascus Gate. We would like to get out of here fast and, if it were possible, to walk slowly towards the desert, where the rhythm of time and the silence are beckoning us. We come back suddenly and Jeannette's voice reaches us as in a dream: "If I had been a boy, I would have been a fighter. My father served in General de Gaulle's army. He was a great soldier, my father, a great soldier." She stares off into the distance towards the bare hills, and I follow her gaze past them to France, her lost paradise, while before us the desert stretches out its first beige carpet and to our left the Mount of Olives opens its arms wide as if embracing and cradling East Jerusalem and all of Palestine until its children are given a land of return. The voice of Jeannette, whom we had thought old, still resonates above the bells of so many churches: "I could be a warrior, you know, I'm thirty-five years old, but on which side?"

In Jerusalem, there are festive birds in the trees, families of multicoloured birds whose names I don't know. I will soon recognize them by their songs, their warbling at dawn and dusk, as soft as silk and linen, and I will give each of them a *nom de plume*—one will be the eastern swallow, another, the olive-tree blackbird, and yet another, with Prussian blue plumage, the King Solomon jay. They are in all the gardens of the luxuriant oasis that is Jerusalem. Jerusalem, set with luminous stones under the constant sun, ringed by arid hills heralding the desert, the ancient wall that once protected it from conquest, and the new wall, which is invisible, its lines drawn high in the sky by the airplanes and helicopters of Tzahal that circle constantly over the city. The birds are used to them, the atonal music doesn't seem to disturb their age-old symphony, while the people here, bustling and agitated, appear to us to be the most nervous in the world and have no time to guide us, don't know which way to orient us when asked for directions—but we are in the East, the nearest of the Easts, where all roads from the Far East end, from which all roads to the new worlds of the West begin. People have no time to stop, can't spare the time to smile. We haven't seen that mark of happy light-heartedness on the faces here, that sign of peaceful welcome on the lips and in the eyes, except in the very rare children we sometimes see walking with their mothers or big sisters, who hold them in their arms and whisper tender secrets in their ears. The children of Jerusalem are like the birds—the war that has gone on uninterrupted for generations has not diminished the joy that only they exhibit, like the warbling of humanity.

She says "I do not want to go with you to the Western Wall—all that affected carrying on, all that bowing and scraping gets on my nerves. I'm Jewish and proud of it, but not of that, we didn't fight for this lunacy." She is Annie, in her early sixties, born in France of parents from Poland, who like so many came to Paris to escape the rise of Nazism. Her family was slaughtered in the camps, except for her Communist father, who, thanks to a *gendarme* in the Resistance, was hidden in the unoccupied zone along with Annie and her brother Daniel, who now lives in the United States. Their mother was caught in the Velodrome d'Hiver round-up, she had gone to visit some cousins that day and she was unlucky. She was taken away with the rest of them and died in Auschwitz. Annie shows us her photograph. These young Jewish mothers are always beautiful, with dreamy eyes, smiling mouths, abundant wavy ebony hair tied in a bun with a few wisps falling on a well-pressed lace blouse. Annie left Paris with her father in 1969, when she was studying international law at university. She never practised here, she became a florist. She loves flowers, birds and children, but not war. She never wanted to marry, she says. "I'm a communist, I'm a Fourierist. How could I accept religious marriage and submission to a man? There's no civil law in Israel, the only law is the law of the Torah. I rejected it on principle. And children, yes, I would have wanted them, I often dreamed of it when I was a young woman. I didn't want to carry a child to death, and death always awaits us with the war." She came to Israel after the "revolution of 1968," when there was nothing happening in France anymore in that respect, she says, nothing being done to renew the humanist and communist ideals that had been perverted. "The revolutionaries of May had quickly turned into sober civil servants." But after the 1967 war, and with the Arab threat, she felt a duty to be in Israel. She and her father finally had a goal—to return, to help their people survive, to take part in building the country. They worked in the kibbutzim. Her aging father, Elias, a cultured, clear-sighted communist, acted as a community advisor, a sage the like of which no longer exists. He died at eighty, disappointed and disillusioned. "He had believed in this country too much, hoped too much, imagined too much that this promised land would be a model of life, of sharing, of mutual aid, for everyone." Old Elias died cursing "this new capitalist country, as stupid, as profiteering, as warlike as the rest." Even Annie could not soothe or comfort him, he was too angry, as if totally despairing. He was against the occupation of Palestine, the murders of Palestinians, the systematic torture in the infamous Khiam prison, the appropriation of land, the denial of the most fundamental rights. Old Elias went "from death to *nothing*. What's the point of life? What a waste, what absurdity!" Her father is the man she loved most, Annie makes no secret of it, he was her guide, her companion in life, her friend. When she touched his cold limbs after his passage to *nothing*, life fell apart for her, she saw Israel swallowed up into a giant abyss. She says, "I don't want to go with you to the Wailing Wall, it's all affectation, bowing and scraping. Come back and tell me about it, come to dinner tonight." Her best friend has a restaurant in an Arab neighbourhood, in East Jerusalem.

Annie has stood up for the Palestinians, along with only a few others. She accepts the enormous loneliness of that choice. All the people in the world who have taken up residence on the continent of this loneliness form a vast "unavowable community." We have recognized it in Annie's gaze, so far off and yet so near.

Amid the strangeness of clothes and languages along the inner wall of the old city, we have reached the Hebrew "Far West," passing through the Armenian quarter, where the dusty stone walls are plastered with gruesome posters that are regularly torn down to be replaced by more of the same, with images of fleshless bodies, corpses discovered in the common graves of villages and towns. They remind us, in case we have failed in the duty of remembrance, of another genocide, one that is little spoken about, here or elsewhere, the opening tragedy of this century: the decimation of an entire people, the Armenians, which has by tacit agreement been suppressed by the other peoples of the world. The afternoon sun beats down on the grey posters, the skeletal limbs and faces that the inattentive crowd passes without seeing. We stop for a bit and give these humble paper epitaphs our quiet attention as a kind of funeral prayer. They are so alone, these witnessing images, mute sheets that everyone crumples with a hurried shoulder in passing. We continue on our way, our eyes drawn by David's Tower and then by the new arch of the Old Temple that was destroyed by the Romans some two thousand and

seventy years ago. We climb as high as possible to take
in the two cities. We see a group of Catholic nuns who
are chanting in prayer, weeping as they chant, in Latin
this time, a language as dead as the sea we will visit
tomorrow. They remind me of other tearful incantations, probably in the sad ceremonies of Good Friday.
The nuns are translating their words as if they know
we're listening, in French we hear, "Jerusalem, I will
weep for thee ... ," we can't hear the rest. The wall is
just ahead of us, but the crowd of tourists is so thick
that we can hardly see it. There are so many people that
you have to go through a little checkpoint, as you do at
customs in an airport, with two police officers on
duty—the war can never be forgotten here. We go
through and come upon not one wall, but two—just as
there is a war with the war, there is a wall within the
wall, that is, there is the long Wailing Wall divided at a
right angle by another, with men on one side and
women on the other. They do not pray together here,
they each wail on their own side. The men's side of the
wall is higher, more imposing, it's the original one, the
real retaining wall of the Temple. The other side is
humbler, lower, and the stones are not as beautiful. On
the men's side, they wear ritual dress and a rabbi lights
the third candle in the nine-branched candleholder. In
six days, Hanukkah, the Festival of Lights, will be over.
The chanting is very loud, the crowd in the area is
huge. A group of American tourists, men in neon-green
caps, goes to stick little messages in the cracks, the
women filming them from a distance with video
cameras. The Jewish mothers and girls, in long dark

skirts, wearing wigs or berets, try to peek through the cracks in the dividing wall at what is happening on the men's side, where the *real* ceremony, the real rituals are seen and heard. Why don't they create their own, why doesn't it occur to them to *really* wail, to form a chorus of contemporary mourners, to beat their heads and tear their nails on the dividing wall of separation. Why don't they smash it to pieces as was done with that other wall in Berlin? They could take pieces home with them, remnants of a time when the first of all wars raged between the sexes. They and their daughters and grand-daughters and great-granddaughters could spend a long time contemplating those relics of a bygone time, they could read the secular novel of a new time that came when their foremothers at the dawn of the third millennium decided, during a memorable ritual in December 1999, no longer to be in fealty, no longer to be subjugated, and when Christian and Muslim women acted at the same time and smashed the same walls and broke the same chains, and no more would any religion sow the seeds of hierarchical discrimination and there would be no more wars, the girls of another age would say, touching the dust of all the dividing walls. We watch the Jewish women trying to follow the ceremony on the other side, their eyes straining to peer through the cracks, their ears cocked to hear the prayers chanted by their men. The tourists of the world attending the spectacle are too noisy, and the women give up against too many obstacles. We leave, the sun is setting, tomorrow is the sabbath, the nuns in the distance are chanting the "Stabat Mater" on the Via Dolorosa.

On the esplanade of Safra Square, we meet Annie and
her friend Benyamin. They are walking arm in arm
between the illuminated rows of the forty majestic
palm trees planted there in honour of the forty biblical
wise men of Zion and the forty pioneers who made
independence possible in 1948. Here, above and
beyond beliefs and allegiances, the ancient story of the
"chosen people" is never forgotten. Moses, Abraham,
Jacob, Daniel, David and Joseph stand like beacons in
the current night of war. There is no division between
Old and New Testaments, no break. The prophets of old
speak in the words of today. We watch our friends
approach, opening their arms, offering their cheeks for
the three kisses, in the magnificence of Safra Square,
between the soft shadows and the light filtering through
the palm trees onto the pink stones. It suddenly seems
to me that only beauty will save the peoples of the
Middle East from disaster. If they succumb to the facile
ugliness of the profiteers who are in a hurry to build by
destroying, it will be the end of what little hope there
is for peace in the negotiations that will soon start again
in Washington. If the negotiators of Israel, Palestine,
Syria, Jordan and Lebanon fail to take into account the
beauty of their lands and their habitats, their
monuments and their ruins, they will sign treaties full
of lies, will initial clauses full of tragedy, will ratify the
death sentences of the peoples crowded into these tiny
territories, interwoven in the depths of historical time,
enmeshed in the same beauties. Will these negotiators
from the Middle East know, when they are sitting

around the table in the USA, that they must make no
concessions, that beauty is salvation from everything,
that the work of creation is the life instinct in action
and that it alone can overcome the other instinct, the
one that destroys, the death instinct? "How did you find
our Far Western wall?" Annie asks us, laughing, and we
tell them. "Those fetishists are in the minority here,"
says Benyamin. "All religious fundamentalists foment
division and war. The ultra-orthodox Jews are no better
than the fundamentalist Muslims or the Christian
fascists, but here, we had dreamed of something
different. My generation, born during or just after
World War II, fell for the utopian dreams, we repeated
the great social illusion of the late nineteenth century
socialists, we believed in a better world. That was our
problem, we brought transcendence down among men,
sort of the way you did with your Christ. Transcendence
must remain a divine utopia for everyone. No Law can
become incarnate without disaster. If God exists, he
must remain invisible, inaudible and unnameable. All
religions, which by definition are man-made, are hypocritical quagmires of conflict. The day all people
understand that God is unthinkable and must remain
unthought will be the day the primordial source of
wars dries up of its own accord." We listen to Benyamin
and look at the stars above the palm trees of the wise
men of Zion. The stars above Jerusalem are so clear. I
look at the star of Bethlehem, where we will go
tomorrow, there it is, the mythic star of our childhood,
the brightest one in the southeast. We see dozens of
Muslims going by in cheerful groups and disappearing

into the restaurants of the Arab quarter. It is the first day
of Ramadan, they have been fasting since sunrise, and
they are hungry. Now at nightfall, they are allowed to
eat, but not to drink wine. How do they do it? The
women arrange their scarves before entering the
restaurants. People are running in all directions, horns
are blaring, and we hear the cacophony of the collective
taxis at the Damascus Gate below. It is always so busy,
so frenetic, so anxious here. Benyamin says, "My
Palestinian cooks have made veal rolls for us tonight.
Come, the Beaujolais nouveau has arrived." Annie, as if
waking from a dream, says, "Benyamin, the fundamental
cause of wars is not in religions, we can always live with
those, leave them to themselves to imagine their gods
and their laws. No, the fundamental cause is in the great
division, the awful separation between men and women.
I dream of an androgynous world—there would still be
two sexes, of course, I'm talking about an androgyny of
the mind and of the heart. Each person would
recognize him or her self in others, the strange would
become familiar, the way it happens when a mother
carries a child. There is another in her, but to her it is
herself. We should imagine the only viable religion on
this model: as giving life to another in oneself. For a
pregnant mother, regardless of whether the other is
male or female, it is Being that she nurtures inside her.
To nurture Being is divinity, *that* is what men have tried
to repress, it is through that repression that the creative
instinct of life was replaced by the death instinct in
action as war. War is hell!" We walk towards her friend
Benyamin's restaurant, gentle Annie's words still

flowing, blending with the din of a Jerusalem full of mysteries and secrets, in the east as in the west. Annie's right, there's no need to look at it from the viewpoint of eternity, it's right here, hell on earth, that's what war has been since the dawn of time.

En route to Bethlehem with the amiable Martin, a young man from Oxfam-Québec who is working here setting up computer systems in the Palestinian schools. Martin will be our guide for the day. He has no problems at the Israeli checkpoints, his permit allows him to go back and forth across the border to the occupied West Bank. Martin is a lively, resourceful young man who approaches life full of hope, he believes it is possible to change the world. In the privileged West, we could use a lot more like him. As we roll along on the battered roads of the occupied territories, I look at him delighted, unable to keep from thinking of another Martin from back home, dead by suicide at twenty-eight out of despair with life—like so many of his Quebec peers who no longer find any reason to go on, who are well educated but have no purpose or plan in a world they find maddeningly irrational, who are faced with a profiteering globalization in which they can no longer even identify the enemy. The Law for them is not transcendent, its commandments seem virtual, invisible, untouchable, faceless and voiceless. They no longer know whom to blame, whom to fight, they no longer see any paths on the horizon, not even a trail through the sand. The

desert within them stretches to infinity, to death. I hear
Martin speak in Arabic to the police officers of the
Palestinian Authority. He keeps a keffiyeh in his car in
case he has problems. His Palestinian Arabic and his
headwear help speed him on his way, protecting him
from the rope that could hang him or the gunshot that
could kill him in an instant. Like so many other young
people in the world, he has chosen to do humanitarian
work. If military service was replaced with this kind of
aid work wherever there is suffering in the world,
perhaps there would be no more wars, I say, and Martin
agrees. On the dry road, the dust blinds us, blocks our
ears and noses, scratches our throats, gets into our hair.
Now I understand the Bedouins, Tuaregs and other
desert tribes who wear clothing of opaque material that
covers them from head to foot. We drive along, looking
at the thousands of buildings under construction,
houses made of white or sandy pink stone taken from
this ground, sparkling in the sun behind the veil of dust.
They are all simple and beautiful, with well-balanced
proportions and lines. Everyone here seems to be
working, carpenters, masons, electricians, plumbers. The
money came from the "international community," an
incentive from the USA at the opening of the peace
negotiations, or, says Martin, from Palestinian exiles
who went away to work in Western Europe, America,
or the Arab countries and have come back with small
fortunes, thinking that Palestine will soon no longer be
a conquered land. The construction is taking place in
some disorder, without any real plan—they don't have
the time, with so much poverty and misery—some-

thing is rising out of that arid ground that looks like a great improvised celebration. I imagine all the women who will be hard at work in the new kitchens—if only one day a liberation movement would sweep them away and they'd become full subjects alongside their men and their children, these women who now are (hidden) objects of desire, vessels of reproduction. In fact, Martin takes us to a centre recently built on Palestinian land, one of the NGOs in the field, this one bringing together women and children—the men don't come to this kind of meeting, and for good reason!— and offering an amazing number of services, with several psychologists and social workers, male and female. Three problems in particular concern them: arranged marriages of girls twelve to fifteen years of age (Muslim families have an average of seven children), marital violence, and sexual abuse of children. "The women here have a long way to go to get out of this war of the sexes," Firiah, a nurse, tells us, "They have no civil rights, marry according to the laws of the Koran, and are the property of their husbands and must obey them in everything and be faithful to them, or else they are beaten, repudiated and sometimes killed, while their husbands have the right to polygamy, to take three more wives. The men do not restrain themselves with their daughters either, they usually deflower them and then have their hymens sewn up and sell them at a handsome price to new owners, their husbands." We hear so many of these stories in the course of the morning, so many accounts of the everyday war beyond the "real" war that men and women have experienced together—mass deportations, collective murders, torture in Israeli prisons—that we are dizzy and nauseous, we no longer have the energy to go to that tourist attraction, the Church of the Nativity. We just walk around it at a distance, and see it assailed by so many temple money-changers, so many pilgrims laden with video equipment and backpacks stuffed with holy souvenirs and postcards. We walk through the streets of Bethlehem, which are being rebuilt with the richest materials of this generous land—porphyries, marbles, gleaming granites and white stones that turn gold in the sun. Thousands of workers are toiling away, working super-fast. Bethlehem will look like a film set, a real setting for a Hollywood film in cinemascope. They are rushing at the last minute, as always here, Martin tells us, they are so excited that they are redoing the streets, the paving stones, the staircases that snake through the maze of the great hill that is Bethlehem. They are paving, sanding, building platforms. They must at all costs finish this masterpiece in time. Tomorrow Abu Ammar (Yasser Arafat)[11] will come and make a speech in front of the Church of the Nativity, and the residents are showing their pride. Abu Ammar owns a second home here, a veritable palace that overlooks the valley. His other house, his principal residence, is in the south, in his stronghold in the Gaza Strip. They must work fast. After Abu Ammar, Pope John Paul II will be coming, in March. He will sleep in Jerusalem, but will come to bless the people of Bethlehem. "If Jesus were to

---

11. *Abu* means "father of"; Abu Ammar is the Palestinians' familiar name for Yasser Arafat.

come back," Martin asks us, "do you think he would
have an old stable built on top of the hill? Do you think
he would chase the money-changers from the Temple
again?" We leave the film set of Bethlehem, it is indeed
beautiful, but no, beauty alone cannot avert disaster, salvation must be sought further, in a land people have not
dared to explore, deep within themselves where the
nameless resides, sometimes emerging stealthily under
the impulse of a creative spark, in the form of a poem
sung, written or painted. There the Other is no longer
completely strange, it becomes familiar to the ear or
touch, one dreams it, grasps it for a fleeting moment,
holds on to it, already longing for escape. In the car,
silence envelops us as we go back across the fractured
territories. We pass the huge Jewish settlement of Maale
Adumin, built twenty-five years ago on the land of the
gutted Palestinian villages of Abu Dis, Al-Azariya,
Issawiya, At-Tur, and Anata. I recite these names very
quietly, even spell them out, like a magic secular prayer
that could overcome this new apartheid that very few
people are concerned about. We drive on with our
unresolved questions, through the loose dust rising
from the reg desert, in a landscape soon set aglow by
the setting sun reflected from the gold dome of the
Mosque of Omar. Jerusalem, another night awaits us.

At night, half asleep, I again see the social work and
psychology centre in Bethlehem, which is affiliated
with the department of psychiatry and social work of
the Arab university in the small city, and I hear the

words of its director, Doctor Eliad Awwad Salem, a Christian Arab. Palestinian Arabs are not all Muslims, but the majority of this largest minority in Israel are Sunni Muslims, they make up a quarter of the country's population. The Christian Arabs are a minority within the largest minority, and on some questions concerning religion and matrimonial and family law, they are closer to other Christians—Roman Catholics, Greek Orthodox and Uniates (Melchites, Maronites, Chaldeans, Syrians and Armenians)—while on political issues related to the Jewish State, they are closer to their ethnic brothers, the Muslim Arabs. The social fabric in this holy and warring land is so complex that it would require the most advanced sociology and ethnology for the peace accords concluded by world leaders to really bear fruit. Meanwhile, with the support of all kinds of NGOs from the rich countries, the pioneers manage as best they can. "While they're negotiating in Washington," says Doctor Awwad, and his colleague Doctor Bojo, from a French NGO, agrees, "we're sitting on a powder keg. Israel has enough nuclear warheads to blow the whole place up, with all the ethnic groups and religions. To us, the only thing to do is help people who are suffering to heal their wounds." He talks at length of the physical and psychological effects of an occupation that has gone on for more than thirty years. There have been thousands of deaths, thousands of persons displaced, houses damaged or destroyed, thousands of exiles, men disappeared whose mothers and wives never heard from them again and cannot mourn, and prisoners subjected to the worst conditions, to mental and physical torture.

It is the women and the children who come to the centre, while the men work at rebuilding the houses or go elsewhere to talk among themselves—they can go out to public places, enjoy themselves, have a drink or a coffee, anyway, they don't believe in those talk therapies with their weeping and wailing. Often the women, confined to the house, make up schemes to go to the centre, they have such a need for help. It is not only the war and the occupation that torment them, they come here to liberate themselves from the other war they are subjected to at home. The war and the occupation seem to have caused an increase in domestic violence, but maybe it was this way before and we weren't aware of it. The women come to unburden their hearts, but also to learn how to defend and protect themselves. There is no social justice for them or their children in the Holy Land, no civil law. The religious leaders determine family law, there's no civil marriage or divorce, men and women go to their priest or rabbi or imam to marry or to unmarry. In Israel, the only marriage laws are Christian or Jewish or Muslim, religion underlies and determines individual—and, inevitably, collective—destinies. These Palestinian women, whether they are Christian or Muslim (there are no Jewish Palestinians, unlike biblical times—that split took place in 1948), have too many children and they don't have enough money to properly educate them. Where procreation is concerned, they are subject to their domestic and spiritual masters, who draw their knowledge of the law from the Koran or from Rome or from the Orthodox popes, each as misogynist as the next. "There are so many problems here," Doctor Awwad says, "with the men absent—dead, disappeared, in prison or away working—we have to help the women and their children. Giving the Palestinians a piece of land is not enough, we are concerned about all these problems that need to be solved, to be healed. The peace process means nothing if we don't deal with the problems related to poverty, ignorance and suffering."

Before falling asleep to the sound of the helicopters and sirens that haunt the Jerusalem nights, I think back to the drawings by the children from the centre, pinned to the wall of Doctor Awwad's office, all beautifully detailed and brightly coloured, all bursting with violence. The young artists are boys and girls from eight to thirteen years old, already preoccupied by peace and war. In the first drawing, armed Israeli soldiers surround a house half in ruins, its stones scattered on the ground, one of the soldiers is uprooting a big tree with a tractor, another one is pointing a gun at a man on the ground who looks dead, and in the centre, there's a woman in tears, her mouth is open, she is raging at a third soldier and pointing to the man on the ground. In the second drawing, there is a jumbled heap of stones and, high in the sky, an American flag in the form of a snake with a dollar sign in its mouth. In the third drawing, there's a camp surrounded by barbed wire, with a padlocked chain, and high in the sky, a dove holding in its beak a bunch of keys pointed towards the padlock.

The next day, we go to Ramallah, the biggest town in the West Bank. We leave Jerusalem in a collective taxi we take in the confusion and commotion at the Damascus Gate, and we travel through still more rocky hills beyond the Mount of Olives and other villages of poverty and misery, but also, everywhere, construction sites. The stones are the same as in Jerusalem, taken from the same generous soil, but the styles are different and so are the methods, the new houses are sober and dignified and they still show the Ottoman influence. Some of them are huge and proudly display their opulence against the surrounding hilltops, massive and incongruous in the humble, almost lunar landscape where the least sprig or puniest tree seems to have done long battle with the rock and dry ground. We follow the bumpy road—the best roads are never on the Palestinian side, they get the land of Cain, with their sputtering old cars, they have to make do with that. We don't understand Arabic; a few words of English are politely addressed to us and we are crammed in with the others. But nobody says much, they have eyes only for anything unusual outside, and besides, in occupied territory, one is reticent with strangers. The jolts of the road do not disturb the soft silence that comes over us, embraces us, we must be in harmony with this perfect blue of the sky, we must deserve this warming sun, despite the many worries we read in the faces of our travelling companions. Until a village that is more orderly and richer appears before us and a cold sweat, a shiver runs through the group. On our left, in the heart of the West Bank, a Jewish "settlement" surrounded by

barbed wire with Tzahal standing guard, as if they had
created their own prison for themselves. We will see
many more of them in the days to come, we will see
their guards, we will even speak to a lot of them, young
soldiers, girls and boys—military service in Israel is
compulsory for everyone—they are magnificent, these
young people, they laugh and sing like all young
people, they are proud to serve their country, Eretz
Israel, glad to give their parents the security they have
lacked for millennia, they tell us, and they are well
educated on their history of tragedies and terrors. It's as
if they all carry in their eyes and their words the
catastrophe of the Shoah, as if, with their big, heavy
rifles, they are pledging to their elders the security that
was so absent, giving them the hope that their fear of
the warlike Arabs will finally disappear. We saw those
young people and we spoke to them. They answered us
with perfect assurance, but they all wanted their names
concealed, as well as the names of the Jewish
"settlements" they had been assigned to protect, "for
security reasons" we were told by a nineteen-year-old
girl for whom the big black gun longer than her arm
"had become a friend." They are proud to serve, to
safeguard, and we understand them—if their people
had been armed against Hitler, there would have been
no Final Solution. In the collective taxi on the way to
Ramallah, thinking about the Jewish village that seems
incongruous and that is afraid, we wish we could talk
with our Palestinian companions, not in Arabic—
although we would like to learn some Arabic and
Hebrew before leaving this land—but in another

language, the one that exists only in the spare words of a poem made up in large part of silences, but eloquent silences, as in music, the pauses just as important as the notes. We would tell them that, after the Shoah, although the victims, being dead, could never give absolution, perhaps their own Jewish neighbours are forgiven in advance for having conquered their lands, perhaps the survivors have a whole territorial eternity yet to live and this credit of lands and weapons will persist for a long time in their bodies and spirits, perhaps the Jews have paid once and for all. But we don't say anything, we let the enigma remain an enigma. The West can spend all the billions it wants to illuminate the triple monotheistic mystery of the Holy Land, it will still be left with its questions. And we, with no billions, are left with ours, faced with the sole choice of continuing on our way, at the jolting mercy of the rickety old taxi, going further into this land of war, towards Ramallah.

We return to our bright little room in Jerusalem, with the window framing a constant blue sky over a garden of palm, cedar, orange and fig trees, where our birds are waiting for us. The white walls are golden with sunshine in these late afternoons devoted to rest. We will see our new friends Annie and Benyamin again this evening and tell them about our expedition into the Palestinian enclaves. But they know, they have gone there often, like others who share their "left-wing humanist" ideals, as they say, they have divided their

time between work, here, in order to live, and forays
into the occupied territories and refugee camps. They
have also gone into the prisons to support the prisoners of conscience and are members of Amnesty
International. Back home, in our peaceful little corner
of the world, Quebec, we are full members of PEN
Canada, the French-speaking section in Montreal.
Against the global ocean of censorship of the written
and spoken word, we have joined this river of freedom
that flows through a valley without borders. Like
Benyamin and Annie and so many others, we are
utopians. Or else we wouldn't be here, we would not
have undertaken this voyage, would not have lent our
ears and our eyes to so much tragedy, wouldn't have
imagined that ink on paper or a voice on the airwaves
might add a few drops to the great river of Freedom,
would have stayed home in cosy, complacent happiness,
as we tell Benyamin and Annie during evenings when
we drink the delicious Israeli Cabernet or Merlot with
them. We have so much to learn from them, and they
say in return that our words and our views, however
naive, refresh their hearts. Like many whose spirits were
nourished at twenty or thirty by the socialist model of
the kibbutzim, they feel threatened by a radical disen-
chantment that has submerged the exuberance of the
beginning and could wreck their lives. Together, we talk
and walk through the streets of central Jerusalem, this
ordinary, rather ugly commercial city that is like almost
all modern cities in the world—the beautiful city is the
rich western part, where renowned architects and
landscape designers have, since 1948, created a dream

out of stone and luxuriant vegetation, but it is also the very old city within its walls and gates, with its ruins and relics jammed with tourists and pilgrims. Together, we prefer to be in the ordinary city, with its insane, uncontrolled traffic. We mix laughter and confidences. One doesn't make such a journey to weep, there are so many sorrows all around that we must avert ill fortune with celebration, so we sing and drink toasts to music, that universal balm.

The ruins bear silent witness to history, their gaping craters accusing mouths that remind us, lest for a moment we forget, of the conquests of successive empires. So do the ruins of souls passing in the shadows on the bodies and faces here, imparting messages we pick up the better because the languages spoken are closed to us. Such are the lessons taught us by these places crowded with people toiling and tested, on the way to Bethlehem or Ramallah or Jericho. Sometimes we meet people who speak languages we know, and we reconcile the lessons they provide with the impressions gleaned here and there. One fine morning (but every morning is fine here), we meet a Canadian woman from Ottawa who is of Palestinian origin, Rahmeh Mansour, a woman of rare strength and lucidity, who runs the Centre for Palestinian Development as part of Oxfam-Québec's community projects. Rahmeh has the alert, practical mind of an activist, she doesn't feel the need I often do to attribute some vague meaning to the ruins, she acts decisively and speaks with the implacable

logic of a person who *changes the world*. We listen
fascinated for a two good hours as she describes her
work with the Palestinian women. Rahmeh is sitting in
her office, where the sunshine flooding in through the
windows illuminates the black clothing she has been
wearing for the past two days. Her beloved father has
just died, the funeral ceremony will take place this very
evening, but Rahmeh takes the time to receive us.
There is as much generosity in this land as war. This
centre in the suburbs of Ramallah is a beehive, full of
people bustling around and machines humming (tele-
phones, photocopiers, fax machines, computers), and
while her bees gather pollen, Rahmeh talks. She has
gone to the trouble of making coffee for us—the
legendary Arabic hospitality is evident in Palestine, and
a host offers something to drink or eat to every visitor,
whatever the reason for the visit. Rahmeh says this
people should not despair, or at least that's what she
believes very strongly, its destiny is now in the hands of
its women, and if the men have left them behind to go
fight for Hamas, the women have taken advantage of
their absence to work together to find solutions to their
two main problems: the general violence against their
people since the start of the Israeli occupation and their
forced submission to their men, from which they are
now trying to free themselves. Don't forget, says
Rahmeh, that 56 percent of the Palestinian population
is made up of women and that 10 percent of them are
dedicated activists who devote their free time to
opening other centres in the villages and doing civic
education on all kinds of questions. The timing is right,

Rahmeh says more than once. "The Palestinian women's movement is part of a general movement for liberation. For the first time a Constitution is being written here, with the Palestinian Authority, and women are taking part, lobbying to make sure it includes family law governing marriage and divorce, and property rights regarding estates and inheritance, which are now refused them, as well as laws on arranged marriage of Arab girls, Christian or Muslim, and also all forms of conjugal violence, and laws on freedom of religious practice." Rahmeh radiates enthusiasm and hope, talking to us about the hundreds of workshops for women that are being organized throughout the occupied territories. She thinks that their secular constitution will serve as a model, even for Jewish Israelis, who do not have one. "We want the Palestinian Authority to become aware of the specific problems of women, to make our demands official, and to turn them into laws. We keep on saying it, we negotiate clause by clause. There is a General Union of Palestinian Women, and we're all working very hard." Tomorrow, December 6, as part of an international week against domestic violence, the Union is organizing a commemoration of the fourteen young women who were murdered by a misogynist madman ten years ago at the École Polytechnique in Montreal. We should also remember, concludes Rahmeh, that Palestinian women have a proven tradition of resistance, that they have a vivid memory of the successive wars (of 1937, 1948, 1956, 1967 and 1973), that they gave birth to the young boys, now men, who in 1987 through the Intifada helped open the eyes of the whole world to the problems of the Palestinian people, which were largely ignored until then. We hear the same thing, the same factual assurances, when, in central Ramallah, we meet Dalal Salameh, a young woman of thirty-three who, along with four other women, is a member of the Palestinian Legislative Council, and who is absolutely convinced that the eighty-three other—male—members of the Legislative Council, as well as Abu Ammar, will understand the demands of the women's resistance movement, if only they can be written into the dreamed-of constitution, if only their "vision"—that's the word Dalal uses—can be translated into written laws and everyday life. "We have a vision not only of independence, but of democracy, of equality between women and men, and eventually, of parity in the corridors of power." I wish them this with all my heart, I hope that no post-modern ruin, of hearts or of stones, will ever spoil their hopes and plans. We go back through the crowded streets of the town, where the misery and violence cry out so loudly that the beauties of the sky and the land are blotted out.

Gaza, Qalqilya, Tulkarm, Hebron, East Jerusalem, Bethlehem, Nablus, Ramallah, Jericho, Jenin, the names of the Palestinian towns go through my head one night when I am myself surrounded, lost in a labyrinth with a Tzahal Kalashnikov trained on each exit. Yet I'm not among the Serbs of Bosnia or Kosovo, and the Israeli soldiers normally have American weapons. But dreams are not the land of the normal. I must have made this connection because of this country's neutrality in the Balkan wars, its reaction to the threat of those other secessionist Muslims in a south-central Europe that, like it, was struggling with its religious boundaries. Whichever way I turn, the exits are blocked, I have to get out, I'll find a way, a trick. Suddenly there is an opening of greenery and water filled with light, it's Independence Park in Tel Aviv, on the Mediterranean. I go out into it without a problem, I'm swimming like a fish, a moment of ecstatic joy when the caress of the wave has overcome all danger, I touch the shore, sit down there, for the moment I'm safe. A woman comes towards me on Ben Yehuda Street, she's from the Women's League of the House of Israel up near Tchernichevsky Street, she has the look of Slavic Jewish women, blond and corpulent, majestic, she says, "I was sent to get you, you will be one of us. Only you have to convert, it will be very simple, I'll explain the steps to you." No time to answer that I have nothing against her religion but I don't want any of them, my own transcendence doesn't materialize anywhere, except sometimes in sparse bits of poetry. No time to even ask her for a coffee, it would be good in the morning sun after this night in the damp caves of cold and fear. She vanishes as she came, I see her shadow slipping away toward the port of Tel Aviv to the north. I turn in the opposite direction, Samia is standing there, very far away, but I still see her, leaning her head against the wall of the Great Mosque of Jaffa, crying. She came back to see her old parents' ruined house in Jaffa, the one on the bay, not far from their mosque, but she didn't recognize anything, everything has changed so much in the half-century since they were driven out. I try to go to Samia, I want to comfort her, but she disappears, everything fades away, and morning is pouring in through the windows. The sleeper, refreshed by a dip in the sea, goes over the day's program in her head.

An appointment in Birzeit, on the old campus of the University of Palestine, at the Community Health Centre, funded by the Palestinian Authority and the UN, as we are told by its director, Rita Giacomin, who speaks freely to us. With one part of my mind, I hear her words while another part unreels the night's dream in the catacombs and ruins of the Palestinian towns encircled by Tzahal, I am myself a town. It is to Tel Aviv-Jaffa that the water and Samia's tears deliver me, I come back to this woman who speaks as one would play a concerto. There's such harmony in this office, as busy as it is, where the telephone is never stops ringing and there are problems of all kinds to be solved. The director, sitting with us at a long oval table, looks like a Goya painting, she has that harmonious beauty, that deep, serious gaze. The thick stone walls of the building turn the golden light of midday to silver, glinting on her black hair in which there are a few shining white strands and on her delicate silver necklace. Her words are fluent, her voice modulated, her hands active, moving in cadence. Yes, a Goya painting accompanied by a concerto, the music is in the air, as Schubert said, no need to look any further. I write down what this woman doctor tells us, and the dream vanishes, goes back to its limbo. Rita Giacomin was sixteen years old in 1967—the women we have met here, in Israel and Palestine, always define the stages of their lives by the dates of wars, not by marriages, children, graduations or books—she was sixteen in 1967. She says, "I don't want to talk politics. War to me means four generations of very vibrant women"—her great-aunt, who lived through the 1937 war, her mother, the 1948 war, Rita herself, the 1967 war, and her daughter, who is nine years old, today's war. That means it's been continuous, this war that's punctuated by three fateful dates and that is still going on, and to which there seems to be no end, no purpose, no hope. She says "The war is the sadness and melancholy of the women—we have joys, of course, my great-aunt, my mother, my little girl, and we love each other, but we don't know happiness." She reminds me of a Jewish man from Austria, some seventy-five years old, that I met at the Post Office the day before, who insisted on talking about his arrival in Israel, in 1947, to the foreigner that I am, who wanted to bear witness to his return to Eretz Israel. His eyes lit up when he spoke of the magnificence of his native Austria. When I asked my naive question, "You are happy in Israel?" he took a good few seconds to answer, looking at me with that air of compassion combined with cynicism of a person who's seen too much and has lived to tell about it, and said, "Poor dear, I am fine, yes, thank you, but the words *happiness* and *happy* do not exist for us." Rita continues the litany of her wars: "The men experience the war as a defeat, because it doesn't end. They are always angry, and we weep, when they recount the history of the Palestinians' wars. They always talk about the men. Someday the important role women play will have to be recognized. During the Intifada, the sons became the sons of all mothers, there was a huge grass-roots movement of women here, a solidarity of poor and rich, which the men do not know. If the peace accords continue to be negotiated by a few men cut off from the people, the women and children, there will be more terrible violence here, both for the Israelis and for us." The women of the Centre have two goals. The first is to transform women's capacity for suffering into power. To do so, they draw on all the social sciences, the bookcase testifies to this, the men and women here do fieldwork and there are numerous studies. "The silent sufferings of women are slowly being turned into speech and concrete political action in all areas." Their other goal is, through a proper civil contract, to give girls the same rights as boys. "If something happens to me, I, like other women, and unlike men, have no rights, no social security." There is a glimmer of hope in Rita's eyes only when she talks about her daughter—and about her husband, who she says was educated in the West and is on the same wave-length—the girl will never become the property of a man and of in-laws, she will be educated and autonomous, and if the war persists, at least she will not know the war within the war. "Everything will change," says Rita, "with my daughter's generation. It is the dream of my great-aunt, my mother and myself that she become independent. With each generation of women, each one marked by a war, we have advanced towards our liberation. Now our struggle is more open, we are becoming feminists. In the West, you do not like that word any more, you are too spoiled. We are passing the torch to the little one, and she is very proud, she has excellent political sense."

At this moment when Rita is perhaps imagining happiness for her nine-year-old daughter, tears flood her sea-green eyes, two suns greeting the two others, the one whose slanting rays are shining down on us and the inner one, the maternal love that constantly strives to give birth to a better world. We must part, each to her own tasks. For a few hours, we will both walk in the streets of the mainly Christian village of Birzeit, filled with women and children, the only men we see are old men, the rest are absent—or dead, or in prison, or away working to rebuild the country—a few Muslim girls are walking arm in arm with their mothers, with scarves on their heads and dressed in the old-fashioned way, they smile shyly and then lower their heads, their eyes on the paving stones. We hear children shouting, girls and boys playing in the schoolyard of the Maronite Catholic school. A fence protects the school and the very new little church dedicated to the Virgin. The children, wearing navy-blue uniforms over jeans, wave to us, talk to us all at the same time in their language, they don't think to wonder if we know Arabic, and we answer in French, which doesn't surprise them, and the bilingual dialogue continues. We leave Birzeit to the sound of their laughter mixed with the songs of birds, the music reverberates very far, to the bottom of the valley, to the silence of the desert nearby, to be brought back with the sand on the waves of a light breeze.

We had already met the Samia of my dream, the one who was crying over the ruins of her old house in Jaffa, and we see her again, Samia Bamieh, a *grande dame* of fifty—in the Holy Land of war, on both sides, women and men always state their age, making a point of marking the time that otherwise might escape them, the vast time that flies from one war to the next—she had said, in the first minutes of our first meeting in Ramallah, at the Palestinian women's centre, "I am fifty years old, the circle of my life is closing. I have lived for the return to Palestine, and the return is here, the purpose of my life has been fulfilled, it is here." She speaks with the hoarse, solemn voice of a Jeanne Moreau, a depth of tone that conveys the invisible. We imagine her in the refugee camps in Lebanon, where her family at first found themselves, we envision her very small, surrounded by family, clinging to her mother's breast. She was born in Lebanon, just after the exodus in 1948, when they were driven out of their beautiful house in Jaffa. Samia shows us photographs and says, "They took the house and the garden, but not this, we carried our images with us." We envision her as a young girl doing volunteer work with the Lebanese women's movement. She didn't want to get married then, much less have children, "Carry children to death, no, never, it was out of the question," she says, using the same words as Annie—those two would get along so well—but she met the love of her life, a Palestinian man her age, also a refugee in Lebanon, and a member of the PLO. They were to love, marry, and have two children, and to become, through sorrows, struggles and joys, "the best friends in the world." She has spent her whole life in Lebanon, lived there through part of the horrible fifteen-year war when nobody knew who was killing or why, who was against whom or with whom, everything was so confused, only in death did the different bloods mix, flowing in one tide over the broken land, the blood of Christians divided among themselves in life, the blood of Syrian and Jordanian Arabs, the blood of Israeli Jews, and the blood of Palestinians, Muslim and Christian. "I was born in Lebanon of refugee parents, and my father and mother died there, having despaired of returning, they died before the Oslo Accords." Her little family again had to take the path of diaspora during the war in Lebanon, they went to Tunisia, to finally return here, to Palestine, in 1996. "I did not fight out of hatred of anyone, not even of those who took our place here, I fought out of love, of my family, of my people, of my country, of our territory. Very early, at seventeen years of age, I knew my destiny was bound to that of my Palestinian people."

"Now my children say, 'This is my country!' It was not always easy for them. In adolescence they accused us of uprooting them, they had to leave their friends and school twice, from Lebanon to Tunisia and from Tunisia to Palestine. Now they understand our decisions, they have become responsible, they have finally come to terms with their diaspora. You know, I know girls who resent their activist mothers for stealing their childhood from them. They never talk about these effects of the war in the media. The war is presented badly, they imagine us all with guns. But we live during war, we make love, we have babies, we mourn fallen fighters, we mourn people who die of disease or old age, we have our loves and hates, our domestic conflicts, and all the same problems as citizens of countries at peace, and we have our dreams, our drives, our desires, our seductions. Women know these things better than men. In the peace talks, economic and political logic always prevails. If women ran the world, there would be no more war. First of all, if they ran it side by side with men, the first war, the war of sexual inequality, would not exist, and then, they would put on the agenda the things that are usually ignored. When women get involved in war or resistance, it is first of all to give their children and grandchildren a better life. I don't believe that is men's goal. They don't even know how to cry, can you imagine, not knowing how to cry? It's like not knowing how to laugh, it's like not knowing how to dream. Men repress their sadness, they keep it inside, and when it resurfaces, it is in the form of anger—their guns take the place of tears and dreams."

Samia, this imposing lady, goes on talking for a long time. She says that, for her people, she had no choice, she had to resist, she says she had to give up a career as a journalist, that she would very much have liked to travel, to bear witness, to speak on the airwaves, to write, she says, "I chose to be an activist while having children. I had to give up certain dreams." She feels old, but I find her young, I tell her. "Reveal my age," she says, "It's not the same for you, it doesn't show, you haven't known war or exile. Here, in my generation, we are all worn out, we have the diseases of old age already, white hair, wrinkled skin, stooped backs." She talks about their current struggle, the constitution that they are in the process of writing with the Palestinian Authority, the fight for democracy and equality between the sexes—it is the women of the land who are leading it, since the men are mostly involved with the struggle for national liberation. The women see the danger, they understand that if national concerns take precedence over social concerns, they will constantly have to start over again, the same old conflicts over the possession of the territory will keep coming back. The women working for democracy see this danger all the better because, unlike their men, they have not created idols among themselves, they have leaders everywhere in the territory, they are linked together without any fixed hierarchical structure, and they are working everywhere, in the Gaza Strip and the towns and villages of the West Bank. Samia continues: "This people that was forced out in 1948 was falling apart. We returned not to conquer a territory, though it belongs to us, but to work for the establishment of a democratic country where women would enjoy the same rights and freedoms as men and would finally have access to the same education. We are making progress."

One evening, Samia invites us to her home in the
village of El Bireh. The stone house, like all the houses
here, has a graceful, sober beauty, it is a humble
reminder of her family's house in Jaffa. "It is not a
luxury, it was a vital necessity to recreate that home." It
has a soul, you can feel it in the tastefully chosen things
brought back from the countries of wandering, the
photograph corner that is like a memorial chapel with
its eloquent images "snatched from the invader." We
contemplate the pictures of a bygone time, a big villa by
the sea in Jaffa with people posing for future generations, regal grandparents, an aunt in a lace dress seated
elegantly in the middle of the garden with splashes of
sunlight in her laughing eyes, a father whose stature and
Sunday-best suit remind me of my own father, a
mother romantic, charming and fresh—she is twenty
years old and has her life ahead of her—and dozens of
other photographs, a movie camera, a painting, some
papers with writing, and then a picture of Samia at
eighteen, by the sea in Lebanon. She says, "Wasn't she
beautiful, that girl with all her hopes written on her
face?" Yes, it's true, they're written there, deep in her
eyes, the film has captured them. She points out those
who are dead and tells us when they died, and names
the survivors dispersed to the four corners of the earth,
in Egypt, England, Tunisia and even Canada. She sings
the beginning of a Palestinian song that goes back to
the dawn of time: "Hard is the diaspora, tender is the
homeland." She takes us to the little garden. She planted
a jasmine bush there, like they had in Jaffa, but it didn't
survive, the earth is dry here—she has planted a jasmine

bush in every place she's lived, as a kind of talisman, a
promise of return for her family—and when it died, she
replaced it with a fig tree, like they had in Jaffa, and that
one is flourishing and producing good fruit under the
new moon of Ramadan. Samia and her whole household are fasting "in the spirit of forgiveness and
reconciliation." She breaks into song, a song of
resistance, which she translates for us:

> At the border, I went through.
> They asked for my identity card.
> I said, It's at my grandmother's,
> At home, in Jaffa, she kept it.
> At the border, I went through.

Abruptly she says, "I was conceived in Jaffa and I was
born in Lebanon. My mother gave me a love of water
and the sea with her milk." Samia does not share our
liking for the desert, she wants water and a garden, she
is in search of an Eden, a paradise lost, a time regained
that would flow like a liquid and wash away the
meanness and stupidity of the world, while her son,
young Maged, at sixteen years of age writes poems to
the time of the desert that flows like sand here in the
West Bank, this strip between the Mediterranean and
the Jordan. We will see Samia again, we have agreed, in
her home or elsewhere in the world, we will write each
other, it's a promise.

In the evening, on the way to Jerusalem, we pass the
village of Beit El, a "Jewish settlement," as they call it.
We see the barbed wire surrounding it, glimpse the
shadows of the sentinels under the crescent moon, the

shining tips of protecting guns raised here and there in the clear warm night.

On our return to Jerusalem, we find this letter from Benyamin:

Very dear friends, when you read this note, Annie will no longer be of this world. She died yesterday. She had lung cancer, but she was confident of getting better and did not want to tell you. The day after our lovely evening together, her oncologist informed her that it had metastasized and she had six brain tumours. Annie knew death was certain. Did not want to endure the suffering of deterioration and a lingering death. Lucid, she chose to leave before. The last evening, she wanted us to drink champagne together, which we did. When I left her in the early hours of the morning, she asked me to come back the next day to see to the death certificate, and gave me a will. She has bequeathed me everything she owned and asked me to take care of the cremation. She wants her ashes to be buried on Palestinian land, in the desert of Judea, not far from Jericho and the Jordan. She would like you to be with me as witnesses to this act of resistance. She always thought Israel should give the Palestinians the whole west bank of the Jordan, from Lake Tiberias to the Dead Sea, as reparations. She believed that the Palestinians would be perfectly willing to sign an agreement to share their water with the Israelis. She said that there are no longer any problems with Syria, or at least that she hoped not, that Syria would get back its Golan and its irrigated areas. She also said that Jordan has the whole east bank for itself, and that in any case it gave up all claim to the west bank ten years ago. You see that Annie died as she lived, caring about those who were oppressed, as her people was so often in history. I am deeply saddened, my loss is irreparable. Will you come with me to bury our friend tomorrow?

We had wanted to see the desert, had so hoped to reach the empire of silence in the endless rolling terrain where the waves of sand lead to more sand, to infinity. We had never dreamed we would make the trip with a burial urn, had not imagined that the desert would open to us when we placed death itself under the sand, had not anticipated that we would have to pay a tribute worthy of it, that we would have to earn our way across it by carrying in our arms something even larger than it, the gaping eternity hollowed out by death.

In the morning, we set out with Benyamin. Crossing the desert is not the same as living in it, but the images of Judea will always remain with us. The desert, like the mountains, is a land of silence, of meditation. All imagination disappears amid the identical dunes, all reasoning vanishes, you have to find a field within you as wide as the sky above to hear its muted song punctuated by the singing of the sand, the occasional rustling of dry grass in the distance where humans have wrested some oasis from this anhydrous world. The ear follows the thread of sound and the eye discovers the goats and sheep that have been grazing there for so long and have learned to subsist on little. Their Bedouin masters, whom we see in their camps of sheet-metal and tarpaulin, to us represent the quintessence of poverty. They are rich with the teachings of their animals; they would die, we are assured by Benyamin, who spends time with them, if they were transplanted to our cities and our comfortable houses. Their gardens are not on land, but in the open sky, their trees, shrubs and flowers are the stars, which they are able to see night and day. Passing dune after dune, hill of sand after hill of stony sand, we drive slowly, encountering not lines of cars, but herds of camels in single file, their hooves not crunching but equal to the silence—going where, we don't know, we have no reference points, but they advance stiffly, as if immovable, towards a distant place of which they are so sure, they follow the same route together with no guides. We drive slowly, and occasionally we see a village on the horizon, a Jewish settlement, says Benyamin, one of these kibbutzim of the return, where men and women worked so hard to survive after the great desert of the Final Solution, wanting to defy the deserts of Samaria and Judea, and they succeeded, they prevailed. Benyamin takes a narrow road between Jericho and the Jordan, as indicated in Annie's will, he turns off the motor, and we get out, carrying the urn, and climb a hill, a dune of packed sand. Benyamin digs with a shovel and we place the urn there and close the little grave of sand again. We place on it a flat stone found lower down, and on the stone, a bouquet of yellow roses, which Annie loved.

How long did we stay there, sitting around the grave without speaking? I don't really know. We drank a few swallows of water, our minds elsewhere, with Annie of course, but also very far away, deep within, each of us lost in that earthly ocean that is within us, from its sunrise shore called birth to its sunset shore called death, there where one no longer knows which way is north or south, where no human compass or sextant can help us steer our course.

On an Israeli road, we sped towards the Jordan and the Dead Sea, first forking upward to greet Nazareth and Lake Tiberias from the distance—you don't come out of a monolithic Catholic childhood without wanting to get close to these mythic places that are the stuff of so many legends—and then back down along the Jordan, catching occasional glimpses of its blue line between the ochre of Jordan and that of Judea, as far as the Dead Sea, whose deadness we saw with our own eyes, saw that it is without birds or fish, a salt bath slowly being consumed by the earth. In five hundred years, it will no longer exist. Having for millennia been the impassive witness of too many tears shed by the peoples on its shores, it is a basin of salty tears. Today the Israel-Jordan border runs through the middle of it—in half a millennium these neighbours will be able to walk over the white desert of salt to each other, will no longer have to turn around or to mourn their abandoned villages. Or else they will die turned into statues like the wife of Lot, a giant crystallized sculpture of whom we later discover further south, towards Masada.

LEBANON

Lebanon

There's no understanding this place, no one can disentangle the complexities of a war that went on for fifteen years but that in fact began long before—but no one knows exactly when anymore—and is not over. You don't know whether this war has ended when you see for yourself that there is still hatred everywhere, on the roads where the beat-up old cars constantly honk and roar by lawlessly at breakneck speed, no turn signals or anything, and pass you on the right or on the left, shouting, coming very close, taking your breath away each time. No one-way streets, no speed limits, no regulations on car maintenance or the fuel put into them. It's polluted, it stinks, it continues the destruction the war began. People on every side were killed—Sunnis, Shiites, Maronites, Palestinians, Druze. No one knows anymore who started it or why, no one knows if it's ended. After the destruction of people, animals, houses and forests, the mindless work of death continues. Once such a beautiful country, Lebanon, source of many waters, temple of cedars, hardwoods and birds of this part of the Fertile Crescent, opened its doors to the surrounding peoples and to the peoples within as well. Not ended, the war. They continue to destroy while building it. Goodbye to the lovely seashore, the coast has been gutted, the ugliness of the buildings like so many slabs crowded together, promoters are the new warriors. Goodbye to the gentle forests, there's nothing to do now but dig, drill, tear up the stone in brutish anarchy, pile it up somewhere else, crush it, make cement or concrete out of it, erect more buildings, more businesses, witness the desertification. Powerless, see a pelican, only one, limping crazily in terror on the highway near Byblos, which was once beautiful. Tourists go there to admire the ruins, while the restaurants serve up the American way of life, while Syrian boys play at being procurers and pimps, while not far away, under the vigilant eye of their army, there are thriving crops that are now worth their weight in gold here—not wheat, not rice, not corn, but opium and hashish, which will take the same maritime route as the girls that are sold. Lebanon, ill-fated country, there's no understanding it, the most learned quit trying long ago, and the women don't understand any better than the men, only they say it, they all say it: "We do not know who started what, we do not even know if it has ended." They say it, write it, weep it, and shout it, and the men destroy while building. The old jalopies drive at breakneck speed, money drives over the hundred and fifty thousand human graves dug by the war—among them twenty thousand Palestinians and as many Maronites, Shiites, Sunnis and Druze—money drives over the ruins, over the remaining treasure of the ruins.

The Israeli army in the south, and the Syrian army in the north and the east hold vigil over this dismembered body, its lungs, heart, brain and limbs torn away, hold vigil in the memorial chapel Lebanon has become, but not in silence, the chapel is so noisy. There's no understanding it! It appeared to be a religious war, but it was nothing less than the image of hell served up to the world. And vultures, yes, we saw plenty of them circling in the sky, biding their time.

No more laws or regulations. What is happening on the roads is a sign of what is happening inside, in the souls and hearts. The law has been killed with everything else, the law of the Father no longer exists, the fathers have been killed, the fathers of heaven and earth, the fathers Allah and Yahweh, the fathers of Christ and Muhammad. The mothers remain, they are in the houses, they cry, they pray, they pray while crying, the Maronite mothers, who are Arabs like the others, like the Sunni and Shiite mothers and like the Muslim Palestinian mothers. It was only their men that killed each other, over factional differences, sectarian beliefs and political lines, but the women took the side of their men, praying and crying—some of them prayed with guns in their hands, but very few. The Maronite mothers did as the other mothers and the other daughters did, but a rampart separated them from the other mothers—they were Arabs too, but Christian Arabs, and Roman Catholics moreover, although their ancestor Maro, saint and martyr, turned his back on Rome over the definition of the nature of God, so long ago that no one really understands what was at issue

anymore, it was at the beginning of the Roman
Empire, when Syria was a Roman province and
Lebanon a province of Syria. A little later, when
Christianity was carrying out its conversions of all these
Semitic peoples, Muhammad, the ancestor of the Sunni
mothers and the Shiite mothers and the ancestor of the
Palestinian mothers, had a series of dreams, which he
came to tell the Semitic peoples of the Fertile Crescent
and the other peoples of the Middle East. He founded
his religion, which the Jewish fathers and the Christian
fathers and the Maronite fathers resisted. There were
murders everywhere, exoduses, exiles, breaks, so that in
this century of ashes, the rampart held firm between the
Maronite mothers and the others, even though they
were daughters of the same Semitic ancestors,
daughters of Canaan or Judea, or daughters of those
Phoenicians who came from the sea five millennia ago,
bringing with them their greatest treasure, the twenty-
two letters of the phonetic alphabet. The rampart of
division held firm, even though they descended from
fathers and mothers who had together experienced
successive conquests by the Egyptians, the Assyrians, the
Babylonians, the Persians, the Greeks and the Romans,
had been bathed in the same ocean of blood under the
Ottoman and Byzantine empires. The rampart between
them held firm in this century of ashes. In their
kitchens or in the washhouses or over the graves of
their men, they all cried while praying. The law of the
Father was irremediably killed. Despite the clamour of
all the Jihads and all the Crusades in the world, the
mothers and the daughters continued to pray while

crying, all of them without exception telling us they had understood nothing of that war, and yet they were not fools. They no longer wanted to analyze the base works of the world, prayer had become their work, and tears. They had become Our Ladies of the Seven Sorrows, it was the only solution, too much blood spilled, too many murders, too many terrorists, and for too long. The Maronite mothers, when they were not praying, had gone with their surviving sons to set up little white and blue statues of Our Lady of the Sorrows all over the field of ruins. There were millions of them in Lebanon, they were left alone, the Muslim fathers and the Muslim mothers didn't touch them, didn't profane these millions of little improvised shrines, they weren't bothered by the Lady dressed in a long blue dress, her head covered, humble, with a long white veil.

The veiled Lady of the Seven Sorrows attacked no one, not the Muslim fathers and sons any more than the Muslim mothers and daughters, not the fathers and sons of the Hezbollah or the more radical ones of the Jihad—like the Maronite Christians, the extremist Phalangists, the Palestinians and the Israelis, they all killed, massacred, pillaged, burned, kidnapped, imprisoned, tortured, but they didn't touch her, the veiled Lad, dressed in white and blue. There she is, enthroned, on the hills, at the end of the piers, in the parks, in the denuded gardens, and they all let her be, enthroned, keeping vigil over the ruins. Her eyes closed and her head bent towards the ground, she doesn't have the air of the conquerors, the emperors, kings or generals in whose honour monuments were once built—no, she stands modestly with her eyelids shut, her eyes that do not look at men are turned towards the ground or are looking within, she sees into things, seems to be looking inside the world, so that you look at her without really seeing her. How could those murdering fathers and sons see her, the Mother of all their prophets, the blessed daughter of the gods for whom they fight, how can they look their own mothers and their own daughters in the eye, when their hands are soaked with the blood of those other fathers and those other sons, how can they gaze at that Lady of the Seven Sorrows when they have all drunk of the blood and sorrows of other mothers, other daughters? How can they follow the inner path of her gaze, turned towards the ground and within, without risking drowning, trapped in the need for tears, milk and blood, seeing themselves very small there in the midst of a huge pool of water rocked by great waves, seeing themselves reflected there, powerless, in the centre of the ocean devoid of landmarks, the ocean that comforts while rocking, that rocks while comforting? They'd rather attack the fathers and sons of other gods, the mothers and daughters of other gods, they'd rather defy all the laws of the earth, the divine laws and the human laws, they'd rather kill, massacre, torture, slit throats and bellies, rape, rather than face that one gaze turned within. That's why She's wearing a long dress, that's why She's veiled, that's why her eyes are closed, that's why her lips are sealed, her eyes must not look at them and her lips must remain sealed, what they would see there, what they would hear from her lips, the words that would finally flow freely, would make them all dizzy, the ground would tremble beneath their feet, the armour would shatter on all sides, old-fashioned warriors or new promoter-warriors who destroy while building would see their weapons and all their possessions tumble into the craters, the crevasses, the pits, into their polluted water where other streams of blood would flow, would see their new ruins piled on the old ruins. And in the post-war reconstruction, that is in fact what they are discovering, old ruins under the new ruins. All the archaeologists in the world are rushing to Lebanon to take advantage of these age-old strata of ruins—since every empire built while destroying, the space underneath is so crowded that Lebanon is one huge tell. But the new warriors don't want to think about that, they even have promoters for ruins. They don't want to risk dizziness, they respect the Lady, tolerate her, but if She were just to remove her veil, they'd kill her, if She were to raise her eyelids and open her lips, they'd go mad. Rather than face that, they prefer arrogantly to rush towards disaster.

The Wazzani, Hasbani and Damour Rivers continue to flow down the mountains of Lebanon to the Mediterranean, as does the Dog River in the valley of the same name, but these veins and arteries that, more than gold, constituted the wealth of the country are shrinking visibly, drying up from year to year, their lungs shrivelled as a result of the death of old tree plantations, their thin trickles carrying human and industrial waste. Nevertheless, after a single day of rain, we saw the Dog River swollen, surging in a torrent through the valley below Zouk Mosbeh, but its muddy waters were bronze in the setting sun, as if it were spitting blood. I went walking where it was possible, where there wasn't a risk of being run down by the careening cars, on the only little street with a sidewalk, beautiful sand-pink stones leading to the Maronite Notre Dame University. I walked towards the blood-red ball of the sun, which would soon drop into the water around the peninsula of Beirut to the south, far from the fury of the traffic, I heard the rushing water of the river down below. A woman who appeared ageless but was perhaps in her forties came towards me on the same sidewalk of sand-pink stones, without looking at me, she said in a loud voice, "Come and sit down, we'll talk." She sat down on a stone bench with her back to the sun, and, paying no attention to me, started to talk. I continued on my way to the goal I had set myself, the end of this little road and of the sidewalk, and when I returned after a good half-hour, she was still conversing, it was herself that she had asked to come sit down and talk. I walked by softly, pausing briefly, not wanting to meddle in her secrets. She was murmuring confidences to herself, seemed calm, happy even, did not have that look of madness that people who talk to themselves usually have. I was going to continue my walk towards my hotel, to slip away quietly leaving her to her dialogue. She seemed enthralled, delighted by the words she and the other-in-her were exchanging. But she abandoned her confidential tone and raised her voice as if she wanted me to hear, wanted me to stay there, as if it was important to her to have a witness. I decided to loiter quietly behind her stone bench, walking unobtrusively back and forth between the rays of the setting sun and the darkness of the mountains on the other side of nightfall. Satisfied, she lit herself a cigarette and continued her dialogue, with lots of gestures and miming. She was nicely dressed, tan suede coat over black slacks and turtleneck, soft leather ankle boots, calfskin bag, no jewellery or make-up, with medium-length salt-and-pepper hair that fell like a veil around her oval face. She was speaking French with some words in Arabic, her expression was one of delight with the paths her dialogue was taking her on, she was hearing voices other than her own, that's certain, so attentive did she seem at times, listening. But as a witness I heard only her remarks and her answers.

"I told you again and again not to go there, but did you ever listen to me? Yes, at the beginning, when you loved me, it was as if there was a magnetic attraction between our bodies, you don't remember, how could you remember? Memory is for the living, memory belongs to those who have bodies, with a head and a heart that beats, I told you not to go, but you had stopped listening to me. When we were joined together, our words, too, were magnetized, we talked for hours, looking into one another's eyes. Against the wishes of your Muslim family, you married a Christian woman, you said 'Jeanne, for you, for your eyes and your body, for your words that stir me, for your eyes that intoxicate me, I would go around the world on my

knees,' and on your knees you asked me to marry you,
you asked my Maronite father, you asked my Maronite
mother, you asked my Maronite brother, and they
refused to give you my hand, they banished me,
repudiated me. We went to see the imam, I studied the
Koran, I converted to Islam, the imam married us, your
family didn't even look at me, they scorned the stranger
I was. If one of your sisters had married a Christian, she
would have had to flee very far away, or else they would
have killed her. They didn't kill me, they spurned me. I
was nothing but a reproductive vessel to them, our
children would be Muslim, that's what they were
waiting for, Muslim children, only the vessel remained
empty of children, week after week, month after
month, year after year, the vessel remained empty of
children, I was *sterile*, you screamed in my ears as you
beat me, because you would now touch this body once
so loved only to strike it, the magnetic force was no
longer love, but rage, you no longer ached with
yearning, you were filled with a desire to hurt this body
that had been so dear to you, you burned to bruise it as
once you burned to kiss it. At times, after falling on it
like a famished beast on its prey, you would plunge your
penis in, to the point of ripping it open, tearing it apart,
I was a patch of land that was raked, wounded, torn
because all the digging, delving, drilling failed to yield
treasure. Then, one fine day, you had no more desire to
touch me, not even to beat me, you became gloomy
and listless, all the fire was extinguished in you, no more
fire of pleasure, no more fire of rage, you were declining
and you wanted to die, you didn't cry, men never cry,

but you wanted to die, that's all you said to me, without
even looking at me, that's what you repeated all day
long. And then you became calm, you would go out
from morning till evening, sometimes you would leave
again at night, but you had become calm. One
morning, you announced to me that you were taking a
second wife, a Muslim this time, she would give you
children, you loved her. But she was like me, an empty
vessel, a "barren womb," you said, cursing, and again
you wanted to die, you called both of us "oysters
without pearls," and you wanted to die, to escape from
yourself, to leave that "bag of sorrows" you said your
body had become, to leave this earth as a free spirit
going to meet its Prophet and its God, free and light
like the spirit of a child, you wanted to bury the "bag
of sorrows" that was your flesh and bones in the belly
of the earth. You had planned your suicide, you had
begun to talk to me again in your final despair, you had
found some scraps of our love that had fallen to the
bottom of the abyss, that the magnetic bodies of our
loving youth had left there in the depths of the crater,
fibres of the vitality that was once ours, that the
anticipation of death brought back to you like the turn
of the tide, you said you were ready for the great leap
into eternity. You talked to me, Rashid, and I, Jeanne,
discovered that I had forgiven you and that I still loved
you, but we had no more life for each other in our
bodies, no more attraction of our flesh. Our bodies had
turned to stone, like two tombstones in the great
cemetery of our two separated lives. I didn't want you
to commit suicide, my own God, returned from the

depths, did not permit it, but I could no longer prevent
you from doing it, it was inevitable, and I was
exhausted, the vessel of my spirit had also dried up. Your
death was written in a great book whose meaning
escaped me, in a foreign language I didn't know how to
read, your death was written, and then the war came!

"Just when you were going to pass into eternity, the
war came! You were no longer the same, from the
moment when your people and my people and all the
rest began killing each other, you were no longer the
same. You regained the fire of your youth, the light in
your eyes, your body became strong and firm and tall
again like the one I had loved so much. You were
beautiful, Rashid, during your training. You were
preparing to leave for one of the fronts, it had been
decided that your division would go to the south. I said,
'Don't go, Rashid.' You didn't listen to me, you rushed
towards war, you rushed towards death. You would
come back to the house with your head stuffed with
religious talk. You had put on the spanking new
uniform of the new soldiers of God, you were burning
to handle your brand-new weapons. I saw a young man
I no longer recognized leave for the front. You had
become the son I had awaited for so long. Answer me
just once, Rashid, do you know in your eternity that
we have a son, that the war gave the two of us a son? It
was you. That is why I never cry anymore. When I
understood that, I completely stopped crying, no more
nightmares, no more depression, no more psychiatrists,
no more medication. I have a son now—you, Rashid—
that I can talk to all the time. I'm still waiting for your

answers, but they will come, I don't worry anymore. You went off to war, to the southern front, and I—like all the women, I cried, like all the women, I lived in the shelters, I slept, ate, spoke, dreamed to the sound of shelling, with the crazy hope that you would return one day a hero, with the crazy hope that peace would return, and more than peace, our love. Until the day I learned of your death, Rashid, until the day I knew it was all over for you, for us. You had fallen, your weapon in your hand, under fire from an Israeli battalion. They told me you were smiling when your comrades retrieved your lifeless body, you smiled when you received that gift you so desired. Someone gave you death, Rashid, the death you had not dared to give yourself, someone finally gave it to you. You must have smiled when you saw the Israeli soldier coming towards you offering that gift, holding the weapon that had the power to give the most abstract thing in the world, death. Giving life is so concrete, it comes from a mother's belly and a father's sperm, life grows slowly in a mother's belly, you can see the belly grow big, then the nourishing placental sac comes out like a bag of guts, with blood and urine and excrement, with the screams of the mother and the child. It's so concrete, giving life, and dying is so abstract, unless a person commits suicide or kills someone else, it's so abstract. So, Rashid, you went away to seek the death you hadn't been able to give yourself. War is a battlefield, but it's also a field of gifts. Men who cannot bear life go happily to the field of gifts, all the murderers, all the killers, all the warriors who are satisfied with what they

are have failed to appreciate the gift of life, they
therefore manufacture instruments that give the gift of
death. When life is not a gift, Rashid, death must be
made a gift. I no longer have nightmares, have no more
need for drugs or psychiatrists, I need only to talk to
you, you see, only to chat with you from time to time.
I love it when dusk comes and the sun is going down,
it's softer, you hear me better. Only, I warn you, if you
do not answer me immediately, I'll go and find you.
They say that in Eternity all gods are equal, and most
important, they say no one is sterile … "

I left quietly. She knew I was leaving, I could feel it.
She began to whisper again, perhaps to hum, it seemed
to me I heard music mixing with the murmur of nightfall in the valley of the Dog. Still, I turned back after a
few paces and said, "Good night, Jeanne," and left again,
my ear cocked for the sound of the river before the
cacophony of screeching cars started up again. The
words she said to me sounded like a moan: "Au revoir,
Madame, Insh'Allah!"

There are few birds in Lebanon, and you don't see
children in the streets of the towns and villages, you
don't see them. No parks for recreation either, not
rebuilt yet, neither adults' nor children's, and the
walking paths and playing fields are too dangerous.
How can they relax, dream, and enjoy themselves
openly and publicly in these once-luxuriant open-air
spaces of freedom that during the long war were arenas
of battle, with barricades set up with felled trees, and

sandboxes emptied into bags to stuff the mouths of trenches? How can they risk the innocence of play there where bullets whistled, shells fell, grenades exploded, and mines were laid? How can they believe in fun again when the war made a mockery of childhood, put its money on death rather than on birth, played games with the end rather than the beginning, made playgrounds into killing grounds? War mocks childhood and conceives children who are no longer able to play, war speculates on death, makes fun of life, hijacks play, and tricks and ridicules children. The children of war came to life through the death instinct—born in pain like children everywhere, they were also conceived in pain, with death so present everywhere, all the time, day and night, outside and in, that at the moment of the begetting orgasm and cry, the thread was broken between pleasure and suffering, and nobody escaped, since death did not come from elsewhere, it was prowling among them, inside, inside Lebanon, and war did not come from some external enemy or some far-off plan of ethnic cleansing or the genocidal strategies of an external enemy. No, the war was "civil," like all civil wars, it drew its lust for death from the entrails of men and women on the same ground, the same territory, the same soil, it was a war of the same, a family war, an intimate war, between factions in the same village and from village to village, between factions in the same town and from town to town, from neighbourhood to neighbourhood. It established its lines of demarcation based on streets and parks, from temple to temple and from church to church, and in the same language, which was Arabic. It was from body to body, all mixed together, a war of same and like, all tangled up, body to body even as in love, where the line of demarcation between life instinct and death instinct no longer holds, where the thread between pleasure and suffering breaks. The mothers of the children of today conceived them in the din of death, in the shelters, and they keep the children in the shelters—who knows what tricks might be played outside in the parks? In any event, no more parks, no more open-air fields to play in. I walk today in Beirut, I want to see the infamous line of demarcation between east and west, between the Christian neighbourhoods and the Muslim neighbour-hoods, where death decided to defeat life, where so much tragedy was plotted, so much happiness was sidetracked, line of murders, arrests, kidnappings, disappearances, tortures of minds and bodies. But you can't see anything anymore, the infamous line is a normal road in the abnormality of the traffic from hell. No more traces of blood and no more echoes of screams, no more barriers or trenches, no more violent, crashing symphony of weapons, only Damascus Street here, with Raouché far to the west on the Mediterranean and El Rmeil on the other side, towards the mountains. No trace of the contortions of yesterday, the convulsions when Beirut, like an enormous beast of ancient times, whelped death. That vanished line of demarcation was called Khutut at-tamaas in Arabic, literally "line of touch."

If you touch this line stained with red, I'll kill you. If I kill you, my double, my brother, you who live just over on the other side, I touch you. Either I cut your throat or I crucify you. We share the same language, with variations, but if you touch it, I'll kill you. The line of demarcation is there, and the Other is so close to it, you whom I will kill are close to me. Those who are distant, the ones that war normally attacks, are not out there, they're right here, very near, intimate and familiar, two steps, two fingers, two breaths away from myself, we brush against the same line of touch. That's why death here came to attach itself to the firing line of life and that's why if I touch you in love, we beget in death. In our breathlessness of love and in the trances, in the pantings of breaking orgasm, our gaze is turned towards the horizon line that is yet so near between our two bodies, and we can't stare at it without it constantly drifting towards infinity, like the gaze of a sailor on a ship on the high seas constantly transported beyond the visible yet continuously riveted on some invisible point, and in the transports of love, what is touched most closely drifts unceasingly towards death. When I touched you in love, my love, each time we begat into death a whole generation of children, but we keep them sheltered in our houses as once in the shelters we conceived them, or else in well-protected schoolyards from which their cries of joy are sometimes heard through so much pain, so much sorrow repressed since they were brought to life in the shelters of our bellies. Some of those cries from the barricaded schoolyards reach my eardrums over the raging madness of the car

traffic. This afternoon, I unfold a note I'd slipped into
my pocket, given to me by Houda, a teacher. I have
without any problems crossed Khutut at-tamaas, the
"line of touch" of demarcation, yesterday red with
blood. I unfold the note, which was written by an
eight-year-old girl who signs with her first name,
Fourate, and I read: "I have travelled around the world
and the most beautiful country is peace."

We have an appointment in the old city, the centre of
Beirut, where for once the new construction is in
harmony with the pre-war city, the engineers and
architects have been careful here, have shown greater
concern for beauty, which, after all, is only a concern
for memory. We are to meet a psychoanalyst and
ethnologist, Liliane Germanos Ghazaly, "the first
woman psychoanalyst in Lebanon," she says with pride.
"Doctor Ghazaly," as everyone here calls her, was born
in 1939 and spent many years studying at university in
her country and then in Paris. After all the commotion
and confusion, I'm looking forward to finding some
balance and logic, some coherence in the muddle. I
need to do some housekeeping, as we often do with
papers, clothes and everyday things, especially since my
house is far away, and besides, I'm rarely given to tidy-
ing up, I say to myself, going down Damascus Street
from the former line of demarcation in order to reach
the old city by way of the Corniche Pierre Gemayel
and follow the Beirut River to its mouth on the
Mediterranean—I've always loved these places where

rivers lose themselves in the sea—and past the mouth,
to walk along the port, to smell its waters, stirred today
by a light breeze from the north, to imagine its boats
going out when the displaced people sought to flee the
besieged south and so many exiles wanted to go far
away to peaceful lands, and then to retrace my steps
back a little way to approach the old city from its
inhabited side, following Fouad Chehab Avenue below.
I want to walk for a long time, as usual, chanting
thoughts and words to the regular rhythm of my footsteps. I think to myself that Doctor Ghazaly is doubly
an archaeologist, since the ethnologist bases her quest
on the ruins of peoples, deciphering them so that these
peoples can gain a specific understanding of their
continuity, and the psychoanalyst works from the ruins
of the body and the mind—it's a single entity, body and
mind—deciphering the inner monument from the
letters that appear erased or illegible to the layperson,
the inner petroglyphs etched by fire, like those
inscribed on stones by the Algonquins of North
America—letters of fire recreated by war.

I enter the downtown area by Fouad Chehab
Avenue, and all the way through the cemetery of
ruins—charred, gutted buildings among the new
housing, gaping mouths from which scraps of metal
hang, their toothless blackness mocking the sky so blue
and the beautiful young women all around—an image
from yesterday haunts me like the frothy backwash
caught in the eddies at the river's mouth. I see little
Said, who has been lost without words since his first
year, when words are born, and has never spoken, and

yet his gaze was intelligent, and so were the drawings he did when at times a glimmer of light seemed to shine on his hidden ruins and carry him away, but he didn't talk and never smiled. A nurse friend had taken us to hospital X, to the psychiatry department—she didn't want her name or that of the hospital published, and we respect her wish. She talked to us about Said and his mother—his father had died in the war and Said had never known him—told us that he was schizophrenic and that science could do very little for him other than administer sedatives from time to time "when he has an attack," which meant he would howl like a young wolf, tear his sheets, eat his pyjamas, scratch his face and body with his nails and then suck the blood, and tear out his fingernails and toenails one by one. But they wouldn't allow him to wreak such devastation on himself, they would give him sedatives and he would fall asleep, and then when he woke up, he would draw, with that glimmer of light in his eye that shows understanding. The nurse friend said: "If only we had a Françoise Dolto here, I'm sure she could do some good with this child," and then she talked about little Said's parents ...

Mariam and Ahmed had met just before the war, at university. Like many students on the left, they had become Marxists and taken part in demonstrations, embracing the cause of the Palestinians—part of the activist Western youth of the late sixties, whose demands went beyond religious beliefs and ethnic affiliations. They joined with the thousands of idealists, in organizations or in the street, who wanted to get rid of the clan system that had existed in Lebanon for centuries, and denounced the Maronite-Sunni power structure, which they felt was corrupt. They wanted to return power to the people, unionized workers and intellectuals, a power that, together, they would cleanse and purify. As part of the movement for democratic emancipation, they also worked for the liberation of women, who were suppressed by religious traditions, subordinated to men, and confined to the home.

Mariam and Ahmed fell in love and wanted to get married, but she was from a Maronite Christian family and he was from a Shiite Muslim family. Despite the warnings of the two opposing clans, they stood firm, freely choosing to love each other and living far from their families, among their chosen friends, with whom they worked for a world free of exploitation, domination and tyranny, challenging oppression with joy and the passionate happiness of living and loving.

In their ardour and high spirits, Mariam and Ahmed had not reckoned with the harshness of their world. Their repudiation by their families went beyond private vengeance. Both clans, which involved dozens of individuals (fathers, brothers, uncles, cousins), attacked them, ridiculous rumours were circulated about them, they were pursued, hunted, threatened, and by the beginning of the war, they had gone from family enemies to public enemies to be killed. They were forced to leave Beirut in 1975, and they went underground in the south, because neither one wanted to take up arms, it was contrary to their idea of revolution, and they lived as best they could, protected by their new friends, Palestinians involved in the struggle.

Little Said was born in 1991 amid Israeli bombs and Hezbollah bombs. His father Ahmed had disappeared during Mariam's pregnancy; at first, she didn't know if he was dead or alive, then she learned that he had died in 1992 in the living hell of Israel's Khiam prison, had spent months huddled in one of the closed cubes used as cells, a windowless box no wider or higher than his own body—when he extended his arms, he could touch the walls—and the only times they took him out of that appalling box, it was to torture him. In 1995, when Mariam learned of Ahmed's death from a released prisoner, she descended further into the depths of silence in which she had been living since his disappearance, she wasn't even able, like other lovers, other wives, other mothers, to undertake a search to find the common grave where the body of her love lay. When she spoke, it was to say to her friends, "I don't want to see my Ahmed's broken body. If the God of my childhood exists, he is in the arms of his mother, Mary." And Mariam took little mute Said in her arms and rocked him, she breastfed him until he was four, she rocked and rocked him, humming Arabic or French songs from her Maronite childhood. Then one day, she left little Said with a neighbour, it was the first time he was ever out of her arms, she took the mountain road to the village of her birth, climbed to the top of the hill of apple trees, and hanged herself from a tree. One of her cousins found the body the next day. "They brought little Said to us. At first he was completely mad. See how peaceful he is now. I'll have him draw something. Look at the glimmer of light in his eye," said the nurse friend.

Before the appointment with Doctor Ghazaly, I sit in one of the cafés on a little pedestrian mall not far from Fouad Chehab Avenue. The cafés in Beirut aren't crowded, unlike those in Jerusalem or Pristina or Skopje or even Sarajevo, few of the residents here seem to allow themselves this pleasure. While the war does indeed appear to be over, you never know, there's been so much violence here over the last fifteen or twenty years, you'd say it hasn't ended, that a monstrous beast is about to resurface. I drink my coffee to the singing of Fairuz, who is adored here—the waiter says, "We like her better than Céline Dion," and laughs and gives me an arak, which I taste in little sips. Laughter, so rare here, is to be celebrated, I think, seeing again in my mind's eye the drawing little Said had given us: a house, but with no doors or windows, it was a completely closed wooden cube, right in the centre of the paper, and beside the black cube there was a human body in the fetal position with the legs and arms tied with a rope, with drops raining from the head and the body onto the ground—are they tears, are they blood? We don't know.

Walled up in his silence, little Said had reproduced for us the rough wooden cube in which his father had been buried alive in Khiam prison, the father he had never seen. How had he come by that knowledge? When he held out his drawing to us, that burning gaze with its unbearable glimmer of understanding, just for a moment, and his index finger pointing to the drops falling from the head and body of the man-foetus ... We don't know!

I continue on my way through the old city of Beirut. We have an appointment with Doctor Ghazaly, not far from the "line of touch."

In the little inn in Zouk Mosbeh, I keep my eyes wide shut to hear Liliane Ghazaly's words. The calm atmosphere lends itself to listening, here not far from the line of demarcation of Damascus Street, which divided the Christians, in the east, and the Palestinians and those with them, in the west: "On both sides, the same violence, and now today, the after-effects on both sides. We shouldn't believe that violence was a male prerogative. Among the women, a rage that had been suppressed for centuries found an outlet in the war. They too killed the Father and the Law. They come here to try to find reference points, because they haven't had any for years, for centuries, in the memory of the mothers and grandmothers, apart from a few exceptions." (The women were oppressed in the deepest depths of their bodies, in the very fibres of their being.) "They were never desiring subjects, neither subjects of desire nor subjects in law. They were objects of the desire of others, of the Other, of men. And they were caught between two models, the Arab and the European, because Lebanon is on the line of demarcation between East and West. In the war they saw all law overturned and they saw the opportunity to kill within themselves the law of men that had so oppressed them." (They destroyed the barriers and taboos, unlocked the locks of the body as they did those of the houses, and in the shelters they replaced the fathers, husbands, lovers, brothers and adult sons gone off to fight or missing.) "They tasted authority. With a rage to live and survive, they directed daily life in the shelters. Others let their rage explode in the street, there was no one more militant than they, no one braver." (They were intoxicated with the new freedom the war gave them, the freedom of loving subjects that had been suppressed for centuries, they seized it in fury, it burst out in all directions.) "After the war, authority was restored, and the women were relegated to their homes again. Nobody had changed. The surviving men once again became the masters of political life, of the external economy and the internal economy. Women's bodies once again took their places as objects of men's desires." (After the upheaval, after the exhilaration of a glimpse of freedom.) "They come here looking for reference points. The law of the Father was killed, but what can they put in its place?" (The desire of before was killed, but how, by what, by whom can it be replaced? Their men have remained the same and they, back in their homes, want the Other, they want to start life again in some other way. At home again they wonder whether the values they learned before the war are still the true ones, all the women, both the Christians and the Muslims, wonder.) "They have a desire for reconstruction, but what they see of the uncontrolled reconstruction of houses and roads appals them and they ask 'How can human beings be reconstructed here?'" (Their rage forced inward, as they have been forced back into their homes, they cry, they have seen the impotence of arms, they see the impotence of their outlaw men directing the destiny of a devastated country, and they cry.) "Some of the women, among both the Muslims and the Christians, become mystical. Accustomed to withdrawal, they choose metaphysical withdrawal. Many choose the withdrawal of depression—but does one really choose this old habit of the female sex?" (The habit of suffering, the depression based on guilt, is so deeply rooted in them because, basically, they are guilty. Guilty of what? Of everything, of having leapt with both feet into the field of freedom and strode across it while the ocean of blood overflowed its steep banks, guilty of having enjoyed the sudden emancipation promised by violence and death, guilty of having enjoyed it without their men, of having joy without their men under the thunder of the bombs, of having savoured their blessed solitude in the shelters, their solitude betrothed to fear, of having tasted death while savouring the delights of the body alone, of having abandoned themselves to the abandoned body.)

"'How can human beings be reconstructed?' they all ask, for a great many of them come for analysis. They are stronger than the men. In their depression, they hold on, stay the course towards another life, whereas the men never go to an analyst, they have certainties. It is the doubts of women that will save the world." (Their thousand-year history has made them uncertain of everything, of themselves and the world, while the men fall apart at the slightest doubt—except for the poets and mystics, that goes without saying, poets and mystics are men's female continent.) "At the first uncertainty, the men fall apart, commit suicide or tear the world apart in war. Women hold on, with their depression, sometimes to the point of madness. At first when they consult me, what happens to them is always the fault of the Other, the Enemy, those who made war against their people, and this is normal, they have witnessed so many barbarous acts, so many atrocities. Then, slowly, over the course of the sessions, they come to blame themselves." (This very private guilt must nevertheless be explored, exposed, worked, all the furrows of suffering have to be surveyed, those of the war but also those that were there deep inside long before the war, the seeds of death that lie in everyone and that war touches to the quick, no analysis will ever be able to dissipate the sufferings of war, suffering is an integral part of life, it is woven into the very fabric of life, the breath in the lungs, the blood in the arteries, the traumas of war will never disappear, but they can scar over when the flood of hatred, anger, rage is discharged with the flood of tears and the flood of words.) "The affect can be healed, but never the representation. The images will never be forgotten—memory is an integral part of life, like suffering—but the person will no longer be submerged by them. The women come here to stop being drowned by their sorrows and to find out how they can become desired and desiring subjects in this huge aggressive world that is theirs.

"'How can human beings be reconstructed?' they all ask." (Analysis is not the only answer, there is no state of perfect clarity.) "In Lebanon there is no meeting place for women and men who want to reconstruct human beings, no place in the clinics, no place of words where people could free themselves from violence, hatred and remorse, no public place for the work of memory—no place of words for the people that invented the phonetic alphabet. Our leaders did, and still do, everything possible to prevent the work of memory that is essential to any mourning work. They said, 'It's over, forget it, kiss and make up and get on with reconstruction.' They went to work on the stones, and the souls were left to their own devices, the souls are adrift in Lebanon. No work of collective mourning, no serious studies, no self-scrutiny, no opportunity to freely express hatred, no reparations, no asking forgiveness or granting forgiveness. They wanted to erase it, to pile up ruins on other ruins, to rub out, to repress. There are false friends and false lovers here, they've made friends with former enemies for business purposes. Nobody faced another person and said, 'This is what I did to you, I hated you, this is what you did to me, I hate you.' They are paving the way for more difficult times in Lebanon, the future will be terrible. I am an ethnologist and psychoanalyst, and I say we have to create a process of collective mourning." (Nobody hears, the leaders are busy pulling strings with promoters of all kinds. Understanding of the war has been jettisoned, no work of mourning, no work of memory, the war in remission, unless the women, from the depths of their depression, finally allow their buried rage to surface like a non-violent army and out of their centuries of incarceration begin this great collective process, leave their shelters, the glimmers of light in their night providing sudden illumination. Otherwise ...)

I'm dreaming. Let us dream, eyes open or shut! I will never forget Liliane Ghazaly's keen intelligence. Or her lilting voice. Or the plan for a national forum on mourning and forgiveness that she proposed to the authorities in her country. Which, of course, was refused! When did war heroes and leaders ever take any interest in the ruins of human bodies and souls?

Mission impossible. What am I seeking through these voyages, what do I want, what was I hoping for? What is my desire? To bear witness, but to what? What got into me, who did I think I was? A witness? Someone who would come from very far away, from the other side of the world of wars, from such a peaceful country, Canada and Quebec, someone who, in the light of a history with no major disastrous conflicts, would be able, from so many testimonies, so many confidences of women immersed in the terrible consequences of the death instinct, to say what war is, what violence is for women, the violence that comes from weapons and the violence that is within—that she, come from the other side of the world, would be able to say, with only the words of writing, that hell is war, war is other people, hell is other people, the men and women who were in it up to their necks, up to their bodies and hearts and minds, very far away there in elsewheres that are like nothing she has ever known.

Perhaps I was more aware of this in Lebanon than elsewhere, here where the "civil" rage broke out and lasted fifteen years, where they all became us's and thems, faction against faction, clan against clan, faith against faith, us's in the same them, the same ethnic group in its diversity and complexity, the same language, the same splendid country that they all cherished and that they, all together, separately, destroyed, and this common agreement to destroy in common disagreements led each one to the Other within, the us's were all the same, all different, similarly different, strangely similar, "I is an Other" became true for each one, and remains so, the drift within the self, madness is at the gates of their minds, war could start up again here, a spark could ignite it, fire is smouldering beneath the ashes, the mothers cried into the hearts of the children but they were tears of rage. And for me, mission impossible, Lebanon pushed me to my inner wall. "I is an Other," once tested and proven in love or in poetry, that war, that of the same and the private, the "civil" war between the self and the Other as I found it in myself, was my own war, and my own violence, the inescapable split, that I came to seek in the four corners of the far-off world, to seek and perhaps to heal with war, which is only an outlet, a gigantic catharsis. The whole land of Lebanon challenges each person in his or her own madness, with the repressed rage that exists in each one. I was going along, proud in the tawdry finery of a witness, fabulating on my own road to Damascus, in the centre of a Beirut devastated by the madness of the Same, by the divided Other-in-the-self. Like that biblical forebear, Paul of Tarsus, I fell off my horse, but, unlike him, I have no divine light showing me the path ahead. No mission. Only, at times, the creative spark of meaning arising out of its own ashes.

History is a tissue of paradox. In some places in the world, people divided all together at times have a desire to make holes in the tissue, to finally cut through the enigma. Mission impossible!

(In the first century of the common era, Paul was travelling on horseback to Syria from Tarsus, in Asia Minor, in what is today Turkey, on business. On the road to Damascus, he saw Christ in the light, and he followed the beam and went to preach the gospel to the Syrians. Later, in the seventh century, the Syrian Christians, fleeing the conquests of Islam, took refuge by the thousands in the mountains of Lebanon, and became the Maronites. Later still, in the twentieth century, there was a major war in Lebanon, and the Muslim Syrian cousins returned in great numbers, with an army of thirty thousand men, and occupied the country. The Syrians were also at war—although it was essentially a war of collusion—with other Semite cousins, who had resisted the teachings and admonitions of Paul of Tarsus, the Jews of Israel, who also occupied a share of Lebanon, in the south. During this "civil" war of the dying century, the people of the land of Lebanon initially divided in two, left and right, beyond ethnic groups and faiths. At the beginning of this Lebanese war that has not ended, the Maronite left and the Sunni left and the Shiite left, together, had supported the three hundred thousand Palestinian refugees who were there following their exodus from Israel in mid-century, but there was so much carnage on both sides and so many profiteers, on both left and right, that it all shattered into millions of blood-soaked pieces, the fabric was completely torn apart, it was an utter enigma, like a black hole of mysteries, all of them in the same mire. The most lucid went mad or scattered to the four corners of the earth, while the mothers, drunk with rage, followed their own warriors, encouraging them with the same cry in the same language, the ululations echoed on all sides in the nights of fire, with their tears that wept in the hearts of the husbands, sons and daughters, they poured out sorrow mingled with the raging waters of vengeance. Hearts were destroyed, and so were minds—on both sides of the line of demarcation, the same delirium, but a red line was needed to mark a difference between these us's here and those Other us's there, too close, here and there, too similar, it's too scary to see oneself so similar to the despised Other, it's the start of the beginning of self-hatred, it's the worst of wars, one descends very deep into the labyrinth of the detestable self, no more beams of light, one lights the way with the fire of bombs, one warms oneself at the fire that destroys, with death the only illumination, everyone, together and alone, loses the way.)

How to write after Auschwitz and why, and how to go on after Srebrenica, Pristina, Grozny? I am neither a Jew nor a Bosnian Muslim nor a Kosovar Albanian nor a Chechen, and yet I go on walking, fearful and disoriented, almost upon the scorched earth of Lebanon, with my total darkness and suppressed rage inside, act of contrition outside, and over it, the tawdry finery of writing. That's the limit, the great *writing* by which the subterranean tunnels of horrors—bodies run to earth, tortured, raped, starved, murdered—suddenly are supposed to be illuminated by death alone. And I put it off, can't even stop anymore and go home, do as everyone else does, live quietly finally, forget. I don't even want to understand anymore, it's too complicated, from every point of view, from every perspective, too complicated, inside and outside. I go on, "rendering the enigma to the enigma," as Valéry wrote, reconciled to human blindness, and to my own. In each little ego in the world, there is a lamento that writing opens up, the score is there, complete, all one has to do is make it sing, a lamento for life because of death, in each little ego, there is a funeral chant, a final oratorio, the first note of which has fallen into the subterranean tunnel with the first breath, in every human being, a symphony of sorrow that only the Mahlers of the world write. We listen to them at times in a state of well-being, at dawn we hear odes to fury, this is called *happiness*. I wonder in passing whether the death instinct in action, which has poured out in war since the beginning of the world, is not an insane challenge to death itself, the death that will come in any case and that we always pretend to forget, whether it is not a cynical staging of the death that has always come to snatch us from life and that will come again, for each and every person. Everyone knows that, everyone knows they don't know why they were created to be no more, put on earth to return to the earth as ashes, everyone knows they don't know what happens afterwards. Except the believers, the lucky ones, who believe they know, they've gambled in the lottery of life, on the big roulette wheel, like Augustine and Pascal, they've wagered on something and above all on someone, and afterwards, the lucky players say to themselves, if there is someone, I'll win everything, if there's no one, I'll lose nothing, since I'll know nothing, since I'll be *nothing*. But the others, all the hordes of people snatched up by the emptiness of nothing, drifting towards absurdity, seeing those who believe kill for their beliefs, witnessing holy wars of all faiths, understanding that those people have faith and hope for themselves but lack what is essential, charity, seeing neither charity nor love in the warriors of the heavenly wager, the divine lottery, all these other sol-diers, involved in pornocratic slaughter and torture, tell themselves, after all, as long as one is created to come to an end, just as well to uncreate life immediately, just as well the activity of death as this state of absurd passivity, just as well the great staging to the music of a macabre orchestra, to break everything, beings and things, before everything is smashed in the unreason and the drift towards *nothingness*.

To go on anyway. I want to see and hear those men and women who, in the fields of fury, still give a meaning to life. I've met them everywhere in Lebanon, people involved in the reconstruction of humanity, women especially—the men refuse to speak of these things, they *know* and they do business, except for the poets lighting the way with black ink, but most of them have gone away elsewhere. The women still have the gift of humanity, they have faith and hope in the human, and often in the *beyond*, but more than anything, they have charity, that is, love and the desire for love. I'm well aware that these words sound sentimental and dated, but here where I am, no word, no term is eternally doomed to obsolescence. In the women's vast loneliness, they have a desire for charity and love in this lifetime, even if there is *nothing* after (many of them, like the men, have kept up the clannish spirit of revenge—no trials and no remorse, and if a spark reignited war, they would again take up their ululations behind their fighting husbands, lovers, brothers and sons—but they don't interest me), and I pay attention to these women, whatever their faith or their clan. I worry about them, would like us to work with them on the reconstruction of souls and want us in our rich countries not to send money only for the bankers, engineers and promoters, most of whom are corrupt. I worry about these women who do not pretend to forget the massacres of Sabra and Shatilla and Damour, who do not pretend not to know about the torture in Khiam, and all the torture, the pornography of wartime, who have it all filed away in their hearts, and who are surrounded by men, women and children who went mad or became alcoholics and drug addicts because in the familiar orgy in which their youth died, it was intolerable, they couldn't help but let themselves drift, because in the surrounding unreason, private reason broke down. Sick to death of missing friends who were unable to tolerate the general chaos and went elsewhere to live in external or internal exile, the women are trying as best they can to close the breaches, but they're so gaping that a big hole, a big crater has formed in place of their hearts. We worry, we know our words can't fill the void, all we can do is pay attention. At times the women's words rise to the top of the crater, at times their words that demand expression through the speaking mouth rejoice, transmuting distress into jubilation, they have found a meaning in what made no sense—we are all floating attention, because this meaning that is theirs escapes us. That's all right, we aren't scholars of misery or of the Magnificats that spring from its soil, that's all right, it's like in poetry, often you don't grasp it at all, the poem itself takes hold of us, we are touched, and we continue the quest, reciting to ourselves, "A throw of the dice will never abolish chance."

To go on, on the roads of survival in this present life, where something is being rewoven over the torn weft, over and under, where a few fallen fibres, a few threads of the fabric, are being painstakingly gathered one by one to make something, no one really knows what, but to make something anyway, to create. *Textus* in Latin is both fabric and text—the women we've met know enough not to fail, in their uncertain assurance, their stubborn uncertainty, they know, and they weave the chapter and the book to come. To go on, only listening and watching, hearing the words of Marlène the Beautiful, who looks like Romy Schneider and who recounts to us—and it's always the same story, she says—the beginning of the war for her, on April 13, 1975, a Sunday. Her husband yelled, "Let's get out of here, they're coming to kill us," and she didn't believe it. She was twenty, her baby in her arms, and then she heard the footsteps on the stairs and the shouting of the militiamen coming up, their boots on the steps, their guns being cocked, the doors being broken down, and she began to believe it was true. She went mad, she says, "I was insane, I don't know for how long," and she shouted and ran every which way, cried out to the Virgin Mary, the mother of all. With her husband, as young as she, she went to the fire escape behind the building and raced down, the baby in her arms, and ran into a militiaman, who stopped her and pointed his gun at her. And then, "even more insane," hiding her baby between her body and the wall—he was very young, that handsome soldier, perhaps he saw himself in the body of the baby between the mother and the wall— she remembers shouting, "Kill me if you want, but not my little boy," his eyes met hers, "an eternity of looking into each other's eyes," she still sees him, and then he went upstairs and let her go. Marlene says, "Ever since that moment that lasted a whole lifetime, I have believed in life. We fled to Qatar and went to Canada, and we came back here. We lost our youth, we started again from scratch, we rebuilt a house, we grew old very young. Our most beautiful words of love are when we say to each other, sometimes, in the evening, in the middle of some activity or some television program, when one of us whispers in the other's ear and the other agrees, that we've come a long way since my baby was saved by two pairs of eyes that really met. I believe in life, life here."

To go to Sabra and Shatilla with a Palestinian friend who insists on taking us there. You can't see anything anymore, no longer any trace of the massacre, they've levelled, erased, neutralized everything. But our friend sees lots of signs, sees clues to what was there before and during the carnage in what remains after, she names them and draws an imaginary geography in the air. I can't imagine it, it's just too much, the vessel of my heart is overflowing, the vessel of my spirit is filled to the brim. Our friend speaks, she still needs to say it, the fabric she is reweaving needs to be remade and unmade again—for Penelope it was while waiting for Ulysses, for our friend it's while waiting for death. We understand her need to make and remake her piece on the loom, her story, we understand the urgency of calling for witnesses as Homer did, we listen, it's her epic, she says, "It's funny, but telling it to you gives me a mad desire to live and to go on," and on the erased ruins of Sabra and Shatilla, *The Song of the Earth* suddenly rises, spreading like a tree.

So we travel through the towns and villages, and we go to Damour, where there was hatred as vast as the hell we imagined as frightened children looking at the illustrated page for hell in the big Roman Catholic catechism, with the most refined, most painful tortures promised to the enemies of Good and the kind of detailed images shown only in pornography. We are in Damour with a young psychologist, who also wants to show, to say, to bear witness. She was fourteen when the monstrous beast struck her village in 1976, she tells us what was there and is no more, the family house gutted, nothing but stones scattered in what was the garden, she describes the trees that were there, in the west, orange trees, in the south, olive trees, a little further north, almond trees and date palms, and in the east, pine trees. "We had the most beautiful garden in Damour, all the neighbours would come to our house and we would go to all their houses, no locked doors, no walls between the gardens." She shows us the most beautiful house, that of her aunt, who died of sorrow, it's at the entrance to the village, not all of it was razed, there are still columns of porphyry and lancet windows, with no glass, in the pure Ottoman style. Under the silhouette of the huge chestnut tree, the only one that remains standing, we see what appear to be evanescent human forms moving from room to room in the gutted house of the dead aunt. We see Damour towering over the heights, its feet in the waters of the Mediterranean, with its plantation of banana trees below, between the road and the sea, in place of the usual sand. Our companion says, "This is where everyone in Lebanon would come before the war to get the best bananas in the world." We imagine her leaving in a little boat, going north, on that night in 1976 when all the villagers fled the massacre, boarding small boats by the dozens and heading to Beirut, where they were greeted by the fire of bombs. "I didn't want to drown," she says, "and the waves were very strong. I preferred the blood-red glow of the city, where we could blend into the crowd, and suffer perhaps, but at least suffer anonymously all together." And she speaks of abundance, driving us high above the village, where the Damour River flows, but there's only a thin stream and she says, "Before the war, this river was a real river." Across the river, we see the villages of the Druze. "I don't know why they joined with our enemies to fight us. Before the war, they were our friends and would come to our houses. The only difference between them and us is that they believe in the transmigration of souls, and also that their prophet is not Moses, but Moses's brother-in-law, the Caliph Al-Hakim Bi-Amr Allah, but should we kill each other over that? I'm well aware that our side also committed atrocities long before the carnage." We are on a rocky mountaintop and we hear the hammering of reconstruction from the village far below, we look for signs of life in this lunar landscape. Some men are rebuilding the village by themselves, but the villagers don't want to come back. Our companion kneels and presses her ear to a fragment of stone, "Do you hear?" We press our ears to it too, and don't make out any sound. She begins to sing softly in Arabic, she says the notes and then the words come from the stone, and we listen without understanding, our eyes turned to the shimmering rays of the setting sun on the ruins reaching their arms up very high towards the lilac sky, and we suddenly hear her voice saying, "You know that in Arabic Damour means *destroy*? And *they* always destroy what they love most."

And to go away, one beautiful morning, far from the towns and villages, far from the sea and its coastline ransacked by the new war of money, to climb very high up into the mountain through the plantations with their espaliers, scraps of life torn from the desert of stone that was once a refuge for all the diasporas and that became their graveyard when the great metal birds dropped their bombs. To climb up to where the two lovers of silence, mountain and desert, meet, to finally glimpse, in the mountains around Faqra, deciduous trees of all kinds, where real birds nest that can still sing, and here where the air can rise freely, to smell the fragrance of orange and lemon trees, the pungency of vines, and the burnt aroma of coffee wafting up from the valley we've come from, to inhale, to touch with our sense of smell the surrounding air. Momentarily turning from the contemporary tragedy of Lebanon, we contemplate the Roman ruins beside the Ottoman ruins, these ruins that no longer hurt anyone, lest, in this century of ashes in which so many things were conceived, so many inventions created, so many geniuses wasted, so many solutions envisioned—until the *final solution*, imagined one terrible time and then carried out with no moral compunction, the only problem being its engineering, its mathematical mechanics—lest we forget the soul of the ruins, and lest even a single ruin, like the tears of rage mothers of antiquity shed into the hearts of their children, transform sorrow into a desire for vengeance—and desire is lack, always—even a single tear of rage in the belly of a single dead forefather all the more reason in this generalized unreason, when an entire people of mixed bloods has too long been subjugated under too many empires, celestial or terrestrial, lest everything always have to be started over when the remorse and the fair trials and the just reparations have not been drunk to the dregs.

To go on, with this one fact in the window of the heart: a single human ruin is worth more attention than these majestic ruins I am contemplating at this moment in Faqra.

PAKISTAN

Pakistan

In the long Pakistani night, groping for anchorage, advancing practically blind in the rolling and pitching, amidst a mass of one hundred and sixty million women and men in the torrid heat and misery, passengers on a huge makeshift boat that is cracking, splitting, taking water everywhere, we try to make out a few glimmers of light on the horizon. Asma the Courageous says, "The only glimmers of hope come from women," and a great many women, and a few men, repeat that promise that comes like a song of dawn in the deep night, like the emerald pools glimpsed here and there in the Thar Desert or on the arid plateau of Baluchistan. "Women's words," Asma says, "belong to a universal language that every woman and man will understand." They are droplets now, but will soon form huge translucent lakes that will once again irrigate these dry lands, or they will crystallize in people's hearts to create those pools of marble of many colours, greens, ochres, pinks, sepias, that abound in this land. "Look further," Attiya says, "Yes, we are an Islamic republic, all the laws of heaven and earth suppress us and make us subordinate to men, our men whom we love nonetheless, in this beloved country of our slavery, Islam-i Jamhuriya-e Pakistan."[12] Yes, millions of women and millions of children are slaves here, working for their masters in footwear and clothing factories or flax and cotton plantations, unpaid and deprived of everything, subjected to physical and sexual abuse. Yes, the masters, with rifles, knives, whips and the Koran as weapons, deny them everything, including the freedom to learn and to love, but, "Look further, get off that boat bobbing on the ocean of dangers and sorrows, leave your eyes behind in the West, abandon your ears in the West, see first of all how the water was brought from the Himalayan heights through the rich valley of the great Indus River in the last century, when the British occupied the country. See how, using the tributaries of the Indus, including the very beautiful Ravi River, which we will clean up when the time comes, we dug with our sweat and our courage the kilometres of canals that today water the large provinces of Punjab and Sind, and understand that, contrary to all appearances, women's daily labour in the present is of a similar nature." And Zubaida says, "We are tens of thousands of activists"—after a few days, we grasp that the word *activist* is not pejorative as it is in our language, French—"You have to realize that we are building canals in people's souls and irrigating their hearts, but it's beneath the surface, it doesn't show, not yet. We are fighting with all our strength against 'Talibanization.' Like the women of Iran, we are fighting, but it doesn't

---

12. Islamic Republic of Pakistan.

show. We still dress as they want us to, from head to foot, we all wear the *shalwar* (pants), the *kameez* (shirt) and the *chador* (veil), but that isn't very important to us—we are getting rid of the opaque veils over our souls and our hearts, we are quietly tearing off the chastity belts and the barbed wire from our minds. We are tens of thousands of activists working everywhere in the towns and villages. See in the distance those glimmers in our dark night of sorrows and terrors, get off this huge creaking boat, hear in Urdu, like the flowing waters of the Indus, our liquid songs of dawn. Press your ear to the multicoloured veins in the pool of emerald marble, do you hear the trickle of the droplets, the memory of the clustered vowels, the solidified words, do you hear them?"

Difficult to hear, difficult to see with our Western ears and eyes, so conspicuous is the misery, the suffering, so suffocating the pollution of sky and land, air and water everywhere in the stifling atmosphere where the dust floats windless and heavy amid the nauseating smells of garbage and cheap fuel issuing in bluish clouds from the thousands of dilapidated buses, cars and auto-rickshaws going in all directions, transporting gaunt humans and assorted merchandise, with pieces of meat hanging alongside cheap jewellery and brass milk cans shining under the fiery sun in a halo of flies and mosquitoes swirling to the same heavy rhythm as the omnipresent vultures in the sky, through the uncontrolled traffic going in all directions from dawn until dusk, when suddenly everything falls silent. The horns, the human sounds and the animals' bleating

cease as darkness falls like a curtain, with hardly enough
electricity to light the main roads, and nothing is heard
but the last prayers of the muezzins coming from the
huge orchestra of mosques. Very soon it's curfew, but
not the one ordered by the army, even though the war
is a stone's throw away, a little to the north in that
beloved Kashmir everyone talks about and for which all
Pakistanis are said to be prepared to sacrifice their lives,
despite the acute awareness of the nuclear threat they
go to sleep with every night. And every sleep opens the
door to the labyrinth of nightmares, they sometimes
talk about them in low voices just-between-us, dreams
here are not part of life, they are dreamed to be
forgotten, erased, obliterated, they belong in the dark
pits paced by sleeping souls, the seven hundred
thousand Indian soldiers stationed in Kashmir often
walk there—but these images must not be mentioned.
There have never been psychologists of the talking cure
in Pakistan, nor in the bordering countries, India, Iran,
Afghanistan and China, much less psychoanalysts. And
besides, the Great Prophet never expressed the slightest
thought on these matters. Here the text of the Koran
governs the lives of men, and of women, their outer and
inner lives, and the Prophet Muhammad made
provision for everything, absolutely everything. What
we could say about the interpretation of the dreams
that inhabit the dark, dangerous nights belongs to the
lunatic imaginings of corrupt Western minds. And in
the morning, after the prayer of the muezzins from the
huge orchestra of mosques, after a meagre breakfast to
the wailing of animals about to have their throats slit in

sacrifice to humans, and the braying of pack mules being whipped to the shouting of insults from out of the nocturnal abyss, everyone rushes for the newspapers, which every morning describe in profuse detail the latest fighting up in Kashmir and provide dozens of stories of sordid murders, rapes, thefts and poisonings resulting from the drinking of illicit alcohol from clandestine stills, because in Pakistan, the consumption of alcohol is illegal, punishable by prison, torture, or death, just as it is illegal to have sex without being married or without respecting the law of heterosexuality.

And then there are the "honour killings," the notorious *karo-kari* murders reported ad nauseam in the newspapers as ordinary news items—in fact they are ordinary, these murders of girls or young women, *karis*, killed by the hundreds, perhaps thousands every year, there are no precise statistics, not yet anyway. Courageous activists work on these sad cases, while the police officers give back to the families or in-laws the unautopsied bodies of these women who "died accidentally," were burned, had their throats slit, or were shot to death by a husband, fiancé, brother, uncle or cousin whose family, most often on the basis of mere rumour, considered itself "dishonoured" by behaviour involving love, adultery, fornication or simply flirting. And sometimes they are bodies of men, *karos*, usually young, that someone wanted to cleanse, by fire or dagger, of adultery, love outside the accepted norms, or sodomy. Prohibitions rain down on any natural attraction of bodies in all the towns and villages, as the dust of the desert sands or the pollution rains down.

The repressed returns in as many contrary forms as there are inhuman laws in the Koran, there's widespread prostitution and pedophilia, with a huge pool of all the bodies disturbed imaginations might want, there are tens of thousands of abandoned children, boys and girls, subjected to forced labour or wandering directionless, famished, idle, ripe for the picking. After the chant to Allah that pulls us from sleep each dawn, after the frugal breakfast of bananas, oranges and banana bread, we are shocked at the accumulation of depravities in the day's paper, we're disturbed by this people that seems to be adrift, so great—and everyone agrees on this—is the political corruption and the social corruption. Against the backdrop of the precepts rigorously and meticulously written down by the Prophet, unbridled hordes take centre stage in a macabre drama, and the craftiest ones feed the beast from the morbid scenarios of the Internet, because, despite the strict imams and the hoarse chants of the muezzins, Islam is on-line.

Before braving the threatening outdoors, where women alone must never be without a chador and a male escort, we are suddenly concerned for ourselves, and with good reason: a short ten-minute walk on the first day, with hundreds of piercing looks like darts on our naked heads and ankles, made us turn back—and yet the two of us are hardly timid! From now on we will have a guide and protector, the good Muhammad by his blessed first name, a valiant taxi driver who will drive us around for our whole stay. We quickly become his confidants, and he can't get over the fact that these "American women," who talk, ask questions and even laugh, who are *free* and have left their children behind, did not jump on him "like whores."

Fate has brought us to Pakistan on March 8, International Women's Day, a day almost forgotten in the West, and celebrated here with more pomp and even more fervour than we experienced in the seventies in the West. Women by the thousands are in the street alongside a few dozen "democratic" male companions, fighting together for human rights, all the rights that are flouted, including those of women. In Islamabad alone, there's a throng of ten thousand activists chanting slogans in the official language, Urdu, but also in English, the language of the leaders and of business, so that the whole world, of which English is the language of communication, can hear them. They also chant poems of liberation by their great writers— here, poetry is sung and learned by heart, even by illiterates, who are able to recite entire stanzas of it. Mixed in with the Urdu and English, we also hear snatches of chanting in the minority languages, which are still quite alive, the sounds of Punjabi, Sindhi, Pashto and Baluchi blend into the general music, the great symphonic chorus a festival of sound, while our gaze follows the many-coloured chadors like sails unfurled on the horizon, undulating in a light, sandy breeze. As in demonstrations all over the world, there are speeches— but we find them melodious, like chanting in close harmony with the songs and slogans of the crowd—and banners, whose colours match the flamboyant fabrics of the dresses. On one banner we read, in French, "No human rights without women's rights," and on another,

"No peace without justice and truth about the status of women." Throughout our stay we hear these words, *justice*, *peace* and *truth*, over and over from all the activists. More than equality, they talk about truth. Because what they are demanding is an end to lying, hypocrisy and corruption. Today, it is the women who are shouting, singing and chanting, working to tear the masks off the corrupt political and religious leaders who, as far back as they can remember, even right after the country gained its independence from the British yoke in the middle of this century, have always kept them down with speeches on purity and sacrifice while squandering the country's riches for their own benefit and indulging their every craving, every excess of flesh and spirit.

People are singing and shouting today in all the cities of Pakistan, in Karachi, in Lahore, but especially in Islamabad, the capital, so that their leaders and the whole world, through the embassies, will hear them; they are chanting the slogans like incantations, but they are not weeping. Unlike what we observed in other countries at war we visited, other countries where human rights are flouted, we have not seen a single woman here crying, probably, I say to myself, because poetry, as omnipresent as the constant sun, has tapped the huge pool of tears of this, one of the most populous, poor and suffering nations of the earth, and poetry gives them back in abundance that singing rain of salty droplets. It comes from all of them, men and women, they see themselves and recognize themselves in it and no longer need to really cry, at least not in

public, or only at night, sleeping at the bottom of the
pit of bad dreams. Poetry bathes these men and women
in the torrent that for millennia has poured out in the
silences of intimacy, their history is so long and their
writing so old, they know the alluvial chords of their
poets by heart from the ancient chorus, and they do not
need to cry in front of crowds, not even when Western
leaders dare to come to their land and admonish them
and give them condescending lessons on democracy,
they do not cry. Other poems and other waters come
down from the north, those ones are red, they are tears
and blood, and they flow from the bodies of the tens of
thousands of their Kashmiri brothers and sisters who
have been murdered for years in the "occupied"
territories controlled by the Indian army—but "India is
becoming more democratic," say Western leaders, India
has its democratically elected Parliament. There have
been countless Kashmiris murdered, Kashmiri women
systematically raped, political prisoners, and people
tortured, and also not counted by the sermonizers from
the Far West are the million of untouchables, out-castes,
murdered every year in India by the high-castes. The
crowds of women and their few male companions of
March 8 do not cry or appeal to external injustice, they
present, their demands, chanting, and this year, 2000,
they have ten of them. The "strong man of the hour,"
General Pervez Musharraf (who is neither less
democratic nor more corrupt than previous leaders of
this country, as all the democratic activists vie with each
other to tell us, adding that he is probably the least
corrupt of all of them), accompanied by two women

ministers who were *appointed*—Doctor Zubaida Jalal, responsible for education, and Doctor Attiya Inayatullah, responsible for the status of women— receives the demands of the women at war against lies and hypocrisy, and the three of them promise the jubilant crowd, as if they too were chanting poems, that they will study and try to solve all these problems "in a few weeks."

Tomorrow these women will be back in their well-protected homes, which they won't leave without a male escort, they'll sit veiled in the back of the car they're forbidden to drive or on the bicycle they're forbidden to ride by themselves, with the man at the handlebars, clinging to him as best they can in the precarious side-saddle position, the only one they're allowed, with their swinging legs hidden under a long dress, trying desperately to hang on to their chadors, which the wind from the frenzied traffic constantly displaces. Do they catch even a glimpse of the road or the landscape, camouflaged like that in their corporal prisons? Are they afraid when they think about the number of fatal accidents caused every day by swerving vehicles? We don't know, don't see their faces, we can only make out the procession of swaying vehicles in the air thick with fumes. We wonder why the right to walk alone on the sidewalks, ride a bicycle or moped, drive an auto-rickshaw or car, pilot a boat, fly a plane, or ride a horse is not part of their demands, since it seems so clear to us that the right to move about freely is the basis of all freedom. Perhaps we're "spoiled Western girls," but this prohibition makes us appreciate the

simple, glorious freedom to walk wherever we want—
it is at a rhythmic pace and in the unhindered discovery
of an environment, in fantasy and without obstacles or
constraints, it is in the liberty of walking, driving or
flying that the first free thoughts take shape. Here,
women cling to their bodyguards as suckling babes to
their mothers' bodies, and that's what their spiritual and
material leaders want. How is it that we do not find this
fundamental demand for autonomy among the ten
presented yesterday, we will ask all the women we meet.
In the meantime, we try to understand the why and
how of those new "commandments" according to
which they say they must undertake their war against
injustice and lies, because, after all, we are not here to
enjoy our Western girls' freedoms—although the
freedom to think is one freedom no disciple of any
prophet will ever be able to take away from us—we are
here to better understand women in war, any war
against bodies and minds, and perhaps to contribute,
through our words as witnesses, to reducing the
violence and the harm, because we do not feel that war,
in all its forms and with all its violence, on the fields of
honour or in family homes, is the inescapable destiny of
this world. We feel that if so many dedicated people are
able to heal in its aftermath, then as many should act to
prevent it.

Among the new "ten commandments" submitted to
the political authorities, at the top of the list is free
access to education for all, but how can this be

accomplished, where to begin, considering that 40 percent of the national budget goes to the military and
only 0.7 percent to education, and that two-thirds of
the population is illiterate and women constitute two-
thirds of the illiterate, and considering that only a third
of children attend primary school and that just a tiny
minority of girls are part of that third, how can this be
accomplished? That is the question all the activists we
met ask themselves, they belong to the educated elite,
are lawyers or doctors, anthropologists or teachers.
"There are so many of us working, we don't know
what to do," we're told by Naghma Imdad, a social
anthropologist who runs the Human Development
Centre in Islamabad, which is funded by two international NGOs and CIDA[13] and oversees twelve activist
organizations throughout the towns and villages of the
country. The reports are there, voluminous, filed
regularly with the government authorities. "We don't
know what to do anymore." Yes, the first thing that
must be addressed is education, but also updating of
electoral lists, which hasn't been done since independence half a century ago; half the registered voters on
those lists are dead. "If women had more education and
there were more of them on the political scene, the
nuclear threat wouldn't be so great, they would not
attend to war but to education and health. Not even
one percent of the national budget is allocated to social
security and health." We spend hours listening to
Naghma in this calm, sunny office in Islamabad on a
street lined with trees and flowers, which is a change

---

13. Canadian International Development Agency.

from the polluted furnace of Lahore where we've come from. She doesn't wear the chador, but when we go out onto the path in the garden, she automatically puts on a shawl that covers her Western-style short-sleeved blouse and slacks. "We have no choice," she says, "When you're a liberal here, you have to make compromises, or else you suffer too much, you'd have to go into exile." Where to begin?

There's education, of course, but also "the right to mobility," Naghma declares, determined. It's not among the "ten demands for 2000," but it will come, "we are only beginning." Then she leaps to her feet, a sunbeam turning her long salt-and-pepper hair flame-colour, as in the contemporary Pakistani paintings all over the walls, she stands like a woman warrior, looking outside where parrots and cocks are singing, her eyes afire with light embrace faraway spaces, she says: "The right to mobility! I would like to ride a bicycle as I did in my teens. Women do not have the right to go anywhere alone, especially on a bicycle. I dream of it! At night, I travel kilometres on my bicycle, and I sing, I hear myself laughing in my dreams. When I was twenty, I could ride a bike, and I wore jeans and let my hair blow in the wind, but since the war in Afghanistan, since the borders were opened between our two countries, since the arrival of millions of refugees here, Pakistan has been 'Talibanizing,' we women have lost the right to mobility." Where to begin? They don't so much fear regional terrorism encouraged by the Taliban—which is the supreme fear of the USA, even though they were the ones who armed the Taliban in its war against the

former USSR—no, they fear the rise of Islamic
fundamentalism, the subjugation and subordination of
women, they fear it, they are suffering from it now, in
their bodies and in their freedom of movement, libidi-
nous and sexual movement, emotional and cognitive
movement, by the millions, they are suffering from it
now, while the spokespersons for the White House and
Congress in Washington are fixated on a single subject,
"the arrest of the number-one international terrorist
and gangster," Osama Bin Laden, and haven't a word to
say about the subjugation of millions of Pakistani
women. Where to begin?

If dreams of moving about freely on foot or bicycle
do not bring Naghma happiness, they at least, like the
actions undertaken in the field, create a density of
existence, a life of dignity within the present pain of
living. "We can't go out without a male escort without
being harassed. To the feudal values that persist in India
and Pakistan—we're the same people, the same ethnic
group, only our religions are different—they've grafted
those of fundamentalism. For twenty years we've been
going backwards. The result? Women restricted to the
home, except for rare highly educated exceptions.
Examples? Look at these documents, these statistics
collected by our centres, with very few results. In the
villages, the women can't leave their houses, not even to
give birth. There are no hospitals, anyway, they have
babies as animals do. No right to contraception either,
and they have to accept their master when he comes,
completely subject to his libido, which is all the more
unchecked because he must never see the least little bit

of female flesh. The infant mortality rate is frightening, as is the maternal mortality rate, because of the lack of proper care. Women's and children's health is part of our 'ten demands.'" Where to begin? "We mustn't spread ourselves too thin," Naghma says, "or pile up chapter upon chapter in the endless book we are working on. We have to go to the heart of the whole question of our subordination." And in the abyss of this land, I imagine a book within a book, whose perfect form within its crucible, like a great oratorio against the desert, the absence, the nothingness, would by its sheer beauty and courage restore dignity to this life, make it bearable—but they are writing it now. Its true meaning still escapes us, it's too far, too deep, we'll read it one day in that "universal language of women" Asma the Courageous talked about. I tell Naghma this and she agrees, adding that "you from the West" cannot yet understand the *freedom* and the *truth* they are speaking of. She believes we've lost our way in the corridors of equality, both women and men, through all our republican revolutions. And now my mind drifts off, we hear the muezzin in the distance and my heart is reassured, that plaintive song that punctuates the solar clock is like a sweet drug until the edge of night. The concept of *equality* has toppled into the void, none of my philosophical guideposts hold here. A music bursts forth in my inner ear with the budding words of a poem in which *freedom* and *truth* would resonate differently. I'm about to ask Naghma to explain what she has just said, what is this freedom, what is this truth they all talk about and that escapes us? Before I even open my mouth to ask my questions, she has started to sing an Urdu poem in a glorious voice. Against the white walls and outside at the end of the garden, I seem to see veiled shadows dancing, I could swear I hear their peals of laughter in the dusk.

Moist coolness of ebony night, nothing moves or rustles, better cover up, we were so hot, mustn't let the sweat freeze on our sleeping bodies. I would like at least to hear the wings of the sleepflying violet butterflies, but it's impossible to open the window, the little inn has no mosquito nets. And I sink into a haze of dreams that are completely unlike the usual stories. I had fallen asleep with the image of Naghma on her bicycle, finally free to travel through her city and the hills around Islamabad, radiant as she was in her youth when luxurious houses and lush gardens were not prisons, and here I am, moving through captivating spaces on a galloping white horse, being carried along at an insane speed, there's a light breeze, its mane strokes my cheek, we speed over the beige sandbanks of the Indus, on its croup I've tied a bouquet of scarlet gladioli for Asma the Courageous somewhere in the desert of Baluchistan. We suddenly turn into the fields, across a huge cotton plantation, I see little multicoloured islands scattered here and there, they're small groups of women pickers crouched among the plants, they're bent and sweating under the burden of heavy baskets strapped on their backs, and under the irate gaze of their masters, their men, who direct their work and shout at them to speed up, whips in their hands. But now, outraged, my horse and I, racing through all the plantations of Pakistan, strike down the idle masters one after another with our fiery eyes alone, they drop like flies, the groups of women rise, they put down their baskets and unfurl a huge banner on which they have written in Urdu some words whose meaning I don't know, they laugh and start to dance. I hear myself shout, "three hundred and eighty, three hundred and eighty!" and I wake up, wondering where I am and why that number.

The day before, I had read that the per capita GNP was three hundred and eighty dollars a year, one of the lowest in the world, and that women and children were commonly used as slave labour—in fact, the abolition of this practice was one of the "ten demands for 2000." Along the roads of the Punjab—but it was the same in all the provinces of the country, everywhere in the cultivated regions—I had seen groups of women bent under their burdens in the blazing sun, I had seen their men, their masters, walking slowly along the furrows, cigarettes between their lips, watching the women, seeing that they kept up their pace. I knew that, like pimps, the men alone would receive money for the harvest from the landowners, and they would dispose of it as they saw fit, but I was also aware that they were petty masters, caught up in the same feudal system of exploitation. The big masters, the few ultra-rich landowners were most often outside the country, living in their luxurious houses and villas in the West, scrupulously praying and fasting according to the Koran between orgies or investments in the global stock exchange, in New York, Tokyo or Hong Kong, taking part in the profitable traffic in weapons or drugs or women for prostitution, with a few dividends of course coming back to the country, so that their politicians would maintain the policy of war. Their wives flocked to the great couturiers of Europe for their clothes, the gold jewellery of just one of them could provide a decent living for a good hundred of those pickers and their children, the mothers could have kept their kids rather than being forced to let them join the thousands of wandering children abandoned to the internal diaspora of unbearable misery.

"Three hundred and eighty, three hundred and eighty!" I awake in the cold sweat of a torrid night, I have slept very little in Pakistan, the frugality of the meals and the complete absence of wine make sleep in the heavy air pleasantly light. But waking also does not have the same consistency, there's a kind of hallucinatory atmosphere probably due to the physical deprivations —perhaps that's the source of that strange freedom Naghma talked about—so much so that I could have sworn the dancing shadows I saw on the white walls and at the far end of the garden yesterday when Naghma sang her glorious poem in Urdu really existed, that the bodies of the women under their long diaphanous veils were indeed real. It was as if I was stoned, but no, it was extreme sobriety that put me in that state, I became receptive to strangeness, lucidly elsewhere, deep within me elsewhere, transported and there, present. And tonight after the dream, it was the same, in the depths of the night, as in Luc Plamondon's song, "I sang in my head," with words that came from me but that I didn't know. I turned on the bedside lamp and let my mind frolic among the brightly coloured images of *Dawn*, an excellent newspaper, especially fascinated by one of them, of laughing women and children dressed in jade green, vermilion, pink, white and pearl grey, with fine lace and gorgeous embroidery, all of them staring at the camera, women, little girls and little boys, it's a party, they're all dressed up, surrounded by flowers and plants. I read the caption: "Karachi: Women prisoners and their children celebrate International Women's Day in the Central Prison here on Wednesday."

So these women are prisoners with their children, so they raise the children in prison—and where do the children come from, where are the fathers? I suddenly remember that one of the demands concerns the women prisoners of Pakistan, who are numerous, they're asking for separate prisons for them, how, why? They're also asking that only women who are real criminals be put in prison. We learn to our consternation that the reason they want separate prisons is that they are regularly abused, beaten and raped by their male fellow-prisoners or guards, and even by civil servants, who, we are told, "come and select certain ones in the evening and take them away and rape them, and then bring them back to the guards, who, like them, call the women whores." So these children who pose smiling beside their moms for this strange celebration of March 8 are mostly the product of rape. We also learn that the majority of Pakistani women prison-

ers are there because they've been convicted of
adultery, because they were made pregnant by some
hit-and-run rapist and then accused of adultery by the
"dishonoured" families and repudiated by their
husbands, that goes without saying. We remember then
what we were told by Salma, our journalist friend, that
rape in Pakistan equals adultery, and that to prove rape
before the judges, the testimony of two men is
required, women witnesses are not credible in the eyes
of the law, it was decided long ago by the Koran. Salma
had added: "There has nonetheless been some progress
in this area. It used to be that these women were
automatically stoned to death in the public square.
Today, as a result of repeated pressure by international
organizations such as the United Nations High
Commission for Refugees and Amnesty International,
at least they are no longer killed, they have a legal trial
before being put in prison." Some trial!

In the morning, we find Naghma at home, on one of
the two patios this time, in the shady tranquillity of
heveas, laurels and tall fir trees, with a garden of
blooming magnolia trees in the distance and, farther
still, the foothills of the Himalayas. All the birds of the
world seem to have gathered around us, we eat almond
cookies and tiny bananas and drink a very sweet, full-
bodied coffee. Naghma looks at the mountains, their
lilac ridges silhouetted against the Prussian blue of a
cloudless sky, she says the mountains speak, "they have
messages, they are constantly changing," from season to
season they say different things. "Islamabad is one of the
rare cities in Pakistan where there are four seasons. And

then, you see, these mountains lead to the Kashmir, they're there with our men who are fighting on the side of the besieged Kashmiris. The mountains are women, the ocean is male." (I would have thought the opposite, put verticality on the phallic side and liquidity on the female side, but this is how Naghma sees her mountains.) "Have you noticed that all mountainous countries are places of war?" and she names Afghanistan, Chechnya, Bosnia, Kosovo. We let Naghma daydream, savouring the blissful moment with our sweet snack on this blessed morning, and then she comes back to us and sings us a poem by the great Faiz Ahmed Faiz, who is practically worshipped here, *The Morning of Freedom.*

Then, just like that, without a pause, she continues speaking. "We don't want war or fighting here, not even class or caste struggle, we've known too much violence. Peace first, we'll solve the social problems later, with the Indian women, we're united with them, we form a broad coalition in a huge movement that brings together all the democrats on both sides of the border, men and women, intellectuals, artists, workers, working together for women's rights and human rights, there are millions of us. I'm not discouraged, things will change. We've been kept in fear and insecurity since India and Pakistan were partitioned on the basis of religion, Hinduism on one side, Islam on the other. It's awful, both sides have gone as far as to make nuclear threats. When the English left, the Kashmir remained a source of tension between the two countries. This problem brings out all that's repressed on both sides. There's been a frightful rise in religious extremism in India as well as Pakistan. Keeping the war going there is the religious fundamentalists' way of dominating the weak, us women first and foremost. I tell you, war is above all the hatred of macho men for women, I'll tell you why." Naghma sniffs the soft air of her mountains, which are watered by a mist that has just dissolved like a cloud of milk, she tastes her coffee, lights a cigarette and continues. "War is the most effective way to suppress the weak, women and children, for men whose only desire is to destroy. And do you know why? Because deep down, the fatherland, honour and power are covering up a feeling of weakness and impotence. Men who are impotent in the social arena are basically afraid of the power of the weak, our power, they know there's an enormous capacity for violence within us, they know we're ripe for rebellion because we've been suppressed, dominated, exploited for too long, so they make war. Men would go as far as nuclear aggression. On both sides, India and Pakistan, rogue regimes are ready to blow everything up, but they're so afraid of our rebellion that they keep us prisoners in our houses and our clothes. But it's all going to change, you'll see, as in Iran, everything is changing."

We talk again, this time to the sound of Beethoven's *Concerto for Violin*, Naghma explains that the isolation in which the West left Iran was beneficial for Iranian women. Change came from within, she says, the women drew their courage from deep within themselves; in their solitude, they were for years speleologists of souls, their own souls, where laments and chants and fragments of texts to be deciphered were stored over the millennia. "You'll see, the same revolution is taking place in us but nobody sees it yet. As well, the Taliban's excesses woke up the most religious women among us. Am I discouraged? No! We're working to analyze and dismantle the age-old patriarchal feudal structure, we're working with the complex social and family architecture, you'll see." And going with us to the bus that will take us back to Lahore, Naghma says, "Things are so bad, they can only get better!"

On the road back, as I looked at the women in the fields working like beasts of burden under the vigilant eyes of their masters and spouses, some other words of Naghma's revealed their full meaning: "I've had the privilege of education. It was the practice of social anthropology in the villages that allowed me to get out of my situation as a privileged, middle-class woman with all her prejudices." That reminded me of the discourse of our Maoists in the seventies. But here, for Naghma, it was true. "I share the lack of freedom of Pakistani women. My freedom is in my head. And I have a great deal of freedom!"

Never mind horses or bicycles, I say to myself, remembering the words of a little girl from a well-off family: "You know, we don't have a right to ride a bike. It's stupid, but we can travel as much as we want and anywhere in the world we want using the Internet."

In the ultramodern bus that takes us from Islamabad to Lahore, we speed along the brand-new highway built

by South Korea, with posh rest stops in a mix of
Chinese contemporary and Ottoman styles, where we
stop to quench our thirst among the crowd of peasants
come to cool themselves in the shade and look at the
tourists. All the travellers are from the well-to-do castes,
including a few women alone, dressed in Western
clothes. For once, there's nobody undressing us with
their eyes, and we rest, immersed in the landscape,
trying to understand the secret geography around the
memory of these places charged with history. The
medieval little mud houses with no electricity or
windows, where both humans and animals sleep, do not
reveal their secrets. Round, with a low protective wall,
they crouch there in the fields like big indolent animals
resting in the sun, dispersed over the countryside,
isolated, apparently lifeless—everyone is inside or else
out in the fields, where human forms move as if in
slow-motion. Some of the houses, in the shadow of
high chimneys of ochre brick that rise up into the sky
like minarets, are located over little mills in which the
sand of the country was moulded into bricks for the
more recently built farms and little houses we spot here
and there. We speed along the brand-new highway that
defies the elements, going through passes and over
rivers like a low-flying plane. The peasants, we are told,
are totally amazed by it, they flock to see the marvel,
which they can never use—this magical road is a toll
road, and anyway, they don't have cars. It's a white
elephant, say the activists, who know that the money
for a single kilometre could have been used to build a
hospital or a school. Others answer that "you can't stop

progress," the diplomats and all the NGOs of the world
have to be able to travel quickly from the east to the
capital, Islamabad, where the political business is
centred, and indeed we meet nothing but diplomats'
cars and the white vans of Médecins du Monde, we're
practically alone on the wide ivory thoroughfare
twisting and cleaving its way through this mysterious
country. At first, we are in harmony with the images
passing by and the sublime song of the muezzin's prayer
the bus hostess plays on a cassette player, but very soon
a James Bond movie on the small screen spoils our
visions. I try to distance myself from the assault of sight
and sound, go back in memory to the image of a young
woman glimpsed the first day in Lahore, walking alone
on a dusty, crowded sidewalk, the thick black chador
covering her completely down to her black shoes,
showing nothing of her except the little rectangular
mesh porthole between her nose and chin for
breathing. She was bent over in her corporal prison that
she seemed to be dragging laboriously in the heat—was
she young, was she old, there was no way to tell.
Suddenly, from my taxi, I saw an old car speed up to
her, and a man got out and forced her in, hitting her
violently on the head. The car sped away, and nobody
in the crowded street had budged, as if they hadn't seen
anything. Now, I imagine her back on the isolated,
medieval farm from which she had tried to flee, tied to
a big rusty nail, whipped by her man, who was
"dishonoured" by the mere fact of her attempt to run
away, perhaps beaten to death. That happens daily in the
remote countryside and in the middle of the

impoverished cities, my imagining it was not disengaging from reality, serious studies done by international or national human rights organizations are consistent with the mad drifting of my thoughts, the "madwoman in the attic" here was not delirious, she was unfortunately perceiving a reality that is in itself mad. My being is seized with nausea, sick of heart and sick of spirit, I gulp mouthfuls of Coke and let myself drift into a half-sleep, lifting my eyelids from time to time to see the rosy ball of the evening sun setting the whole countryside ablaze, caressing the veiled shadows of the women returning to their thatched houses. I must regain my strength. I have a full agenda for tomorrow. God, how far away my native land seems tonight!

From the outside, Kinnaerd, the private college for girls, looks like a well-protected fortress, with its wall and its guards in a sentry box at the entrance. Not just anybody can get in, nor can the schoolgirls come and go alone, certified drivers or their husbands—some of them are already married—drop them off every morning and pick them up at the end of the afternoon. Since we never see them in the city, we are glad to finally meet some young women, and in fact, we have an appointment today with three of them designated by one of their teachers, Dr. X, who does not want to give her name, and whom we've spoken to beforehand, so we will see these "representatives of the elite," as they describe themselves. Besides chatting nicely about this and that under the arbour in the large luxuriant garden where pink and white petals fall like rain in the slanting rays of sun to the wingbeats of green, orange and blue birds singing unknown songs, we have one subject in mind for these charming young ladies in their regulation uniforms of silk, fine cotton and fancy lace, we want to know what they think of the practice of arranged marriage that is common here, for them as for all the women of Pakistan, of all classes. We know that liberalization in this area is one of the "ten demands for 2000" submitted to the leaders, that arranged marriage is not based on free choice between two people in love, but on a legal contract between two families of the same clan and caste, in the pure tradition of endogamous patrilinearity, that certain girls are thus married at puberty, for example, to the son of their father's brother, which is in a sense the ideal union for the families. We don't want to shock or offend them, only to understand how they perceive their situation. Do they submit to their inevitable fate or do they rebel? Is adolescence for them, as it customarily is for us, a time of turbulent transition marked by a distancing and even rejection, at least internally, of adults' rules, which are felt to be unbearable constraints? We are astounded by what they tell us, totally taken aback ...

Either the girls selected for us were perfect, docile representatives of the prevailing fundamentalist Islamic ideology, parroting the official discourse on the need for women's obedience to the protective husband and provider of material security and the necessity of submission to the Koran, in light of which they vigor-

ously condemned "the false freedom of the West and
the generalized American pornography," or else all the
schoolgirls at Kinnaerd have been brainwashed, which
we doubt. Other meetings, many, will lead us to choose
the former hypothesis.

One of the girls met her husband on the day of their
wedding, he was abroad when the two families agreed
to the terms of the contract, he came to her loaded
with gold jewellery that she shows off proudly. The
wedding festivities lasted the whole day and late into
the night, the men together, the women among themselves, and then the married couple found themselves
alone in the privacy of a room arranged for them in her
in-laws' home, a house she knew no better than she
knew her companion. She was a little afraid, she says,
but everything was fine in the end, she blushes and
touches the wedding band proudly displayed on the
third finger of her left hand, gold and diamonds. By
noon the next day her husband had left, taking a plane
to Vancouver, where he's an important businessman. He
"gave permission" for her to finish her college
education, she will join him in Canada this summer, she
will "join him for life," she seems a bit anxious but says:
"It's best this way. We don't believe in love the way
young people practise it in the West, it's immoral.
Parents here are responsible for our lives, they know
better than we do what's right for us. We owe them
respect and obedience." The other two girls agree and
one of them, eighteen years old and also recently
married, adds: "My husband gives me protection and
security, a beautiful house with servants and a

chauffeur, all the clothing and jewels I want to buy. In addition *he lets me* go to school. What more could I want from life?"

What do they think about the poverty in their country, the *karo-kari* killings, the women raped in prisons and homes, how do they see the demands for freedom and truth championed by the democratic activists? All three become tense and angry, voices are raised, those activists are going too far, they name them, condemn them, would be ready to see them placed under a fatwa, they deserve the same fate as Taslima Nasreen and Salman Rushdie. "Freedom of expression"? The "right to choose whom one loves"? All "false Western concepts ... American depravity," says the little one who hadn't dared to speak yet, trembling with anger, and suddenly her voice rises, pure, her eyes are misty with tears, in this sumptuous Eden with a flock of birds circling above, she sings some verses of the Koran in Urdu. I remember the dark days of my Catholic adolescence in the grey boarding school, when I could recite by heart the encyclical *Rerum Novarum* or Aquinas's five proofs of the existence of God, and at night, on the sly, in the chaste dormitories, to the rustle of the long black robes of the nuns guarding us, forbidden flashlights in hand, we would delight in Gide's *Fruits of the Earth* or Rimbaud's *A Season in Hell*—they had not totally clipped our wings of rebellion.

Policemen armed to the teeth, standing at attention,
stare at us, fingers on triggers, in front of a huge
armoured gate over the façade of the building, they
activate an iron curtain that clangs shut over the
armoured gate, keeping their eyes on us, and motion
authoritatively with their free hands to our taxi driver
Muhammad, ordering him to clear out. Muhammad
opens the car door and tells them politely that we have
an appointment and are expected at the office of the
lawyer Asma Jahangir. After verification of our papers
and the usual questions, the policemen lower their
weapons, raise the iron curtain, and open the armoured
gate and we enter, accompanied by Muhammad, who
takes his role of bodyguard seriously. We climb the stairs
to the third storey and are subjected to searches and
identity checks on each floor—we submit to them
gladly, knowing that this is essential protection for
Asma, a courageous human rights activist whose life is
regularly threatened, who alone with her lawyer sister
defends the cause of women and civil divorce, and who
has seen a woman she was defending killed right before
her eyes in the law court by her mother-in-law, who
was furious over her divorce action. Finally we enter a
small waiting room teeming with women and children
and drenched in sun and sweat. The full gamut of
marital failure and violence is written on the women's
tired faces, the whole litany of fears and defeats, but
there are also some notes of hope and deliverance in
this immeasurable earthly purgatory where the scrawny
children cling to the skirts of the heavy mothers and
the babies in weary arms cry in chorus for nursing—

not now, not in public, the good, calming milk, each mother seems to be whispering in her baby's ear. The mothers look at us, some of them smiling.

Suddenly Asma the Courageous comes towards us, her arms open as we have seen her in photographs in the newspapers when she speaks to crowds of peasant women in the villages, explaining to them with passion and patience the virtues of freedom and truth and the courage they'll need, the strength to denounce misdeeds and corruption, and the honour of casting off feudal oppression, comes towards us with the same enthusiasm. I had imagined her tall and sturdy, but instead she's very small, yet she radiates strength. Without a veil, bareheaded, with short hair, she has sparkling eyes despite the circles etched by too many hours of work—this woman has the largest private clientele of all the lawyers in Pakistan—she has a luminous fragility. She's a secular saint, a lay Mother Teresa, she's known throughout the country and far beyond, she was president of the Human Rights Commission of Pakistan and a United Nations delegate to Kosovo. Yet she makes time to talk to us, faces our questions and our tape recorder, doesn't even keep track of the time, with the ringing of the telephone, which she has muted, with the echoes of animated conversations and the laughter and crying of children on the other side of the door of the study she has ushered us into. We breathe in the smells of cigarettes and old leather, antique wood and old books of this very old continent, the centuries of history bear witness to the long history of women that she recounts for us. But a "new century of new freedom" is coming, she says, filled with wonder, suddenly looking like the innocent, spirited girl she must have been. Her eyes throw off sparks, her cheeks turn pink, fatigue vanishes from her face at the mere mention of the victories wrenched from the tyrants in patient, daily struggle. "We will overcome 'Talibanization.' Women are capable of being flexible and negotiating, they are more courageous than men, greater in peace, they don't need wars to demonstrate their strength and courage, I saw it in Macedonia, where I spent hours with the Kosovar women in the refugee camps. And they're also more candid, they don't talk doubletalk the way politicians do, they don't go in for Politics with a capital *p*, I've seen it at all the world conferences on women's rights. And so I place my greatest hope in the universal language of women— which some men are beginning to learn—this language has the same vocabulary and grammar as every one of the languages of all peoples, but speaks of things and events and human beings in an *other* way. See how easy it is for the three of us to understand one other, we didn't know each other barely an hour ago and yet we understand each other as if we were old friends, we communicate in a common language that seems very far from our mother tongues, and even those very different mother tongues understand each other better simply because of their special connection to our universal language."

(Isn't it poetry she's talking about, isn't it poetry that makes an *other* way of living and thinking resonate in words? Can the sentences of this language, like the lines of a poem, navigate among streams that would otherwise be inaudible?)

To understand the activists of the East, the kind of people we sometimes describe in the West as *engagé* intellectuals, we have to think beyond ourselves, to move away from the central continent of philosophy, to forget for a time our reasons—even our unreasons—to think about war and peace in an *other* way. I doubt that we, in all our arrogance, are capable of it, because our philosophical masters are European, they belong to those peoples that have colonized not only the physical territories of all the other continents, but also the thought, the mythologies created by their inhabitants.

"You know," Asma continues, "the war here isn't between men and women, but between people, both men and women, who are fighting for the secularization of the country and those in power, who are being pulled by the fundamentalist forces of Talibanization. Those forces have been growing astronomically for some time, there are even doctors—this would have been unthinkable before—who advise their patients to read the Koran instead of taking medication. Do we not have every reason to fear, given the political instability, the great poverty, the enslavement of millions of women and children, the lack of education and health care? Should we not expect the most harmful consequences, the worst degradations from the perversity of a religious ideology combined with fascism? We are fighting very hard on several fronts: drafting laws on civil marriage and divorce and the decriminalization of homosexuality, writing articles on the freedom of young women to choose their own husbands. We talk to them wherever we are invited, yesterday I told some of them, 'If you think it's essential to see and touch a fabric before buying it, don't you feel you have the same right in the choice of the man with whom, in principle, you are going to spend your whole life?' You know, very simple things about the individual right to freely choose one's destiny. While I was speaking to those 'young girls in flower,' I saw that some of them were dreaming, gazing off into the distance and smiling rapturously, and I said to myself, this is my work, and that's why the death threats don't really frighten me anymore, especially because my children are grown up now, this is my work, giving girls the ability to dream of a free and true world! Giving abused women a way out."

We leave Asma to her many clients and promise we'll see her again. In the packed corridor that separates us from the outdoors, a veiled woman who is a stranger to me hands me a note written in French on a scrap of newspaper: "We have offered men the olive branch of peace. They answered us with the weapons of their sexes and their guns." Who is this woman and where did she learn our language? She has slipped away quickly. We will probably never know.

"To survive, if you want to stay here and not go into exile, you have to make compromises," says Swaleha Niaz, a young woman of twenty-four who has not yet consented to an arranged marriage. She is a painter and free, and wants to devote her life to her art, talks about her artistic quest like a true philosopher. We see her paintings, which would not be out of place in the major galleries of the world. Her "liberal" parents, she says with delight, allowed her to set up her studio as she wished in the big family house where we are invited for an elaborate dinner. They're "liberal," it's true, but they are still astonished to see "the images that come out of my head" and to hear what she has to say on freedom of expression. They gave her a year of art study in France, from which she returned "emancipated," she says, determined to explore fully the paths her art has opened up for her. "When I came back from France, where I had freedom of movement, I was bothered by the attitude of the men of my country. They ask us to cover ourselves from head to foot, our clothes are statements, religious flags, but they're always staring at us, undressing us and raping us with their eyes. I realized this there, where staring like that is the exception—here, it's so common you don't see it anymore. That's alienation: no longer seeing your own body, which has become the object of the obsessive gaze of another. When I came back from France, I understood that there was a war here between men and women, I saw that this war was pornographic. They have their eyes aimed at us like guns. We are bodies that they force us to veil in order to conceal the objects of their obscene desires."

Working "around the theme of pornography," trying to find her centre, "to exist in spite of the system around me, to find my freedom inside myself," Swaleha was able in France to have nude models, men and women—here, that's impossible, prohibited, criminal—and she photographed them for her work. Now she can surf the Internet, she says, "The bodies of the women exhibited there, open and disarmed, are a metaphor for the situation of women in my country. The bodies of women here are disarmed and conquered lands, men penetrate these territories, violate them and kill them as in wars. We are at war among ourselves, I want to show this in my paintings of women's bodies. Men do things women don't want, I want to show this in my painting. Every woman has to see this, every woman has to understand that she is at war against herself because of pornography. In order to find a way out, she has to first go inside herself and fight that war. I'm fed up with politics. I want to work on these questions. Here, all the intelligent young people are disillusioned, all those who aren't brainwashed by religion are disillusioned, we don't believe in politics anymore. Our politicians have always been corrupt, the religious leaders are sex-obsessed hypocrites. I don't have the energy to shout in the public square, all my energy goes into creating, my commitment is to my painting. It's my way of saying I don't agree, I don't agree with this war of men against women. I say it through the images in my paintings. I've abandoned realism, it's less shocking."

We see the series of images through which young Swaleha expresses her vision of the world, those related to the sexual body (uterus, vagina, hair, anus, breasts, mouth, eyes) and those related to women's everyday lives (iron, baby bottle, fabric, utensils, basket, vase, fruit), dozens of series, each including dozens of painted or engraved images repeated obsessively, each fragment of the sexual body, each everyday implement shown as deformed, in a quest for a new meaning—for example, the vagina or the iron will have hooks or claws, their function is no longer to soften, but to lacerate, and juicy fruits are presented behind barbed wire. In her search for "inner truth," as Swaleha puts it, before any composition of a "subject," there is a war to be waged involving breaking down and taking apart. "Even if we are changing society," Swaleha says, "even if we are moving towards freedom and truth, we will have to take with us all the shattered and fragmented parts."

With her we go to an exhibition at the National College of Fine Arts in Lahore, where she studies. She says, "You'll see that the young people here are free to dress and paint or sculpt as they wish," and it's true. Like poetry and music, painting knows no borders, and what we see here is totally stateless, all these pieces could have been done by young people in Western countries, you couldn't tell where they come from by the style alone, inside the frames or in the installations these young women and men have gone around the world, and we've never seen so many smiling faces, nobody has given us that piercing stare, we've strolled freely with Swaleha, finally seeing young people who have found their path to truth. In the middle of an interior garden bathed in sunlight and the majestic shadows of century-old chestnut trees, there's a sculpture inspired by Rodin's *Kiss*. "It's a couple kissing," says Swaleha,

"You can't tell what sex they are. If this were seen outside these walls, we would all go to prison."

The same day, we cross the city of Lahore from east to west, to its well-to-do suburb Model Town, where we meet Salima Hashmi, whose paintings we want to see. We've heard she's a talented painter and respected teacher, and it was the works of her students that we had the pleasure of seeing at the College of Fine Arts. Those young people owe to her—and they say so with enthusiasm—the freedom of exploration and expression that allows them to endure the constraints of the world outside without too much suffering. She is also the daughter of the great poet Faiz Ahmed Faiz, a hero to all Pakistanis, who died in 1984 and whose luminous last words, Salima says proudly, came in those very dark years when "the only goddess was named corruption: women will save Pakistan." "What a wonderful heritage!" says his daughter fervently, surrounded by her paintings, in which the light itself is a character. On her knees is a leather-bound, gilt-edged book of her father's poems, from which she reads us extracts. I see her slender artist's hands poised on the ivory sheets of cotton fibre paper, her fingers following the lines written in black India ink. Writing Urdu, like Arabic, is an art, the page is like a painting, and the lines presented to the gaze and the voice chanting the poem are a gift, beyond all understanding, the gift of a meaning I immediately discover—only my own poems could have the same effect on me. While in my mind's eye I see a procession of fragmented images detached from any known reality, Salima says, "In Pakistan, there are two languages, that of diplomacy, which is lies, and that of metaphor, which reconciles the people with the truth." (I suddenly think of the twenty thousand people, men and women, who the day before attended the great Mushaira[14] in the national stadium in Karachi, to listen for hours to their favourite poets, Inayat Ali Khan, Athar Shah Khan, Taj Baloch, Meeruthi, Krishan Bihari Noor, Ahmed Faraz and Tabish Dehlavi. These lovers of words declaimed like music had planned ahead, because the festival lasted late into the night, they brought drink and food, cushions and blankets, and in some cases, little writing stands on which they themselves could write poems. Yes, it was a festival night for poets from all over the country—and even from India, don't they speak the same ancestral language and chant to the same music? I was dazzled by the intimate understanding of the audience captivated by these sung poems, incantations that they would all chant in chorus, applauding and asking for encores, and the rhapsodies would begin again readily, with passion and delight.) A complete feast for eye and ear in this big house of Salima's, where every object seems to have an ancient soul. As if waking from a dream, I hear Salima's voice say, as she puts her father Faiz's book on a small mahogany table, "There are two lights in this rotten world, but basically they're both the same: that of women and that of poetry." Then she explains to us why there is not here, as there is in the West, a right and

---

14. Literally, festival of the word.

a left—they are Western concepts, she says. "What you call the left is in our country neither communist nor socialist, it is those who fight for peace. That's all, the rest will come later. If India and Pakistan would put the money for weapons into education and health for everyone, the rest—justice and respect for human rights—would follow."

She says, "On both sides of the Kashmir border, the little boys who play with their nuclear and other weapons are equally stupid. And the West is hypocritical towards our peoples, the West lectures us about nuclear weapons and human rights violations when the big problem here is the corruption of all the governments since independence—and even before. The *haves* maintain endemic poverty and shameful illiteracy. Your spokespersons in the West know that and they're hypocrites. This truth has never been put on trial either in your countries or in ours."

We look at Salima's paintings, which tell tragic stories with light emerging from shadows, they're absolutely dazzling, she uses mixed techniques with acrylic and pigments on paper tinted with tea. Made by women in Bangladesh, the painted linen fibre paper is "fragile as a woman's sex." We are contemplating a series on domestic violence—a servant in long white robes, moving with the lightness of a shadow, has placed the paintings in the sunlight flooding in through the windows, another one has served us tea and cakes— suddenly, a painting that completely captivates us, *Poem for Zena*, that, in its blackness shot through with the fire of a lucid wound, tells the story of Zena, a young woman whose fundamentalist husband, a mullah, a "holy man," had tortured his young bride in order to purify her dangerous sex and prevent any adulterous pleasure, had punctured her vagina with an iron rod heated red-hot in a forge. The young woman was taken to hospital by some local women, who had found her at death's door, and "only Benazir Bhutto went to her bedside, and no political party would comment." Thanks to Amnesty International she was able to have surgery in London, but that's not in the painting. There's only a gagged mouth at the bottom in an obsessively repeated series (and only repetition and variation, as in fantasy, can convey the obscene), the rest can only be abstract, it is the light that speaks in the colours, which seem to be in constant polychromatic movement—the brown blends into the garnet and, touched by a splash of yellow, becomes dried blood that flowed long ago and seems to end in a mouth open to the desert, because the dried pigments so clearly seem to be moving. Salima says, "To me, Zena is the symbol of all women, you see, that's even a photo of my own mouth there, at the bottom of the painting. When Zena came back from London—her 'holy man' was in prison—do you know what the first thing she did was? She took the only child she would ever have in her arms and she smiled. She smiled! That's why I put a gag on my mouth. They can stop us from speaking, they can violate our bodies as they did in the Kashmir, Kosovo, or Chechnya, but they will never be able to kill our spirits!"

All along the bumpy streets back to our hotel at the end
of the day, the poems and paintings fade before the
scenes of the city, which has become a field of animals,
there are so many of them in the area where tomorrow
the animal-keepers of Allah will be working. There's
going to be another festival, the Eid, the big day of this
moon of March of collective sacrifice, the peasants from
the surrounding region will sacrifice to an angry God
as many animals as the sins they have committed, then
they'll sell them to the rich, whose sacrifice will be the
money given and the reparations, all the meat
distributed to the poor, and so everyone will have
"killed the animal within," as commanded by the
Prophet a millennium and a half ago. The preparations
and all the rituals tonight and tomorrow will be the
same as in the past. In the middle of the field of animals,
the horrible, stinking traffic punctuated by their cries,
the suffocating heat of the long day ending in bleating,
bawling, braying and bellowing, I remember the sad
festivals of sacrifice and forgiveness of my childhood,
the Good Fridays when everything seemed dead
because Everything was dead, it was cold and rainy in
the heavy silence of penance in which everyone cried
out their pain, but inside, we didn't see the blood
spurting from the cut throats of the sheep and ewes,
goats and kids, cows and calves that we see this evening
by the hundreds tied to their posts awaiting execution,
those scenes were not actually played out before our
eyes, the mysteries of heaven and earth were kept
abstract, the blood would be drunk by an officiating
priest in the form of wine and we would eat the bodies

in the form of unleavened bread—we didn't really understand why—it was so long ago, my mind falters in the murky limbo of remembering. Our taxi driver Muhammad tries as best he can to make his way through this huge field of animals and their peasant masters who are soon to be separated from them in the revulsion and jubilation of their murder, as commanded by all the prophets and the Prophet. It's better not to look too much, there are the many dangers of the road and the unbearable bellowing of the animals, we close our eyes, letting everything jumble together in a post-modern cacophony from which, in the furrows of our night's dreams, we will try to extract some meaningful syllables.

At dawn on the last day, the aftermath of the animals' field of death is spread out in the open air, bellies, guts and excrement that will flow nauseatingly until it all dries up in the sand and dust after the vultures have come. We would like to leave for the Gulf of Oman, to walk on the water, stretch out on it, wrap ourselves up in it as in a light, downy quilt, bathe our hands and our cheeks in its salty nectar. We wish it could by a miracle become champagne that we would drink until no longer thirsty—or the miraculous Easter water that was given to us as children after the melting of the blue ice, when we'd say goodbye until next year to the snow on which we had slid all winter, bellies and chests immaculate white. But now we have to leave again, to go away from Pakistan and the Gulf of Oman, to embrace friends with a thousand wishes of courage and hope, to get on the plane for Karachi among the white-

robed crowd going to Mecca, in Saudi Arabia, for the
ultimate festival of the Hajj, the mystical meeting with
the Prophet. To Mecca, yes! To drink the water of the
same well where He quenched his thirst, yes! To place
their bare feet on the path where He walked barefoot,
it was so long ago but at the same time it was yesterday.
But a last sight tears us away from the sublime scene,
one that will stay with us until takeoff—and forever—
the vision of hundreds of bodies stretched out in the
suffocating heat on the ground at the airport, wrapped
in long, soiled robes, right on the hard, dirty ground,
they've come to spend the night outdoors, they all
appear to be asleep, side by side, looking like rows of
shrouds, they don't have the money to go with the
others. Are they perhaps dreaming that they're there in
the blessed East, curled up against the white stone wall
of the Great Mosque of Mecca? Do they hear in their
dreams the words of the last sermon given by their saint
in that faraway city? Does a woman—each one's own
woman—who would tear the veil from their long dark
night appear to them in a dream?

SRI LANKA

Sri Lanka

The plane that takes us from Karachi to Colombo is
crammed with cheerful men in Western clothes, we
don't recognized them anymore, they no longer stare at
us with eyes that pierce like darts, they're completely
involved in their business, some are typing on portable
computers, all seem happy as if they're going to a party.
They've left their wives in Pakistan, and except for a
young Frenchwoman from Médecins du Monde, we're
the only ones of our sex. Yesterday's Eid al-Hajj, the
bloody commemoration of the sacrifice of Abraham-
Ibrahim is already a thing of the past, already so far
away. What will they celebrate in Sri Lanka, a land of
Sinhalese Buddhists and Tamil Hindus, light-years from
the Islam of Pakistan? Our questions plummet into the
long desert of the Punjab, dotted with emerald lakes,
pools of marble and tribes said to be warlike. Now and
then we spot processions of draft elephants, but from
here they look like columns of ants, I wish the plane
could set down for a moment, for just an hour, say, so
that we could meet these men and women of the
desert, talk or sing with them, grasp a little of their

amazing knowledge of the world, I would like it if an
exchange of thoughts or emotions between us were
possible (will we not cross paths even once in this world
where chance has landed us in the same century?), but
supposing this meeting were to take place, wouldn't we
each be plunged into the chasm of mysteries where the
Other takes us, each writing, deep within, a private
indecipherable poem of absence and, ultimately,
abandonment to the Other, wouldn't it take several
centuries of living together and crossing the sands on
our draft elephants for a spark of presence to occur?
Coming out of my reverie, I hear my neighbour to the
right (he's a charming old man who's crossing the
border wearing the beautiful linen costume of his
country) say in a low voice, as if he had read my
thoughts earlier: "You know why they are all going to
spend the weekend in Colombo? Half to buy alcohol
and drink undisturbed in the fancy hotels for tourists,
the other half for the traffic in arms, since they make as
much from the war in Tamil Eelam as from ours in
Kashmir. War is a thriving business in our two Third
World countries, both bled dry. Pick your side. All the
pacifists in the world will never get the better of these
gangsters. There's no hell after death. Hell is now. On
earth. And it always has been: now on earth! Except for
the oppressed who use war to defend themselves—like
the Tamils in Sri Lanka, as you will see. Those who
make war for profit have no souls. After their deaths,
they will no longer exist. Only those who have souls in
this life will survive eternally. The others will become
nothing. For the time of their earthly life, they are the

devils of the present hell. Only the peace of just souls and heaven are eternal."

On landing, we see at least one of our companion's predictions borne out, as soon as we get inside the terminal, our men in their Sunday-best clothes rush to the liquor store. When we've gone through customs and are waiting for our baggage at the carrousel, we see them come out, weighed down with bags of bottles, grinning from ear to ear. It's the poor Pakistanis who die every day in makeshift distilleries, these men today have the means to come here to go on a binge, there's nothing these men who have no right to a drop in their own country won't drink. Our companion tells us that they don't sing or laugh on these drinking bouts, they scream and shout, they get smashed and wreck everything, and the Sinhalese or Tamil neighbours stay in their houses, close their windows, would rather swelter in the torrid heat of the late monsoon season than hear the din of the orgy. The neighbours will shut themselves in tonight and pray to the moon, and in fact the moon is full this evening. Tomorrow will be another holy day for the Buddhists and the Hindus—every full moon heralds a holy day, thirteen times a year the Sinhalese and Tamil peoples give thanks to the moon in abstinence and silence: for a day, no meat, no alcohol and no arguments in the house, for the Moon is the mother of all the female deities of this earth that, for the day, is heaven, as expressed by the thirty-one letters of the Tamil alphabet, of which the thirteen vowels, *uyir*, are souls and the eighteen consonants, *mei*, bodies. And we, this evening, address a very secular prayer to the moon: that she light our way and guide our steps in the opaque blackness of this small, strangely vast country in the shape of a teardrop just below India, to which it was attached until the reshaping of the continents of the southern hemisphere centuries ago. But a long time before the break-up of the land masses, in the Stone Age a hundred thousand years ago, two Dravidian peoples, the Iyakkar and the Nagar, lived side by side on the southern subcontinent, and these peoples gave birth, over millennia of mixing, to "two races," as is commonly said in Sri Lanka, that of the tigers, the Tamils, and that of the lions, the Sinhalese, and gradually over the course of migrations, to two languages, Tamil and Sinhalese, the former derived from Malayalam, Telugu and Kannada and the latter from Elu, and through religious conquests over some ten thousand years before the common era and in the first millennium of the common era, to two religions.

Let us ask the moon for a path for our dreams in this tiny teardrop, this jewel of land and sea, this vast country where we find ourselves tonight, for a diabolical war is going on here between two peoples, one of which, the Sinhalese people, has parliamentary political power and the power of money and an army, while the other, the Tamil people, has gradually been dispossessed of everything since independence from England in 1948, when the island was called Ceylon, lacks adequate education and health systems in a country where the Sinhalese language of the Buddhist majority has been declared the only official language, and has seen thousands of people killed and shops and houses burned down in pogroms since 1983, which the Tamils call "the beginning of the holocaust." The Tamils voted in 1977, in a proportion of seventy-five percent, in favour of territorial autonomy for the northeast, Eelam, which is today immersed in fire, blood, rape. And yet these two peoples, each with its own history, religion and language, and even its kings, had survived conquest by the Portuguese, then the Dutch, and then the British between 1505 and 1948. Despite four hundred and fifty years of occupation, conquests, and sporadic wars, they had maintained their respective languages and cultures. And in this Sri Lanka, literally "resplendent island," as it was named twenty years ago by the Sinhalese, one of the two peoples is dying; since 1983, sixty thousand dead or disappeared; five hundred thousand civilians displaced and without resources following the invasion of the Jaffna Peninsula in 1990 and indiscriminate bombing by the Sri Lankan army throughout the territory of Tamil Eelam and its capital, Jaffna, and the deportation of civilians from Jaffna; eight hundred thousand Tamil refugees and exiles, in England, France, Switzerland, Germany and Canada; systematic rape of women, young girls and little girls by the soldiers of the Sinhalese army and the police of the regime.

Total censorship of the media, which get all their information from the military authorities; self-censorship by the newspapers, radio and television in the south, where very few people know what's happening in the north, and also by the foreign media, which, of course, faithfully report every suicide

operation by the LTTE[15] in the headlines, so that each
time a bomb explodes in the south, the international
community knows about it. This happens cyclically. In
December 1999, President Chandrika Bandaranaike
Kumaratunga lost her right eye in an explosion, and in
March 2000, twelve civilians were killed in Colombo,
the work of suicide bombers, men or women—they're
called the "Black Tigers" because their bodies are
burned. This is "the ultimate sacrifice," we are told by
N., a Tamil woman involved in the struggle. "It is more
than giving life to a child, it is giving life to a whole
people, and moreover, dying by fire is the ultimate
purification, the attainment of nirvana." But nobody
knows about the thousands of civilians of Tamil Eelam
who have been killed by daily shelling and bombing
over the years, and yet the international community
knows, all the international organizations, the UN,
Human Rights Watch, Amnesty International, the
NGOs on the ground, know. The murders and rapes of
civilians—they have figures and sworn statements—the
population displacements, internal and external, the
economic embargo imposed on the northeast for thirty
years, the loss of freedom, the systematic torture—all of
it is known. And we continue to read in the newspapers
of the "free" world that the war in Sri Lanka is between
the legitimate Sri Lankan army and the "LTTE
terrorists," the same deceptive propaganda we've seen in
Kosovo or Chechnya, while an entire people is dying
and has no other choice to respond to state terrorism

---

15. Liberation Tigers of Tamil Eelam, an illegal military
organization of the Tamil separatists.

but to put its trust in the only group that can defend it and protect it, the Tamil Tigers, even though it is also known that there are madmen and gangsters among them, as in any corrupt war. But the evidence is accumulating in the UN commissions and other international organizations whose mission is to protect oppressed peoples. There's a Sri Lankan president and a Parliament, pushed by fanatical Buddhist extremists, who are waging what they call a "war for peace"— there is no war more dishonest, no war more smugly assured of its rightness than one waged in the name of peace, in Tamil Eelam as in Chechnya—with the blind support of the international community and extremist religious leaders who've traded Zen for racist violence, as well as that of the arms dealers of East and West, the temple money-changers of modern times.

Let us tonight ask the moon for a path for our dreams, for on this teardrop of blood in the Indian Ocean, in the steam bath between monsoons, protected from the mosquitoes that carry dengue and malaria, windows tightly shut, we can't hear the song of the waves or the rustle of the broad leaves of the coconut trees, have glimpsed the moon between two palm branches, just above a herons' nest—a path for dreams, because the path of our thoughts is confused, gone far to the north where we're not allowed to go, along the Kilali Lagoon where, in 1995, in the first exodus from Jaffna, five hundred thousand panic-stricken Tamils fled the bombing of their city, or to Kilinochchi where, in July 1996, in the second exodus under savage bombing, two hundred and fifty thousand civilians sought refuge in the forests of Wanni, deprived of everything, including aid from NGOs because of restrictions imposed by the government. I finally fall asleep with these words of Desmond Tutu, quoted in the very courageous book *Let My People Go*, by Father S.J. Emmanuel, Vicar General of the diocese of Jaffna and "witness of the lives and sufferings of its people":

> Non-violence as a means towards ending an unjust system presupposes that the oppressors show a minimum level of morality. I doubt however that such a Gandhian campaign would have saved the Jews from the Nazi holocaust.

Then I wake up, turn on the bedside lamp, pick up S.J. Emmanuel's book again, and read:

> How is it possible that peoples and nations cry out so loudly against a single bomb in the Colombo city or in any part of the world ... but do not condemn the Sri Lankan government, when its forces, under the pretext of attacking the terrorist bases and under the cover of a strict media blockade, drop not one, but hundreds of bombs and fire thousands of artillery shells over civilian areas day and night and cause indiscriminate destruction of churches, temples and schools and kill many thousand of civilians for so many years?

I turn off the lamp and return to the shores of Kilali Lagoon, the moon with its secrets suddenly melts into the feather pillow, and I fall back to sleep with those words. In this room at the edge of the unknown sea, in

the middle of a strife-torn country that is a tear in the
Indian Ocean, south of India, of which it was once part,
a vowel emerges, immense, it is soul, it says (such
concision is possible in the Tamil language): "I am a
woman in war."

Sri Lanka is a paradise for tourists from all over the
world. Along the beaches of golden sand in the south,
there are transplanted bits of the Côte d'Azur, Florida
and the Costa del Sol, while nearby in the background
are the people, in Third World poverty, emaciated in the
heat, in search of food, bodies often sick, filing by in the
shadows like shadows, suffering from malaria, AIDS,
tuberculosis. There are not enough drugs, clinics, or
hospitals, they don't have the resources anyway, no
national vaccination program, the vaccines too
expensive, how can they afford it when thirty percent
of the national budget goes to the war, the "war for
peace," how can they permit people the luxury of not
dying from a disease when they have been dying from
ethnic war for fifty years, and when the annual per
capita GNP is approximately seven hundred American
dollars (with the population of the Tamil northeast not
even included)? Every morning granted by the various
deities, the daily newspapers contain page after page of
names of the dead with the causes of death—I've never
seen such a long obituary section in any country and
the number of young faces is frightening—but never
any discussion, they're in no particular order. Nor is
there ever any news of the dead at the front in the

north, the civilians who've fallen under the army's
bombs go uncounted—in Tamil Eelam, they only
cleaned up the field of honour, uprooted the
"terrorists" like weeds. Nor are the bodies of the
women raped and then murdered by the soldiers
counted, nor the bodies of the members of their
families or neighbours who had the misfortune of
being witnesses, nothing is said of the collective rapes,
always by soldiers or police officers, of mothers,
daughters and granddaughters, nor of those explosions
of bodies when the rapists, to erase any trace of the
crime, put grenades in the vaginas, none of this is
reported in the obituaries of the morning newspapers.
But the names of the women, young girls and little girls
torn open with the male sexual weapons, guns to their
heads, those names are known, those women have a
paper monument at the UN, at the Commission on War
Crimes and Crimes against Humanity, and they have
paper monuments in the files of the British Refugee
Council, Human Rights Watch and Amnesty
International. They were from Tamil Eelam, from the
towns and villages of Thiyavattavan, Vellaveli and
Pathmeni or from the forest, where they were driven
and tried to survive. They were ten or twelve or twenty
or forty years old. Sometimes they were raped as a
group, grandmother, aunt, mother, daughter. Their
names are there in the common grave of the archives,
they're called Verani, Sinnarasa, Sivasothy, or
Chavakachcheri, hundreds of cases recorded. But the
tanned, muscular, blond tourists to the resplendent
island, who dive in the coral reefs, sail or read insipid

brochures for organized tours under the palm trees, sipping their punch served on a silver tray by a waiter with a big smile and such white teeth—at least this one has a job—don't know those names, they've come here to relax, they work so hard in the West, they don't know that behind the scenes a human tragedy is taking place that looks like genocide, they don't know. After the diving and swimming, the weight-training and massage sessions, and the obligatory sunbathing, they'll go in a luxury bus to visit Kandy, the "cultural city," will eat at a well-known Chinese—or Italian—restaurant, then take pictures of the elephants and storks, pomegranate trees and hibiscus bushes, frangipanis and orchids—of course, the island is an earthly paradise—and will tell their friends when they return home, "What a wonderful vacation we had in Sri Lanka!"

The Tamil northeast was barred to us, but in the south, in Colombo and Kandy, we met activists who have worked on the ground and members of NGOs involved in the defence of human rights and the protection of threatened populations. However we cannot write their names here, they are in such great danger, whether they are Sinhalese or Tamil, of being captured and tortured by the forces of order, soldiers or police, or simply murdered with no one ever knowing, as has been happening to large numbers of people throughout the south for the past ten years, with hooded gangs breaking down doors and dragging out presumed terrorists to take them away, nobody ever knows exactly where—in fact, nobody knows who those armed, masked men are, are they police, army, religious extremists? nobody knows—so that in the south, too, the disappeared number in the thousands. Many women suddenly find themselves heads of households—not even widows, who could receive a government pension, since they don't know if their husbands are dead or disappeared, and they "are deprived of the chance to mourn," as M., a social psychologist, tells us. "There are only five psychologists in the country," she adds, "and a few psychiatrists, who administer antidepressants. And in the north, nobody. We're trying to train a few for work in the field." No mourning possible, and "no possibility of blaming an enemy," the violators of homes and often of bodies remain faceless and nameless. "The women and girls do not associate their subsequent psychological and physical disorders with the macabre orgy, and don't talk about it, it's taboo. They go to the temple burdened with their karma, it's fate. In spite of their economic problems, they scrimp to buy sacrifices, flowers or lanterns so that a husband or son will return, spend hours at the temple every day, bowing at the feet of the Buddha or the deities dedicated to human suffering." As for the rapes, so frequent here that they are no longer counted, they may occur at the many army checkpoints or in police stations, under the threat of the soldiers' or policemen's rifles and revolvers, but nobody says a word, it's the ultimate taboo. "We start by telling the women they're not responsible. They have trouble believing us, the shame is so great that they sometimes prefer suicide to disclosure." We go through the well-documented reports of national and international organizations citing the proven suicides and the murders committed, alas, by "dishonoured" family members among both the Buddhist Sinhalese and the Hindu Tamils. The bodies of the women and deflowered girls are purified by fire, the "dishonoured" men of the caste, clan, or family burn the profaned bodies and piously deposit the ashes in small alabaster urns—honour restored for the men and nirvana for the women, at the price of a human life. Isn't their religion based on the principle that "existence is suffering" and the quest for nirvana, or liberation from that suffering?

"Psychology is taboo here," M. tells us, "Feelings are not expressed through words. We are working—we're a small team trained in the West—on all the effects of violence against women, with the women we can reach. On the absence of mourning, the absence of aggression, the endemic depression. On all the psychological and physical aspects of post-traumatic stress syndrome—nightmares, bleeding, anemia, asthenia, frigidity, all of them. We train women who will go and lead 'talking groups' throughout the country, in both the north and the south. No borders for us. We know both languages and both religions. One day, we'll go and meet with the women rotting in prison. Most of the time, they don't know why they're there. Like all the others, they have no right to a trial. They don't have lawyers either. We're working on it. In prison, they're tortured and raped. We're compiling files. There are so few of us. So alone!"

That evening, we met a Sinhalese woman working in
a store in the centre of Colombo, she was from the
south, where her husband was kidnapped ten years ago,
has five children to feed, that's why she chose the
capital, where it's easier for older teenagers to find odd
jobs and ways to get by. The children go to school, at
least there's that—Sri Lanka is the most educated
country in the Third World, it's a "socialist" republic,
after all, education and health are, in theory, free for
everyone (except in Tamil Eelam, where the people
have always been literate, with an extremely rich
language and literature and two highly sophisticated
grammars that date back to before the Christian era,
but now, since the government embargo of the north,
there's not a rupee for these things). This beautiful, tall
woman, wearing a sari from the south made from a
long draped piece of turquoise cotton, never smiles and
doesn't cry anymore, she says, "not in ages," but she
thinks. She says: "I think all the time, even at night, I
don't dream, I think. I think of my husband. At times I
blame myself for his going away and I scream. At times
I blame him for going away and I scream. It has
happened so many times since he disappeared. The
children do not even wake up anymore when I scream."

We came back before nightfall. In the air, there was
a mixed smell of camellias, cinnamon and red pepper.
But more than the smell, and more than the waves we
heard in the long white corridor open to the sea and
the garden, there was the screaming of Chagrina—that
was her name—driven into the eardrum of my soul,

shattering everything in its path. All the way to the purest heaven.

We are in R.'s garden, she introduces us to her shrubs and flowers as if they were people, she talks to them too, names them, and kisses them, "my rock violets, my lilies and irises, vine of my heart, jasmine my love, my cactuses and orchids, my hibiscus, my cotton blossoms, my frangipani bush, my lemon tree." She says that a large part of her life is there, they're all in the chain of reincarnation, so you have to take care of them like people. She says, "I am Buddhist in my mind, but my soul is Catholic." Her family was converted to Catholicism under the Portuguese occupation, and one of her ancestors was a Buddhist king, "it stays in your veins, you know, royal blood." She shows us one of her proudest treasures, a wood rosary dating back seven generations, bequeathed by her maternal grandmother. "When nothing happens, I am Buddhist, merged with the elements and the beings around me, in close, quiet relationship with the great Buddha sitting under his holy Tree fourteen centuries ago when he attained enlightenment." She also knows Rimbaud, whom she recites by heart through the peaceful days, "he was a contemporary Buddha," she says, amused. And when she's happy, when she gets up in the morning "at the edge of enchantment, I am Catholic, I take my rosary out of its case, I touch it and recite it." But "when trouble knocks on my door, then I am Hindu, that religion has all the deities for suffering, each misfortune has its god or goddess." We suddenly hear the sea, as if all three of us, in the way that people sometimes agree on something, had decided to listen to it together, it's right in front of us yet we hadn't heard it, as if there were bubbles of silence in the air. She listens, eyes closed, and says, "I love the sea, eternity speaks in its waves, it brings me closer to God, and also, the sea is like my people, so calm and yet so violent."

She remembers the pogroms of 1983, the whole country was in flames, the gentle Sinhalese had come out of their houses and, one very long day and night, had attacked the Tamils, destroyed everything, set fires, injured, killed, raped, with rifles, clubs, or even their hands and feet, had broken bones, gouged out eyes, torn off ears, cut off heads, eaten hearts. The police had let them do it, the army had stayed in its barracks. And then everything had calmed down, the tide had ebbed, the Tamils had buried their dead and left, some had gone abroad, others had taken the road to Tamil Eelam, walked for days through forests and lagoons to the Jaffna Peninsula, where war has been waged against them ever since. But some of them had stayed, not wanting to believe what they had seen. R. knows some who still say, "it was a bad dream, those things didn't really happen." She doesn't understand why her people, so gentle, normally so calm and pleasant, went mad like that, she says, "I believe it was the propaganda, decades of propaganda and lies that held the Tamils responsible for all the hardships my people had suffered for centuries."

She says, "Racism is ignorance of the Other. The love of my life was a Tamil—now exiled in America—but the families prevented the marriage. If mixed marriage had been possible here from the start, there would never have been a war. I'll soon be sixty and I still love my Tamil lover of when I was twenty. Whenever happiness crosses my threshold, I take my two-hundred-year-old rosary out of its case, I think of him, I caress the soft polished wood of the rosary, I say the beads, I recite my Hail Marys, I cry for joy, and I love him." And when, in class—R. is a teacher in a college—she hears the sound of an ambulance, she tells her students to "stop everything and pray. Whatever their religion, Buddhist, Hindu, Moslem, or Christian, we fall silent, we pray. And the screams of ambulances are frequent here. I tell my students, we stop everything, the blood of our people is flowing!"

It's hot, as in Marguerite Duras's *India Song*, our bodies sweat, listless on white sheets. This evening we will eat bananas, pineapple, cheese, basmati rice, drink water, perhaps have a piece of chocolate with a cup of tea. Ceylon tea is mellow, grown since the days of the British colony, and since the death of the old coffee plantations after some insect or pest, no one is sure what, destroyed every twig, every speck of the previous beverage, once the glory of the island. The English brought abundant cheap labour over from Tamil Nadu, in southern India, to do the hard work in the coffee, first, and then tea plantations, in the mid-nineteenth century. So Tamils in a sense consist of two peoples, those of Sinhalese stock, usually of the higher castes, and those descended from the labourers from Tamil Nadu, who belonged to the untouchables. They formerly fought with each other but today the war against them has bound them together in the same ordeal of fire and blood. This evening I imagine the planters of the last century, worn down by the heat, bent under their baskets loaded with seedlings, sometimes falling under the lashes of their Western masters, hardened colonists whose mission was to increase profits for the British Empire, or collapsing in the sun, consumed by malaria, dengue, or tuberculosis, while the delicate lips of the West sipped the delicious nectar from china cups, dreaming of the tropical paradise where it would be so good to go and rest. Dripping with sweat, I drink my tea slowly. From the window I see some tourists still out in their long white wooden chairs, glasses in hands, it's happy hour, they've spent the afternoon roasting on both sides between dips in the cool swimming pool, they don't have to suffer in the blazing sun, won't die burning, barefoot, ragged, under the yoke in the fields of exploitation, will probably be struck down by skin cancer one of these days. Privileged people who don't know the horrors of war or forced labour still imagine gloomy fates and frivolously dig their own deathpaths—in war or in peace, the death instinct rears its head.

(During the night, I dreamed that the English colonists of the last century had systematically burned the coffee plantations of Ceylon to replace them with

tea, which they preferred. In the morning, I told myself
that maybe my dream wasn't so crazy after all.)

It's not easy to meet with the president of a highly
militarized country in a state of war. There are soldiers
everywhere, at the numerous checkpoints both in the
city and in the countryside, there's one at every
intersection in Colombo, standing straight as a
mannequin, staring impassively at potential enemies,
rifle barrel trained on the people walking by. You
pretend you don't see them, hurry by, instinctively
pulling your head into your shoulders like a bird
sensing danger. It's not easy to be received at the
presidential palace, but when we arrive there after
clearing many barriers (our taxi was x-rayed, its every
nook and cranny searched, and we were subjected to a
thorough inspection of our things and papers and a
body search—after all, we could have been suicide
bombers), Mrs. Chandrika Bandaranaike Kumaratunga
tells us she approves of our project on women and war.
She agrees to see us early in the morning between a
press conference and a cabinet meeting, because we are
women—men often don't understand our language,
she says—and we will understand what she has to say to
us. This woman brought children into the world during
"the LTTE's dirty war," who lost her right eye in a
bloody attack in December 1999, saw her father, the
"liberal and democratic" prime minister, killed by an
extremist Buddhist monk—her father had "wanted to
negotiate with the Tamils," she was fourteen years old

(it was then that she decided one day to go into politics and put an end to this "dirty war"). After studying political science in Paris, married an extraordinary artist and activist for Tamil rights—he was killed too, they don't know by whom—he was her love and the father of her children, she was forty-two years old, today she's fifty-seven.

But on the current war, the one being waged against an entire people, on the daily bombings, the pogroms of twenty years ago, the mass deportations, the systematic rape of Tamil women, the creation of Sinhalese colonies in Tamil Eelam, the denial of political rights (since independence, hundreds of thousands of Tamils of Indian origin—"not old stock"—have had their citizenship and voting rights revoked) and language rights (it was, after all, under the rule of her father, S.W.R.D. Bandaranaike, in 1957, that Sinhalese was decreed the only official language of the country), the economic embargo against the Tamil northeast, the total censorship of the media, Chandrika Bandaranaike has set answers, cast in stone in her head. Like all the successive leaders of India with regard to the Kashmiris, the leaders of China with regard to the Tibetans, Karadzic with regard to the Bosnian Moslems, Milosevic with regard to the Albanian Kosovars, Putin with regard to the Chechens, the Turks with regard to the Kurds—and at one time with regard to the Armenians—all the war leaders of dominant peoples say the same thing about the "little" peoples fighting for their physical and spiritual survival, the same fights, the same words: "They want war, they are terrorists. We want peace, so we must eliminate them!"

Chandrika says: "The LTTE is a bunch of terrorist bandits. They do not want to negotiate. Or rather, they pretend to negotiate while they kill behind your back. They say one thing, think another, and do a third." (I've heard that many times. About Arabs. About Moslems. About Jews!) "They want war? Well, I'll give it to them. And I'll win. I never do things by halves."

My gaze is attracted to the enclosed garden where a little footbridge arches over a pond filled with swans and water lilies, like so many little white moons strewn over the water golden in the morning sun among the big mournful birds, it's beautiful, no other word for it, like Monet's gardens in Giverny or the Métis Gardens in my country. I suddenly find myself drifting off to all the places without war, where one doesn't even think of peace, it's so there, vital as the breathing we never dwell on. I come back to Chandrika, this beautiful, intelligent woman, who, in another place, might have been a friend. In this luxurious setting—a barricaded oasis of luxury in a desert of misery—she radiates a quiet strength combined with gentleness. I continue taking notes while my colleague records: "I suppose women are more sensitive than men. When my father was assassinated, violence was state policy, the government used terrorist killers. Fifty thousand people, Sinhalese and Tamils, were kidnapped by hooded men and died or disappeared, no one knows which, and my husband was killed in front of my eyes. We were centre-left, we were working for a democratic alliance with the Tamil organizations, that was in the eighties. After such bloody events, either you become embittered and filled with hate or you want to destroy the root causes of the evil. I made the latter choice. Initially I went away to London with my children. I went through a kind of personal psychoanalysis while doing my doctoral research on the origins of political violence in my country. I didn't understand how, in a country that is so civilized, educated and politicized, there could be such brutishness. I came back at my friends' urging, I wanted to change things. I appointed my mother Prime Minister. There was a jingoistic minority in my party. I eliminated it. I brought together all the parties, including four Tamil ones, to negotiate. I extended the hand of friendship as no male politician would ever have done. I wrote to the head of the LTTE several times. He answered. We talked for eight months. Signed agreements, which he broke. He betrayed us. They forced us into war. They dragged us into war. We are fighting the war. To win. I want to wage this war well. As a woman, I'm a perfectionist."

(I think back to what we were told by S., a pro-Tamil activist: "The President talks peace but she makes war. Basically, we know she's powerless against the racist Buddhist extremists, the corrupt, feudal landowners and shady arms dealers, who also control the lucrative traffic in drugs and prostitution. Those forces, together, are not interested in the survival of a people. Only war suits their purposes, and all the corruption that goes with it. They want power and money. They are not even in the country, for fear of bombs. They live elsewhere. Their assets are invested in tax havens. They don't give a damn that one people is dying under bombs and the other in misery. Human beings don't exist for them. They don't see the evil they do, they are within the evil. I believe the President when she talks of peace. She's an idealist. The dirty war is being waged without her. She is subjected to the same propaganda on the LTTE, the same censorship that is imposed by her government. She's blind!")

The parliamentary leader and his secretary come in several times to tell her the interview is over, but she wants to continue the conversation, it's as if she doesn't even see them, they smile at us with the gracious affability people here, from both groups, have more than those anywhere else. She leaves her official desk, comes over to us, and we talk some more, off-mike, for a good half-hour. She wants to say, wants us to know that the war she is waging is not against the Tamil people, she is not a murderer, the war for peace is being fought against the "LTTE terrorists," those soulless bandits, she really wants us to understand that she is not just the product of high caste and a major landowning family with ties to political power: "I am working with the people. I was an activist for land reform. For twenty-two years, I worked four days a week in the poorest villages. The people know it and they love me. I am a mother. I suffer seeing death everywhere here. I have two children. I have only one message for the daughters of my country: the only thing that counts is understanding. Humanism of the head and the heart.

Seeing and feeling big. So that women and children here can be happy!" She kisses us.

We go back through the barriers, retrieve our passports, and leave that gilded prison, our minds absorbed in the other prisons, so many of them, where thousands of "terrorists," mostly Tamils, are rotting, locked up without trial—nobody has precise figures on the number of prisons or of prisoners—subjected to physical and psychological abuse, to every conceivable torture. We think about the huge prison that today is Tamil Eelam, about this people that for thirty years has undergone cruelty, deportation, exodus, about the women and men who have fled into the forests and are fighting to survive, weapons in their hands, belts stuffed with explosives, amulets of cyanide around their necks, we think about the systematic rape of women and girls, which is a war crime—but there is no international criminal court for Sri Lanka. And we have an impression, because the blazing sun here, the exuberant flora and fantastic fauna, the aromas of cardamom, cinnamon and other spices, and the symphony of paraphernalia adorning the strange temples are real hallucinogens, we have a foreboding, among the little moons of the water lilies, an image that follows us to the white haven of our hotel, a foreboding of the shadow of absolute evil like a huge human body with the entire planet in its grip.

Mangalika does not conceal her name, anyway she's known throughout the world, and in spite of her youth—she's in her thirties—she's crisscrossed the planet, going wherever there are conferences on peace or human rights. She receives us in her bustling office at the Social Scientists Association in Colombo. She defines herself as a "researcher in the history of women and their struggles since the beginning of history," is interested in "nationalist and feminist women pioneers, Sinhalese or Tamil, those who have defied colonialism and patriarchal society." Her words are quick and seem inexhaustible, a continuous flow accompanied by lively gestures, no time to lose, life *prestissimo*, she seems to be saying to herself, life is too short, let us quickly find as many solutions as there are problems, even more—that's what I see behind her shining eyes and bright smile. She moves like lightning among the boxes of documents and the posters and notices on the walls— the 1999 Hague Peace Conference, Picasso's *Guernica*, a calendar with the days of the year circled in red or marked with big blue *X*s, weekly schedules in Sinhalese (I'm fascinated by the roundness of the writing of this language, made up of circles or semi-circles, its alphabet like a series of notes and silences lined up on an invisible musical staff). I'm struck by a nice coincidence: Sri Lanka is the last country in our travels, and in the first one, Macedonia, in Olga's office, there was also a poster of the famous *Guernica*. The rays of the sun this morning, reflected onto the walls through the huge ferns outside, dance to the Republican cry of the Catalan painter, and the Spanish Civil War of the thirties stretches out its shining arms to the civil war taking place here in the year 2000, which Mangalika discusses solemnly. She also works in the Centre for Women's Studies, such generosity will ultimately bear fruit, I have absolutely no doubt. "There are a lot of us women," she says, "and there are male companions with us. We are as concerned with the fate of Sinhalese women as Tamil women, they are all dominated by their men, all denied free choice in love and career, except the privileged women of the high castes. But the Tamil women, who have been mobilized by the war and have greater freedom beside their companions in struggle, are better off. They occupy important positions in the military hierarchy and can use weapons to defend themselves against sexual assault. After the war they will have gone through major changes, will have had different relationships with their male comrades, their sex lives will never be the same. It may very well be that their families will not want to take them back, but they will be free to determine their destiny and there will be peace."

Mangalika tells us of the birth, during the war, of the Human Rights Committees, the broad interethnic coalition Women for Peace, the Movement for Inter-Racial Justice and Equality, and the White Lotus Movement, in which religious and lay Buddhist intellectuals are working for peace. She says the latter "want to go back to the Zen spirit of finding peace in the heart of war," and that the spirit of Buddhism today has been perverted by a thirst for political power that has extinguished the flame of the *bhikkhu*, or clergy, and their mission of meditation and teaching of the Buddha's doctrine. "The monks in the senior clergy do not want peace, and our president, despite her good intentions, is paralyzed against them—her government is a sterile eunuch. The majority of the political monks have lost the state of *kalyanamitta*, the ability to enlighten one's neighbour through spiritual knowledge." Mangalika believes that is the main cause of the war, the collapse of the moral values that have always given her people a quiet strength, through conquests and the vicissitudes of history. "There is a schism, a split among the Buddhists of my people, but it is a test, a kind of crucible in which the conditions for peace will be created again." But the time has not yet come, "Time is so slow, slower than our desire for change." Too many Sinhalese extremists do not want to negotiate for peace, do not see their interest in it. And the government is blind when it fights both the LTTE and the people working for the recognition of human rights, all human rights, including those of the Tamil people and those of women belonging to both peoples. "The laws here discriminate against the Tamil minority and women."

Mangalika continues, despite the constant ringing of the telephone, "There are so many activities in this life," and she tells us how many. Since the pogroms of 1983, the horror and fear have awakened activists, democrats, oppressed people and women—so many disappearances, so many murders and kidnappings in the streets of the cities and the roads of the countryside, so many bodies "drifting in the rivers," their blood mixing with the water. "They have awakened from the nightmare," are working now, hardly have time to sleep, "don't want to dream anymore anyway, it's too horrible," no longer take part in the festivals, the elaborate meals to which their lavish cuisine has accustomed them. Suddenly she stops, her thin, nervous body becomes calm, she gravely scans the horizon beyond the fern garden, staring at a far-off point in a geography we do not know, and she says, "I understand the sacrifice of the Tamil women suicide-bombers. I understand that of the raped women. Since they have lost the purity of their bodies, the fighters come looking for them to join the suicide commandos. Those men know, and so do the women, that only the ultimate immolation by fire can restore the innocence and chastity that were swept away with the wreck of their flesh. Only the black smoke of the burnt offering can give them back the dignity that was taken from them in rape. Suicide is the offering, the supreme sacrifice of the victim. You know, Hindus—and Buddhists too—do not share the Western concept of *identity*. Besides, such violence was injected into the bodies of the raped women that only war and murder can eradicate its seeds."

Coming back to us, Mangalika explains why she fundamentally does not believe in the violence of terrorism: "There are other options. I think feminism can give these women tools to better understand the violence within themselves and their age-old tendency to sacrifice themselves—as the slaves of the world have had to do from time immemorial. To escape. I believe it is better to analyze and campaign than to kill by killing yourself."

We go back by car through the poor, flower-lined lanes that took us to Mangalika's office. There's a scent of lilacs, the same as in the northern hemisphere but spicier, the thud of a bomb in the distance, and then the crack of a rifle shot. I see a woman in a long cornflower blue sari running as fast as she can, as if panic-stricken, she disappears into a shady street behind a little white house, there's burning dust everywhere. After the terrified woman has disappeared, I remember, as I pray for rain, René Char's words in "L'Abri rudoyé," from *Le nu perdu*: "I have always loved on a dirt road the nearness of a trickle of water fallen from the sky that comes and goes chasing itself alone and the tender awkwardness of the median grass that a load of stones stops as a dark reversal puts an end to thought."

Yes, at this moment, in this country, there is an end to thought for us. But no rain, no grass. Dust. A terrified woman running away. The dull thud of a bomb and the crack of a rifle suddenly silencing the birds. As if under a spray of stones, the trees seem to have emptied. We go back.

During the long Colombo-Karachi-Paris plane trip, I think again about what President Kumaratunga said at the very end of our interview. More women than men participate in the country's economy. A million women work as domestics abroad, where they are often mistreated, beaten and sexually abused. They send money home to their men, who don't work and who drink and have sex with their children. Within the country, two-thirds of the workers on the tea plantations —tea is Sri Lanka's main export—are women. The men beat them and rape them at will, drink and loaf at home, assault and rape the children. "We've set up a training program for the women, for both those going overseas and those working within the country. We comb the towns and villages for them. It's a beginning. I have understood that a true agrarian revolution will come about when women are no longer slaves. The same with peace. There is a cancer of violence, a devastating decay that is spreading among the men of this country. Women will save us from disaster."

We have an appointment with the association of Tamils in France, in the twentieth arrondissement. The office is as poor as the neighbourhood, it is the very image of the poverty of the refugees of this diaspora throughout Western Europe and North America, a dispersed throng engaged in the hard labour of survival. Propaganda accuses them of coming to the rich West for money to feed the Liberation Tigers of Tamil Eelam, but they haven't dreamed of a gold rush or a fabulous conquest of the "Far West," they're here because they can't stay there any longer, their lives would be in danger. Not to mention the misery, people spend days there struggling merely to obtain the papers that will give them the right to work and to housing, and hours every day trying to find odd jobs and come up with schemes just to be able to feed and clothe themselves. It's so cold here in the mythical rich northwest, so freezing in the constant humidity of the grey sky that the mere thought of the icy Far North way up in Norway and Canada gives them a fever, they shiver with it. In the evening, after the children's lessons and the modest supper—but like children all over the world, the kids are at ease in this new culture, swimming like little fish in the French language, in which they already know how to sing—after tucking the children in, in their long, soft pyjamas provided by Emmaus, after singing them lullabies from their own far-off country that they've never seen—they don't even have those marvellous comic books our spoiled children can't get enough of—after the children are finally asleep, the tired parents spend the last hours of the evening going down into the bottomless well of memory that leads to horror. They try in vain to drive out the images of terrified flight into the depths of the jungle when they kept falling down and getting up again amid a thousand mysteries and threats, they hear the bombs and see their houses on fire as if it were yesterday, they bring back to life their dead, holding them in their arms again and again to hear their last breath, they see again their clothes stained with blood and vomit from the bodies of their dying loved ones. They count on their fingers the number of their disappeared and put a name and a face on each finger, summoning sleep with this macabre procession as others count sheep, and finally giving their bodies to the night, but the nightmares return, because repetition is the eternal mission of bad dreams.

In the shabby but very tidy offices of the Tamil association, there are two icons on the wall, a portrait of the
leader of the Liberation Tigers of Tamil Eelam,
Velupillai Prabhakaran—who does not look like a wild
animal but a strong, determined man, there's a great
sadness in his eyes, the same sadness we saw in the eyes
of all his people—and one of a totally emaciated
woman named Poopathy—who died in 1989 after a
hunger strike she undertook in sheer despair at the loss
of her family. She had seen the soldiers of the Sinhalese
army capture her husband and children, had gone to
inquire about them, had received no response other
than sniggering and rebuffs, had retreated home and
started the hunger strike that ended in her departure
from that thankless land, and when she arrived in the
other world, she became a saint. "She's our own Mother
Teresa, she's a heroine!" we're told by Revati, a young
woman of twenty-four who is already running the
Tamil women's association. She has come to meet us
with a friend, Rajani—both of them are so happy that
two women from North America are interested in
them, they say, and express their gratitude again and
again, because nobody here seems to be concerned
about the fate of their people, here or elsewhere. They
compare themselves to the Kosovars or the Chechens
and say, "The newspapers and television cover their
wars, though, is it because they're closer to the rich
West, is it because there's more curiosity about Islam
than Hinduism?" They don't know the reasons for the
silence and rejoice in the thought that someone in
Canada, on the radio or in a book, will talk about their

people's struggle for liberation. They're dressed modestly, in western clothes, but the care they've taken in their dress (with a few sober pieces of jewellery) is touching. Revati is beautiful and marvellously alive. Rajani, a little older, has suffering written all over her face, and when she smiles, it's as if a stormy sky is being split by lightning, suddenly illuminating the shadows. She was nineteen when she left her country, she explains, "All I saw between the ages of eleven and nineteen was atrocities committed by the Sinhalese army, my adolescence was destroyed along with every-thing else." She speaks Tamil and Revati translates as she talks, a requiem in two voices under the portrait of their heroine Poopathy. "I saw my father beaten up, the schools closed, houses burned down. I hid in the forest. I knew fear every minute of every day and every night. I didn't even have nightmares anymore, the constant fear blocked my imagination. My own brother died in a suicide operation, gone to Eternity, a burnt offering for my people, for me. He's a saint, I'm proud of him. That pride helps me to live!" The women suicide bombers? "They are goddesses. They are the people I respect most in the world!"

They both say they are sad but at the same time confident about the outcome of the fighting, they are sure that one day peace will come, they have "no feeling of hatred towards the Sinhalese people." They say that peace will mark a double liberation, for the Tamil people and for Tamil women, who "will be ahead of Sinhalese women, because they have been fighting beside their men, have known equality, freedom to

choice their partners, sexual freedom. It is unfortunate
that we had to go through the war, and fire and torture
and rape and death, to get to that point. For centuries
and centuries we were kept in the kitchen." These are
Revati's words, and Rajani nods in agreement. "And
when peace comes, the Tamil women will say 'Never
again!' It will be a true revolution." Revati came to
France at five years old with her refugee parents, at first
it was a struggle to adapt and survive. She remembers
the school where she had problems in all the subjects
because she was behind in French and her parents had
neither the money for private tutoring nor the time or
knowledge to help her. She speaks excellent French,
but says she doesn't write it very well, which is why she
never went past high school. "I would have liked to be
a journalist or, better yet, a lawyer, I could do more to
promote my people's cause." (And if I had the money,
I'd pay for the studies she so ardently desires, and I ask
the rich of the world to create a foundation to provide
scholarships to the best schools for intelligent refugees
who want to learn.) She also remembers the scornful
laughter of her little classmates because she was "badly
dressed," never had treats to share, and was barely able
to get through the school curriculum. But one day, she
became "a naturalized French citizen"—her eyes light
up with pride and she smiles a dazzling smile. "I became
active then. I was fourteen years old. I decided to
defend Tamil identity, my country, and my land with
every means at my disposal, and to fight for the
liberation of the women of my people." She has just
married a man of her people, whom she chose freely

and loves, but in answer to our question about happiness, she says the word does not yet exist for them, being happy belongs to another world, one she has never known. "If I were in Tamil Eelam I would definitely take up arms, I wouldn't even hesitate to sacrifice myself in a suicide mission," to which Rajani agrees without hesitation. Oh, how they would love to go back there, both of them say in a single breath, when peace is restored, but in the meantime, they "are working to survive," and their situation is desperate: "Nobody cares about us, not the UN or the Red Cross or Amnesty International. Nobody cares about our fate!"

Revati suddenly begins to dream, tells us of the images she has kept inside since early childhood, talismans carved on the walls of her soul, which help her fall asleep each night, slipping into her dreams like a nostalgia that heals the melancholy of the day. She remembers the house her parents built—burned down in the nineties—the field of grain like a big garden, where as a small child she would walk with her grandfather, and the rice paddies—also destroyed by the Sinhalese army, but she *refuses* to think about that—remembers the palm trees, the beach, the fine sand and the path to her grandparents' house, which she would run along "because we were always afraid," still breathes in the smells so penetrating that they went from her nose down to the soles of her nimble feet—the smells helped her to run. She again sees her grandfather climbing the dizzyingly tall coconut tree as he did every night at dusk, and bringing down a long shirt full of coconuts—those trees were also bombed, but she *refuses* to think about that—and her grandmother rocking beside the pink peonies, smoking her fragrant cigar as she did every evening after supper, and singing.

Revati's grandparents "no longer even rest in peace" in the cemetery where their urns had been placed side by side. Because the cemeteries of Tamil Eelam were systematically desecrated in the war, graves exhumed, smashed, the ground dug up, trampled—as if they had wanted to kill death itself. The souls must have crossed the dark, icy waters of the Styx under the murderous blows of the angry living. I imagine them meeting thousands of sea nymphs along the way, weeping in chorus with them for Tamil Eelam in chains.

RETURN

Return

On my return home to Montreal, there were two letters waiting for me. One was from Anna announcing her departure from Toronto. She was returning to her country. The other, from Israel, was from Benyamin.

I wanted to catch up on the news at home, and I watched the two major events of the week on television: the ceremony marking the repatriation of the remains of an unknown soldier of the war of 1914–1918, which were taken from France and buried in Ottawa with earth from each of the Canadian provinces and territories, and the death by suicide of André Fortin, of the Montreal band Les Colocs. Despite the smug complacency of people here and their apparent indifference to the great ills of the planet, it seemed to me that underneath the forced hilarity of a whole generation of young men, something repressed was making its presence felt and that this was not unrelated to the alarming suicide rate in the same age group. These young Quebec men are no longer unknown soldiers going off to war to defend a cause. They are at war with themselves. And they are killing themselves! As if they have never exploited their "capital" of compassion for the Other. Had they been able to test reality in places where people torture, rape and kill, and to do so not with weapons but with their knowledge, fed by the desire to change today's humanity—inhumanity, in fact—they would surely have succeeded in converting their terrible private suffering into a capacity to support the Other. But to cure the Other, one must first know the Other. And there is so little information here on anything related to Elsewhere. To know the Other, one also has to have met the Other-in-the-self. To "know oneself" implies an internal shift that involves taking the measure of the distance between the self and the Other, surveying the areas of fallow land where the instinct of death and destruction weaves the very fabric of life. To heal the Other, one must first heal oneself.

As in countries at war, the women and girls here weep for their companions who have died by their own hand, have disappeared into the eternal Elsewhere from which no one returns. A period of civilian service abroad or at home would also be beneficial for these women and girls, many of whom suffer from depression. Albert Jacquard recently said that if we want humanity to survive, we must devote the twenty-first century to cleaning up the planet, because the last two centuries of unrestrained industrialization have turned the earth into a huge garbage dump. It's true! The earth is a garbage dump spinning through the galaxies. But it still has its beauties, and nature everywhere moves us. However, if we want our descendants to enjoy its splendours, we have to leave our romantic souls aside, to notice, under the seemingly clear water of the stream or river, the toxic residues polluting the ground water, to sense, under our feet as we cross the bountiful fields and forests, the hell of the soil contaminated as a result of unchecked industrialization. As part of the clean-up of the planet—which is possible—there should be a clean-up of the bodies of people killed, which must be given decent burials. An enormous job. But do-able. We need to do more than just honour one unknown soldier who has fallen on the battlefield. War, in this century of ashes, has changed. It no longer takes place man-to-man on a front defined by generals. There are no more fronts. Or rather, the front is everywhere. War is waged by extremely well-equipped armies or militias against civilian populations: old men, women and children.[16] We would need a huge memorial to the unknown civilian. A human race that is no longer capable of burying its dead surely has no right to exist.

For all our young people asleep amid the false hilarity, cosily covered with the soft quilt of peace from sea to sea, there are also, in addition to the planet to be cleaned up, souls and bodies to be healed, wounds to be bound. Right now on this earth, there are millions of slaves bent under forced labour, dominated by drug traffickers or pimps, thousands of people rotting in

---

16. According to figures from the United Nations Population Fund, a century ago 90 percent of people killed in wars were soldiers and military personnel; today 90 percent of the victims of war are civilians, and three-quarters of them are women and children.

prison, subjected to torture—and torture has become pornographic, rape in all its forms is part of it, as if the unbridled imagination no longer had any limits, as if the old warriors' codes of honour are no longer in effect, as if today's wars have pushed the barriers against acts of collective perversity further and further back. In the prisons of Chechnya, the Russian soldiers did not only rape the women—so that, as in Bosnia or in Kosovo, they would carry within them the child of the enemy—they also systematically castrated Chechen men. Thus "ethnic cleansing" is carried out through sex, pleasure perverted into sadistic suffering, and the life instinct associated with the sex act warped into death-dealing power. There would be plenty of work for our idle youth in all the organizations concerned with the flouting of human rights in the world. Work with our leaders who conduct negotiations abroad, very often with terrorist states as their partners. Work in all the NGOs involved in the lands of fire, blood and rape. There is so much to be done. We are so poorly informed here!

In France, where I've just returned from, and where I lived for the whole year between trips to these major destinations, there is more information in circulation— the French are more numerous, have more resources, are closer to the conflict zones, and have experienced war on their own territory—but it is not uncommon to hear (or read) intellectuals denounce the "so-called humanitarian work" of organizations dedicated to the defence of human rights or NGOs in the field, on the grounds that their "good works"—this is always said in a condescending tone—have only one purpose, "to appease the consciences of those who support them," that they smack of old-fashioned religiosity, that, basically, they don't do much good, not the campaign against anti-personnel mines or the work of the International Criminal Tribunal or the many UN commissions dedicated to the defence of rights and freedoms, Amnesty International, the United Nations High Commission for Refugees, Human Rights Watch, or PEN International (which, incidentally, at its last congress, in Moscow, at the instigation of the Russian writers, condemned the genocidal war in Chechnya), or all the work being done among the devastated populations of the world by the hundreds of NGOs of the rich West. We can answer these intellectuals by pointing out that their cynicism is their own way of keeping a clear conscience and that by not taking a stand they do not risk guilt. Or not answer them at all, and continue to act.

Before setting out, I asked myself a lot of questions, which have remained unanswered. But in the field I understood why I wanted to write this book. Beyond the reading and the interviews with experts, which were often enlightening, something happened to me one day in Kosovo that I would call an epiphany. It was in Malisheve, the village in the ravaged valley of Drenica where we went with Henriette, the dedicated French midwife working for Médecins du Monde. In the poor clinic where dozens of women in distress were waiting, one of the women came over to me. She had noticed my notebook and pen in a pocket of my jacket.

She didn't speak my language and I didn't speak hers. The interpreter was occupied elsewhere with my colleague. But the woman had plenty to say to me. Seeing that I didn't understand her, she took the notebook and pen from my pocket herself, opened the notebook to a blank page, uncapped the pen and put it in my hand, and, moving the pen on the page, began a long monologue, all the while holding my left hand tightly against her belly. As she spoke, she moved my right hand along the lines of the paper. Under my left hand, I felt the warmth of her belly. It was from there that she wanted me to write, from that belly under attack that she wanted to see me acting with the tool she knew to be mine, writing. I spoke in my turn. Told her I understood. That I had come here to bear witness to the suffering of women in war. That I would write it when I returned to my country. Later the interpreter told me: "That woman was raped by a gunman from a Serb paramilitary group. She does not want to carry the child of the enemy inside her. She wants an abortion. She already has eight children. Her husband was kidnapped. No house or animals, everything was burned down. She wants you to write that. She says you understood, she saw it in your face. She says that she felt it in your hand on her belly."

(Yesterday, a young friend from here who is very involved in community work said to me: "It's true, Madeleine, what you write about foreign countries. But don't forget the war being waged here against women and children, the rapes of women and children. There are a great many cases of incest. Go and see what's going on in the reception centres for juvenile delinquents, girls and boys. A lot of rape and physical and psychological abuse. Learn about it. Write about it! You don't have go to far-off countries to understand the source of war. The war being waged against children here by adults who have power is appalling." She's right, of course. That's what I told her.)

Anna writes me a long letter in which she tells me she's going home:

> You can say it, I'm going back to Lebanon now that I'm not afraid anymore. The Israeli army has withdrawn from the south that is my country, and the soldiers of the SLA[17] have surrendered. I'm not afraid anymore. On television I saw my people break down the walls of Khiam prison, I cried for joy. I want to return home. I was well received here, you know. But I find this peace insipid. You live in Quebec, a country that is not a country. You seem to have adapted to that in-between place. It is as if there are no more dreams here. As if there's a great political vacuum. Everyone seems to make do with this.
>
> ... And then, how can I say this? I hear the cries of my people rising from the street, I open my window, deaf to the Toronto traffic, I hear the lament of all the hearts wounded by snipers

---

17. South Lebanon Liberation Army, an auxiliary of Tzahal.

and war. Like a long sigh from the earth worn
out by hatred and death, the earth laid low, its
back to the wall ... I have read everything you
sent me and really thought about it. Our
compassion, dear friend, keeps us warm amid
the cold darkness of the world. And keeps us
curious amid the general apathy. And keeps us
talking amid so much silence and resignation.
And keeps us intense amid the drabness
covering the world. And gives us respite from
the ugly face of the earth. And bestows on us
the warm balm of the world like twilight falling
over the sea ...

Anna is returning to Lebanon with her family, she
will see her Mediterranean again and her liberated land.
We will write each other, of course. Perhaps we will see
each other again, as perhaps I will see some of the
exceptional individuals I encountered in the countries
I visited, because in every one of those countries,
beyond the atrocities, a few true friendships were
formed in the test of reality and took root in the soil of
courage and the passionate drive some people have to
rebuild life differently. On these travels, I have surely
learned more about these forces than the forces of
death and destruction. I touched with my heart what
Blanchot called the "unavowable community" that
exists throughout the world. It reaches across borders. It
flows without barriers or checkpoints, as rivers flow to
the oceans that encircle the earth. It surrounds people,
and does not need to form a political party to recognize
itself. It is self-evident and speaks its own language. It

creates its own interpreters who transcribe it in paintings, dance, music or writing. It is!

The same day, this long letter from Benyamin. From Jerusalem:

You know, I am slowly healing from Annie's death. I know she would never have committed suicide if she did not have terminal cancer. She loved life too much. She simply overtook the death that was trying to catch her ... I sometimes go back to that patch of land in Palestine where we buried her. I think of the two of you then. I sing the *shabbat* songs of my childhood. Did you know that *shabbat* means "sunset"? I go there, to her grave, at nightfall. When I sing, time seems endless, as vast as the universe, time sweeps over me, and I melt into Annie's presence. I remember the hours after the assassination of Rabin, in 1995, when Annie and I and a few others decided to do something with our Peace Bus. We travelled across the country to tell Israelis that tolerance, on all sides, was our only guarantee of survival. We met with settlers in the occupied territories and talked to them about the fact that the Palestinians make up 18 percent of our population, are deprived of a state, and have no rights as citizens. We had two slogans: "Occupation equals violence" and "Peace equals equality." We also talked with our representatives in the government and with soldiers in Tzahal. The Peace Bus mobilized thousands of women—

women active in Bat Shalom, of which Annie
was a member, and in the Women in Black
movement. I was with them with a few male
companions. For years, we crisscrossed the
country. Our work bore fruit. The army
withdrew from southern Lebanon. Khiam and
its tortures are no more. Peace agreements are
being negotiated with our Arab neighbours and
with our Palestinian brothers. I am no longer
hopeless. I have decided to stay here. It is my
country. When I sing the *shabbat* melodies for
Annie and the sun goes down over the dry
sands of Palestine, I love this country of Israel
like a living being …

It is not necessary to travel to far-off lands to change
and to move within yourself. I have always known that.
Confirmed it each time with my friends when I
returned from my peregrinations. Back in Paris from
Asia, I learned that my old friend of eighty-eight had
departed this world for the Heaven she invoked every
minute of her slow dying. "She wanted so much to go
there," her old companion in shopping and housework
told me, "that she was radiant with joy at her last
breath." Before taking to her bed, she insisted on
destroying all her personal files on rape that she had
accumulated over the years, burning them herself at the
back of her little yard. She wanted her friend to witness
that extraordinary *auto-da-fe*. She wanted the ceremony
to take place at dawn, on a day when the sun of the

cool morning caressed the hills of Ménilmontant. That March morning, seated on the wobbly bench in the little garden with bowls of hot café au lait, two old ladies silently contemplated the bluish smoke rising to the heavens, offering the outstretched arms of the sun's rays the consumed work of an entire lifetime. "She did a good job. That's all that counts," her friend tells me. "She did a good job!"

As for Rabia, the Kosovar refugee I met in September, I also saw her again at the end of my travels. This time, knowing her country a little, I thought that perhaps we would be able to talk. She and her family, all twelve of them, were still living in her cousin Zake's little apartment in the Paris suburbs. Since I had just come from their country, they welcomed me as a real friend. Cousin Barbuka had made a mutton stew, I'd brought a good wine, and we talked late into the night. Rabia ate, drank and smiled, but she didn't speak. When I was leaving, on the doorstep, Barbuka said, "I'd like to walk with you a bit." After a few steps, she told me in a low voice that Rabia did not speak any more than she had before in Kosovo, but that she was cured. "Cured!" she said, this time very loud, and the word echoed in the night. Suddenly one day Rabia had asked for a sewing machine, had gone back to work on it, and, most of all, had stopped raving in that strange language nobody understood.

What had happened?

At first, she had agreed to see a psychiatrist, in fact it was a psychoanalyst, who only asked the family for a few francs. Rabia went and all she did was cry during the entire first session, and all she did was cry again during the second, this woman who hadn't shed a tear since the tragedy. After that, she didn't want to see the analyst again. She just said to them, "I'm cured. I've cried all my sorrows. I'm not going back. That woman is very nice. I want to sew now. I would like a sewing machine."

They took her at her word! They all chipped in. The next Sunday at the flea market, they found "the beautiful old machine you just saw. Since then, she has been sewing. For us, for friends, for the neighbours. She doesn't rave anymore. She sews. What happened with that psychiatrist? We don't know. Is it magic? Sorcery? All Rabia did there was cry. She's working. She's not crazy anymore, you understand?" And Barbuka adds pensively, "What's really beyond us—but after all, it doesn't matter—is that when she sews, she sings in a foreign language, the same one she used to rave in. We understand absolutely nothing of what her songs say, and the music is also made up, and I swear to you, it's beautiful!"

I'll come back, I tell Barbuka. I want to hear Rabia's foreign language and her made-up music.

During our travels through the Balkans, the Middle East and South Asia, we heard the victims of war describe the horror in languages that were foreign to us. We asked questions without answers, held on to the thread of our doubts through the weave of what escaped us. It had seemed necessary to get close to the faraway in order to penetrate the enigma of war. The madness of the song from elsewhere or the totally new image is always threatening to the sedentary. But wars have been nomadic since the most ancient times. For the space of a book, I wanted to become a nomad. I wrote the book so that the victims would not be forgotten.

The duty of memory imposed on us by the Shoah has multiplied. The women and children of Sierra Leone, Chechnya, Algeria, Guatemala, Chiapas, Tamil Eelam, Rwanda, Bosnia, Kosovo and Palestine ask that we keep the light of memory alive. We live in a country of peace and well-being. But without real solidarity, that peace is an empty shell that will shrivel and our well-being will burst like a bubble. Are we aware that four big diamond-trading companies in Great Britain, Belgium and Canada are pulling the strings of the war in Sierra Leone, making profits on the Toronto Stock Exchange while gangsters are massacring the civilian population on the ground and diamonds, weapons, drugs, and women and children are being traded in the money-laundering markets?

If we have a duty of memory with regard to the Nazi horror, we also have a duty of knowledge with regard to the horrors that are occurring in the world today. And the two are connected. The Holocaust deniers are the same people who don't want to see what is happening now. They are the real warmongers. There is not yet an International Criminal Tribunal for them. Rape has only recently been recognized as a crime against humanity. One day, through advances in international humanitarian law, those who pull the commercial strings of conflicts from far away while reaping profits from assets invested in tax havens will be recognized as guilty of war crimes.

In our travels, we were not war correspondents and did not go to see the war on the ground. We went to the victims, those who survived the horror. They spoke to us of their dead, of all the deaths that have torn pieces of life from their bodies and minds. The victims wanted us to bear witness to the terrible consequences of the conflicts, but above all, they called for the perpetrators to be tried and convicted, and demanded that they ask forgiveness and make reparation. I join my voice with those of all the victims throughout the world who are demanding just sentences. With them, I say the following words to the masters of war in thought and deed: conviction, reparation, asking forgiveness. By choice, I did not meet with the killers. I have nothing to say to them. With them, silence. The place to exchange words with them is in the courts. However, I recognize the need for experts to study the minds of war criminals as is done in cases of murder or rape by individual criminals. In order to understand. In order to prevent. In order, perhaps one day, beyond the justified wailing of the victims, to hear *The Song of the Earth* rising up out of the terrifying depths of today's abyss.

But already, all over the world, there are voices making themselves heard, inaudible to the masters of war. We have picked up a few of them, they provide wings to anyone who wants to go to a time before the wounds, beyond the daggers carving borders, they are saying, "All the children of the earth are mine, and mine are all the oppressed lands of the earth." We go down the St. Lawrence River to the great open sea of the Atlantic, or, in the opposite direction, cross the Rockies to the great open sea of the Pacific, and cock our ears to the horizon. Thoughts come to us in defiance of space and time, for now they're all inside in a strange ceremony, they are saying in a very low chant—we catch a few fragments—"One day, we must imagine the victims happy!"

Facing the great open sea, which is no longer an impassable Wailing Wall born of disaster, we remember the words of Albert Camus: "One must imagine Sisyphus happy." Sisyphus had put Thanatos in chains and forced him to go with him to the Underworld. We imagine the Medusas of the great open sea chaining Eros to their bodies, escaping murder by Perseus, and with their gaze alone, the gaze from their souls, reducing any master of war to dust. In the same way, women rebels, of whom there are a multitude in this world at war, may perhaps reconcile themselves to the absurdity of their human condition.